The Philosophy Student Writer's Manual

Anthony Graybosch

California State University, Chico

Gregory M. Scott

University of Central Oklahoma

Stephen M. Garrison

University of Central Oklahoma

Prentice Hall
Upper Saddle River, New Jersey 07458

Library of Congress Cataloging-in-Publication Data

Graybosch, Anthony J.
    The philosophy student writer's manual / Anthony J. Graybosch,
Gregory M. Scott, Stephen M. Garrison.
        p.   cm.
    Includes index.
    ISBN 0-13-237371-8
    1. Philosophy—Authorship.   2. Philosophy—Study and teaching.
I. Scott, Gregory M.   II. Garrison, Stephen M.   III. Title.
B52.7.G73 1998
808'.0661—dc21   97–2305
                                                        CIP

Editor in chief: Charlyce Jones Owen
Acquisitions editor: Angie Stone
Production liaison: Fran Russello
Editorial/production supervision: Bruce Hobart (Pine Tree Composition)
Cover designer: Bruce Kenselaar
Editorial assistant: Elizabeth Del Colliano
Manufacturing buyer: Tricia Kenny

This book was set in 10/12 New Baskerville by Pine Tree Composition, Inc.,
and was printed and bound by RR Donnelley Company & Sons.
The cover was printed by Phoenix Color Corp.

© 1998 by Prentice-Hall, Inc.
Simon & Schuster/A Viacom Company
Upper Saddle River, New Jersey 07458

Printed in the United States of America
10 9 8 7 6 5 4 3 2 1

ISBN: 0-13-237371-8

Prentice-Hall International (UK) Limited, *London*
Prentice-Hall of Australia Pty. Limited, *Sydney*
Prentice-Hall Canada Inc., *Toronto*
Prentice-Hall Hispanoamericana, S.A., *Mexico*
Prentice-Hall of India Private Limited, *New Delhi*
Prentice-Hall of Japan, Inc., *Tokyo*
Simon & Schuster Asia Pte. Ltd., *Singapore*
Editora Prentice-Hall do Brasil, Ltda., *Rio de Janeiro*

To
Divna
Jeremy
Melissa

and thanks to:
George Berger
Scott Mahood

Contents

2 Writing Competently 54

PART TWO: *Conducting Research in Philosophy*   *81*

PART THREE: *How to Think and Write Like a Philosopher*   *153*

Preface

TO THE STUDENT

One of the most frustrating tasks students face is mastering the requirements of the different disciplines they encounter in their college careers. Philosophy presents a particularly difficult challenge since most students do not study philosophy in a formal manner until they reach college. I know I find myself sitting all by my lonesome self in the auditorium during summer orientation when we set up information tables for incoming students who have declared interest in particular majors. My colleagues in other disciplines are swamped, but I have time to catch up on some reading. So before I get down to describing how this book is going to benefit you, let me just make the following unpaid commercial announcement. Philosophy majors score significantly higher than all other humanities and social science majors on standardized tests for admission to graduate and professional study. This includes tests for business, medical, and law school. Majoring or minoring in philosophy or including philosophy as a double major is one of the wisest investments you can make in your education. Think of the personal attention you will receive!

Philosophy is an un-American discipline. As Americans, we are entitled to believe anything we want to believe. But philosophy actually challenges your entitlement to a view. It is impolite. It asks for reasons for even our most cherished and "private" beliefs such as those about religion. Perhaps this is because philosophers do not believe that there are any views that are truly private. Or perhaps the philosopher you encounter in your first class is devoted more to the validity of the process by which you arrive at a belief than the truth of the belief itself. It does not matter. The challenge to private views many students face for the first time in adulthood is disturbing. Obviously I wish philosophy were taught at an earlier age, in elementary school and high school. But there is significant opposition to including religion in public schools, let alone the critics of religion.

Many students take courses in college that encourage them to describe their feelings. In one of the first undergraduate courses I taught a student wrote in the first person about the morality of abortion. She told me that she had been impregnated by a man who was not her boyfriend, that it was difficult for her current boyfriend to accept her pregnancy, and that she had considered abortion and rejected the option as not right for her. However, she was concerned that other women have a right to abort. Her paper went on for several pages. I kept reading, looking for an argument that never appeared and ended up feeling that I had inadvertently invaded her privacy. And any grade I would be tempted to put on her papers would be a negative evaluation of her life.

In philosophy, we are not really interested in people but in arguments. I did not want to validate or condemn the author of the abortion paper. I was interested, and left uninformed, as to why she felt her boyfriend had a right to an opinion on her abortion, what reasons had played a significant part in her decision, and why the reasons that were not good enough for her might be good enough for those other women whose choice she was inclined to protect. In other words, I would never want to tell her that her decision was wrong, but perhaps I would say that she had no right to her decision.

If you have just come from a composition class in which expression of feelings and exposition of life history and your inner voice were emphasized, then you may be having the reaction I alluded to above. You are realizing that expectations in philosophy are different than they are in some other disciplines. But rest assured, if you learn how to write good argumentative essays this skill will assist you in many other courses, your professional career, and your life as a citizen. You will not be an easy mark for the various hucksters—whether politicians, salespeople, or religious exploitators—whom we face in our daily life.

The Philosophy Student Writer's Manual contains all the material you need to write successful philosophy papers. The introduction explains the different major perspectives found in the contemporary philosophical community. While aimed at beginning philosophy students, the introduction will also be a useful refresher for more experienced students. Chapters 1 through 9 focus on the basics of good writing, research, and philosophical argument. The lists of sources in Chapter 4 provide descriptions of major reference works like the *Encyclopedia of Philosophy* as well as specialized reference encyclopedias such as those devoted to bioethics and philosophy of religion. Chapter 5 presents sources available through the internet, such as discussion lines, and the American Philosophical Association's home page on the World Wide Web. Chapter 6 discusses the format expected of philosophy journals, and so should be of particular interest to those preparing for a career in philosophy. Chapter 7 offers a comprehensive description of source citation and bibliographical formatting procedures for research papers.

Chapters 10 through 14 are, for the most part, devoted to specific types of philosophy papers. Philosophy is such a broad field that it is virtually impossible, not to mention costly, to include chapters on every philosophy course you might encounter. Some attention has been paid to writing for the most popular undergraduate courses. But the chapters on philosophical argument, ethics, and history of philosophy should provide guidance even when your particular course is missing. Obviously, there will be much of interest to the student of legal ethics in the sections on criminal justice ethics and the philosophy of law.

A glossary is also provided and I recommend that you scan it for the occurrence of terms you feel you already understand. One difficulty philosophy presents is that it uses terms from ordinary language and other disciplines in a technical manner. It is not uncommon for terms like *idealism, pragmatism,* and *utilitarian* to be bandied back and forth between class participants without any communication going on at all. I have included a section in Chapter 2 on the most common equivocal terms.

When I am introduced to people socially they often remark, "I took a philosophy course once." And the once receives emphasis. The goal I set for myself as an instructor is not to turn students into philosophy majors or minors. I just want them to take a philosophy course more than once without the second course being a result of failing the first time. My best undergraduate instructor told me that his goal was to instill an appreciation of philosophy that would lead students occasionally to return to philosophy over the course of their lifetime. (Thank you, Robert O'Connell, S.J.) I hope this manual removes one of the roadblocks that can thwart appreciation of the discipline that I love. If I have but one life, I want to live it as a philosopher.

The Philosophy Student Writer's Manual will help you write with precision and clarity. Assignments are included that illustrate the skills required in a large variety of philosophy courses.

TO THE TEACHER

I dread correcting the first writing assignment of the semester. There are always a few students who have shown interest in philosophy and have made good contributions to class discussion who demonstrate that they have serious trouble with the written word. Perhaps your students are consistently better prepared than mine. But you probably find it difficult to justify the class time it takes to explain the different expectations they face in philosophical writing from the more exegetical approaches of other disciplines. Or you may teach courses in professional and applied ethics that have no prerequisites. I do. I teach Ethics and Criminal Justice. Students come in ready to discuss questions like police use of deadly force, corruption, discretion, and undercover work. But if any real philosophical thinking is going to occur in the course we must first spend considerable time, if not money on an extra text, on the basics of ethical theory.

I could not decide if I wanted to write a basic introduction to philosophical argument or a writer's manual or a short text on ethics that I could use to supplement anthologies of professional ethics. So I combined the three. If you are teaching business ethics you can direct your students to material that explains basic ethical theories, references to business ethics journals, explanations of common logical fallacies, suggestions on drawing up an outline, basic guidance on using electronic research tools, and a glossary of philosophical terms. The purpose of this text is to allow you to spend more class time on your subject and less time giving instruction on the basics of writing or philosophy.

I have also included chapters on writing papers for specific areas of philosophy. I could not include all the areas I would like but I hope you will find enough suggestive material to make the text worthwhile. I have tried to keep an upbeat tone throughout and have sprinkled occasional humorous remarks in the text to keep readers looking for the next joke. And, of course, your comments and corrections are most welcome. My e-mail address currently is graybosc@ecst.csuchico. edu.

Lastly, I would like to extend a special thanks to the following Prentice Hall reviewers for their invaluable comments and suggestions: Marya Schechtman, University of Illinois at Chicago; James E. Maffie, California State University, Northridge; Robert L. Simon, Hamilton College; and Charles L. Reid, Youngstown State.

Anthony J. Graybosch

An Introduction to
the Discipline of Philosophy

There will be no end to the troubles of states, or indeed, my dear Glaucon, of humanity itself, till philosophers become kings in this world, or till those we now call kings and rulers really and truly become philosophers.

—Socrates (Plato, *Republic*)

Philosophy! We are in it for the money.

—Chico State University Philosophy Club Motto

I.1   PHILOSOPHY IS NOTHING NEW

Even if this is your first philosophy class, you have been doing philosophy all your life. All of us have thought and even argued about the big questions of philosophy: free will, the existence of God, the nature of knowledge. If you are partial to literature or film, especially science fiction, you have considered such questions as these: Can there be a thinking machine? If so, does it have a soul? (*Do Androids Dream of Electric Sheep?* asks the title of a novel by science fiction writer Philip K. Dick.) But you don't have to be a moviegoer or a science fiction buff to "do" philosophy; it permeates all aspects of our lives.

Children seem to be born philosophers. Like any good philosopher, they are always asking embarrassing questions. Perhaps it is this embarrassment that causes us to teach our children, as they grow, to avoid philosophy. We prefer to sidestep conflict, and we still follow the old adage "Don't discuss religion or politics." (How many of you have been told something like this at one point or another in your life?) But to reject this advice, to refuse to avoid the conflict that always attends a worthwhile argument, is to begin to practice philosophy.

What you learn in this book about constructing arguments and writing critically will serve you well in other disciplines. Your psychology course, for example, may have different writing standards than those discussed in Chapter 4 or 6 of this book, especially regarding footnoting and bibliographical formats, which in a psychology paper will probably correspond to the guidelines prevalent in the social sciences and not the humanities. But good argumentative writing in psychology shares fundamental characteristics with good argumentative writing in philosophy, and the same is true for the writing you will do in your history class, your economics class, or your class in American literature. Since the fundamentals of argumentative writing are always the same, why not learn them from the originators and the experts—in other words, from philosophers?

A few of you may have some trepidation about studying philosophy. You may fear that by considering the arguments of professional secular humanists you are going to lose your faith. I will be honest with you. Philosophy challenges the dogma of traditional religious faith. It certainly is possible to be, like Alasdir MacIntyre, a respected philosopher and at the same time a believer in religion. But know this: philosophers argue about nearly everything. When you study philosophy, be prepared to face challenges to your most cherished beliefs.

The official purpose of this book is to introduce you to the basics of philosophical writing. We will be concerned with how you should, and should not, engage in doing and writing philosophy. Along the way we will do quite a lot of philosophy. Studying philosophy without actually philosophizing would be like taking a course in aesthetics without ever listening to a piece of music or reading a poem or a short story. In fact, even before we move on to Chapter 1, we are going to explore a standard philosophical question in order to give you a feel for philosophical argumentation.

To those of you who have studied philosophy before, let me say a word about this introduction. You could indeed skip the beginning of the book and read just the chapters of interest to you. But no matter how practiced you are in the discipline of philosophy, I would strongly encourage you to read the introduction anyway. It is often useful to refresh your memory of a subject you have studied. Besides, few things can be more rewarding when you examine something than to find a way to come at it from a new angle. This introduction may give you that new angle.

First things first. Let's do a little philosophy by looking into a classic question.

I.2   ARE YOU DREAMING?

How do we know that we are not dreaming? This question, once raised by the French philosopher René Descartes (1596–1650), always sparks a variety of answers when I ask it on day one of my Introduction to Philosophy class. One student will say that we can determine we are not dreaming by pinching ourselves. Sometimes another student reports that she does not dream in color, so if she is having visual presentations—in other words, if she is seeing something—in color, then she is not dreaming. There is always one student who says that he would ask someone else. And then after a little discussion someone says it is a stupid question.

These commonsense responses are so natural that they must be valid in some context. What I mean is that, in a rough-and-ready manner, the type of knowledge they illustrate and support is, in most situations, good enough. Someone asks you if the New York Jets will be in the Super Bowl next year. You reply, "No." If the person then asks "How do you know?" your first response is not to assume that he is asking you the question "How do we know anything?" which is a question about the foundation of knowledge. Rather, you ask your interrogator if perhaps he would like to make a wager on whether the Jets will be playing in the Super Bowl or watching the game on television.

"Are you dreaming?" is, in most contexts, like the question "Are you paying attention?" asked by a teacher. The proper response to your teacher is to sit up straight and reply, "Yes, sir, I was just thinking about the Pythagorean Theorem," or whatever else the teacher is trying to teach you. In ordinary contexts, these two questions are not taken literally. The former is really a challenge to your seriousness about whatever topic is being discussed. The latter is a request for a promise that you will begin paying attention, or at least look like you are.

But despite its oddness when taken literally, the question "Are you dreaming?" raises some serious questions. It is not enough to offer the replies given by students in my intro class. Some of us do dream in color, or at least report that we do. And even if we had visual presentations at different times of two types, colored and shades of gray, we could not justify saying that one was an experience of reality and the other was not simply on the basis of the variety of pigments.

Nor is the idea of pinching ourselves to see if we can experience pain a good reply to the question. I have had dreams in which I experienced a great deal of pain. When I woke up I was very pleased to realize that I still had my arms and legs. But while the dream was going on I "felt" like I was in pain. So when I pinch myself now and do feel pain, I have to realize that I might just be dreaming and, in the dream, dreaming that I feel pain. After all, when I am dreaming and am pinched, I do dream that I feel pain.

As to asking someone if I am now dreaming, that will not help at all. People in dreams are no more reliable than people in real life. The person I ask may be a liar, or the dream person I ask may be dreamt as a liar. And in any case, what person could be reliable enough to know if I am dreaming if I cannot know it myself?

All you biology and psychology majors out there are dying to tell me that someone else could tell whether I was dreaming by looking for REMs (rapid eye movements). You might not be able to tell me while I am dreaming that I am dreaming, but you certainly could tell me when I woke up. We could imagine a lab in which someone is asleep. The lab instructor—let's call him Professor Skinner—says to psychology student Freud, "Mr. Freud, go determine if Jung is dreaming."

Freud goes over and peeks under Jung's eyelids, discovers REMs, and reports back to Professor Skinner, "Yes, Jung is dreaming." So Skinner says, "Remember to tell him he was dreaming when he wakes up. Now, Mr. Freud, look at the next patient, Mr. Adler, over there on the other slab."

How valid is our lab approach to the question of whether or not we are dreaming? Suppose that, when Mr. Adler wakes up, he explains that he never dreams. Even though Mr. Freud tells Mr. Adler that he had rapid eye movements while he was asleep, Mr. Adler will not agree that he was dreaming and is now awake.

This lab scene we have invented is similar to commonsense contexts. The lab instructor and his student Mr. Freud have a tacit agreement as to what counts as grounds for saying that a patient is dreaming: the presence of REMs. Our lab inhabitants are no different, really, from the commonsense reasoners that I get in my classes, those advocating pinching or some other proof. The lab just has its own set of rules for being justified in saying that so-and-so is dreaming. Does this mean that a good answer to the question of dreaming in your perceptual psychology class may not be a good answer in your philosophy class? Yes, it does. It also suggests that the philosopher *is asking a different question,* or at least emphasizing an aspect of a question that is usually taken for granted elsewhere.

I probably have no need to point this out, but our Mr. Freud has no way of knowing that he is actually in a lab performing an experiment. He cannot ask Professor Skinner. Skinner might be just a dream. And Jung, he is asleep. And Adler, he does not dream, so the question makes no sense to him.

So what is the *philosophical* question that Descartes was asking when he raised this dream issue? Printed below is what he said. But before you read Descartes, try to answer the following questions to your own satisfaction:

- How do you know at this moment that you are not dreaming?
- Does it make sense to look for a proof of your own existence?
- Do other people have minds, feelings, dreams? How do you know?
- If Kasparov had lost his chess match to the computer program Deep Blue, would you have thought that either the program or the machine had ideas?
- What is the philosophical question that the dream argument points toward?

DESCARTES' FIRST MEDITATION

It is now some years since I detected how many were the false beliefs that I had from my earliest youth admitted as true, and how doubtful was everything I had since constructed on this basis; and from that time I was convinced that I must once for all seriously undertake to rid myself of all the opinions which I had formerly accepted, and commence to build anew from the foundation, if I wanted to establish any firm and permanent structure in the sciences. . . .

Now for this object it is not necessary that I should show that all of these are false—I shall perhaps never arrive at this end. But inasmuch as reason al-

ready persuades me that I ought no less carefully withhold my assent from matters which are not entirely certain and indubitable than from those which appear to me manifestly to be false, if I am able to find in each one some reason to
doubt, this will suffice to justify my rejecting the whole. . . . [F]or owing to the
fact that the destruction of the foundations of necessity brings with it the down-
fall of the rest of the edifice, I shall only in the first place attack those principles
upon which all my former opinions rested.

All that up to the present time I have accepted as most true and certain I
have learned from the senses or through the senses; but it is sometimes proved
to me that these senses are deceptive, and it is wiser not to trust entirely to any
thing by which we have once been deceived. . . .

I must remember that I am a man, and that consequently I am in the
habit of sleeping, and in my dreams representing to myself the same things or
sometimes even less probable things, than those who are insane in their waking
moments. . . . At this moment it does indeed seem to me that it is with eyes
awake that I am looking at this paper; that this head which I move is not asleep,
that it is deliberately and of set purpose that I extend my hand and perceive it;
what happens in sleep does not appear so clear nor so distinct as does all this.
But in thinking over this I remind myself that on many occasions I have in sleep
been deceived by similar illusions, and in dwelling carefully on this reflection I
see so manifestly that there are no certain indications by which we may clearly
distinguish wakefulness from sleep that I am lost in astonishment. And my astonishment is such that it is almost capable of persuading me that I now dream.
(*The Philosophical Works of Descartes.* Vol. 1. Ed. Elizabeth S. Haldane and G. R. T.
Ross. New York: Cambridge University Press, 1911. 144–146.)

Much of this passage is written in the first person, but Descartes is hoping
that his confession will strike a cord of recognition in his readers. He is hoping that
they, too, will say that they have had a similar experience. Descartes is searching for
agreement to several important premises he needs to launch his dream argument.

A premise is a claim that is used to support a further claim. Philosophers
would like all their premises to be supported by good arguments, to be born out as
conclusions of good arguments. But no matter how supportive a premise can be to
a particular claim, there is always the question *what supports the premise?* In other
words, no matter how far we go in any investigation, we tend to feel a need to find
support for each new piece of evidence. Look, for example, at this argument:

Premise 1: The Bible conveys God's message for man.
Premise 2: The Ten Commandments are found in the Bible.
Conclusion: The Ten Commandments are the moral law of God.

The two premises in this argument support the conclusion. But how trustworthy
are the premises themselves? It is possible to test them, at least up to a point, by re-
arranging the terms of the argument:

Premise 1: The Ten Commandments are the moral law of God.

Premise 2: The Ten Commandments are found in the Bible.

Conclusion: The Bible conveys God's message for man.

In this second argument, a premise from the first argument becomes the conclusion. This shows us that two premises can be used to support each other. But does this fact convince us of the truth of either conclusion? Do we accept the arguments simply because the premises support the conclusions? Or do we feel the need to find separate support for the premises before we allow ourselves to trust the conclusions?

This problem of the justification of ultimate premises has led many philosophers to embrace the view that there are some ultimate premises that do not depend on other premises for their justification. Such philosophers are generally called foundationalists. Descartes is a foundationalist. You are a foundationalist, too, if you were irritated when Professor Adler in our laboratory example above claimed that he never dreams—not because you believe that Adler forgets his dreams when he wakes up, but because you believe that everyone dreams and Adler is just being argumentative. Foundationalists believe that some truthful premises are just given.

But Descartes is a foundationalist with a mission: he wants to make sure that the ultimate premises he believes in are error-free. Although he does not explicitly state it, in the first paragraph of his meditation he accepts a tacit premise that it is very hard to discover all possible sources of error. So although he may have become aware of some false premises he accepted in his youth and is now suspicious of anything else he learned from the same sources, he simply may not remember where all his youthful premises came from, and so he knows that he may still discover further false beliefs. The only way he can be sure that his knowledge, which he compares to a building with a foundation, is reliable is to tear it down and begin again with a new foundation. This leaves him with the problem of how to build a new, error-free foundation of knowledge. What tools should he use? What sorts of "knowledge" should he discard?

In his second paragraph Descartes asks us to accept the reasonable premise that we should withhold belief not only from false premises but also from those that we have any reason to doubt. Then he moves on to consider how trustworthy his senses are as tools for discovering trustworthy beliefs. He knows that he cannot investigate each individual premise we have come to accept through our sensory experience of the world of trees and automobiles. That would be an impossible task to complete. But if there is some reason to doubt the reliability of the source of all these empirical beliefs, then we should doubt the whole class.

Descartes is not arguing that sense always gives us false beliefs. Rather, he argues that, because sense is sometimes confused with dreaming, we cannot sort out those contexts in which we are being given false sensory beliefs in dreams from those contexts in which we are being given reliable sensory beliefs by our actual, waking senses. The fact that we cannot determine when we are dreaming rather than sensing throws doubt on the fact that we are sensing, not dreaming, now and in each context in the past when we thought we were sensing.

At this point in the argument, Descartes's "reasonable" premise about when we should withhold belief seems to suggest that we should believe nothing that is based on the senses. Sure enough, it is possible to come up with situations in which the senses don't seem completely trustworthy. For example, your senses may tell you the first line below is longer than the second. When you measure them, however, they turn out to be equal.

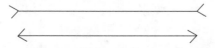

But do such examples really mean that you must doubt all the data supplied by the senses (including the measuring)? Not necessarily. This is not a knockout argument against the senses because, odd as it may sound, you must accept the reliability of the senses (your ability to make a measurement) in order to cast doubt upon them. Descartes cannot, after all, call the senses into question unless, at least in some contexts, they are beyond question.

So far, Descartes's question about dreaming has led him to question some of our most basic assumptions about life, such as the validity of cherished ideas and the trustworthiness of our senses. His argument about dreaming goes on, becoming more complex, implicating still other assertions that we commonly make about life. Ultimately, Descartes cannot claim with certainty that he knows whether he is dreaming or not. But what was his point in entertaining this rather odd question in the first place? Remember that we began looking at the dream argument in an attempt to see the philosophical—not psychological—issue animating it. What a philosopher wants to discover by considering dreaming is different from what a psychologist is interested in determining. Descartes has not undertaken his question in order to establish a laboratory definition of states of consciousness. He is looking, ultimately, for a way to determine those premises that belong in the foundation of knowledge. He is looking for an acid test of certainty.

The criterion for this test is not a psychological one. Imagine you receive a call from Walmart saying your mom has been picked up for shoplifting. My response would be "Not my mom! You have the wrong number or the wrong Graybosch." And if they showed me a videotape of my mom putting Star Wars figures into her purse, I would think the tape had been doctored. I am *psychologically* incapable of thinking that my mom would steal anything. And I hope you have that type of certainty, also. But psychological certainty is not what Descartes is looking for. By doubting everything, Descartes is looking for premises there can be no reason to doubt. Those premises, if they exist, are the ones that will provide the foundations for the sciences—the ultimate premises. He is looking for *evidential,* not *psychological,* certainty. (By the way, eventually Descartes came to believe that he had established a class of "clear and distinct" premises that are safe from doubt.)

So, in a sense, the dream argument is not really about dreaming. It is an example of an argument that allows us to enter into a philosophical discussion of the nature and possibility of human knowledge. Philosophers often approach questions very indirectly. We begin with a common question that embodies or provokes a philosophical discussion, such as: Are you dreaming? And we see how deeply that question leads us into understanding ourselves.

Used by permission of Benjamin Graybosch.

Within the discipline of philosophy you will find philosophical activities classified according to how they are carried out today or how they were accomplished in different times and places. You will become familiar with the names of philosophical movements such as pragmatism and idealism and even movements associated with particular eras and geographic locations such as Anglo-American (Analytic) philosophy and Continental philosophy. One basic contrast you will run into in much philosophical talk is a distinction between Western and non-Western or Eastern Philosophy based in prevailing conceptions of reason. I hasten to add that there are representatives of so-called Western philosophy in non-Western philosophy and vice versa.

Many non-Western philosophers have been interested in the nature of dreams and dreaming. But a common concern with a phenomenon, even one as familiar as dreaming, does not guarantee a common interpretation or perception of its nature. Chuang Tzu, a Taoist philosopher who lived in China sometime between 400 and 295 B.C.E., used dreams to raise important metaphysical and moral questions. Here is a passage from Chuang Tzu's "The Equality of Things," in which Tzu conceives of the relationship between dreaming and reality in a way different from Descartes' conception.

> Once I, Chuang Tzu, dreamed that I was a butterfly and was happy as a butterfly. I was conscious that I was quite pleased with myself, but I did not know that I was Tzu. Suddenly I awoke, and there I was, visibly Tzu. I do not know whether it was Tzu dreaming that he was a butterfly or the butterfly dreaming that it was Tzu. (*A Sourcebook in Chinese Philosophy.* Ed. Wing-tsit Chan. Princeton: Princeton University Press, 1963. 189–190. I have profited from the discussion of this passage in Gary Kessler. *Voices of Wisdom.* Belmont, CA: Wadsworth Publishing Co., 1991. 1–3.)

For Chuang Tzu, the experience of dreaming leaves him unable to tell what kind of existence is properly his own. Is he ultimately a butterfly or a man? But what is important is that, whether he is a man or a butterfly, Chuang Tzu still undergoes both experiences. There is a fundamental underlying unity that holds the two ways of life together. Chuang Tzu does not take the road either Descartes or Aristotle travels. He does not try to distinguish reality by separating illusion from truth. Instead, Chuang Tzu embraces all experiences as equal and sees the truth in a way that accepts all experience as equally real. The common experiences of being a different entity yet the same person, of being unable to distinguish dream from waking life, lead him to seek a view of reality in which conflicting claims are reconciled in a deeper unity. And if this unity exists within the self, the microcosm, then it will exist for reality as a whole, the macrocosm.

Descartes, Aristotle, and Chuang Tzu all use dreaming as a kind of launch pad for a larger argument about the nature of reality, but their approaches and their conclusions are different. You may not want to accept Chuang Tzu's conclusion about reality, in which knowledge of a part is knowledge of the whole. Perhaps you are more inclined to Descartes's view of reality, which holds that reality can be comprehended in separate, discrete parts. I can imagine someone reading Chuang Tzu and becoming very upset. Chuang Tzu's way of looking at dreams introduces the possibility that all of our most ordinary experiences may be illusions. Tzu's conclusion attacks us psychologically. Such a philosophy can lead us to change our lives.

Our brief exploration of the ways in which philosophers have used the phenomenon of dreaming as a springboard for argumentation provides us a hint of the diversity within the discipline that I love. Let's stop here and do a little philosophy. Answer the following questions:

> Should Chuang Tzu's story of the butterfly be taken seriously?
>
> Does it make sense to compare our ordinary relationships to dreams? Are some of our personal, emotional, sexual relationships akin to dreams?
>
> Isn't Chuang Tzu's attempt to reconcile conflicting perspectives by asserting an underlying unity a case of circular, and therefore flawed, reasoning?
>
> Are philosophical questions worthless because they are incapable of being answered once and for all? Does philosophy ever make any progress?
>
> From what you have read so far, do you feel that philosophy is hostile to religious belief and loyalty to your country?

I.3   WHAT IS PHILOSOPHY?

Philosophy is both a discipline—an area of study—and an internalized mode of doing something. Philosophers are guided by the principle that nothing should be allowed to stand in the way of inquiry. Since many of the ideas worth inquiring about are the ones that people feel a great deal of attachment to, philosophers often either seem silly or make people angry. They question beliefs that many of us take for granted, such as the existence of an external world. And they want to discuss questions that our culture has labeled private and immune to polite challenge, such as the existence of God.

The British philosopher and historian R. G. Collingwood said that if you ask people questions until they get angry, you uncover their philosophical beliefs. Collingwood is using the term "philosophical" here in a general way to refer to a person's worldview, and not in the specific way, preferred by philosophers, to refer to beliefs we arrive at after rigorous investigation and discussion. Although I expect philosophy will get people angry at times, I am always slightly surprised at my students' reaction to Socrates. They read about Socrates' trial for a charge of impiety and corrupting the youth and feel sorry for him. They wonder how a cultured state like Athens could execute—via their equivalent of lethal injection—a man as cultured and entertaining as Socrates. I ask them to imagine that an unemployed senior citizen has set up a table in the local shopping mall. Perhaps he adds a sign that says, "Hey kids, want to discuss questions like the existence of God for free?" How long would it be before a group of concerned citizens attempted to remove this free thinker from a public place?

So one concept of philosophy is that it is a discipline committed to a reasoned investigation of any significant area of existence. It tries to uncover presuppositions of cherished beliefs and subject them to further discussion. Consider the following exchange between Socrates and the theologian Euthyphro, in which the concept of piety, or reverence shown toward a deity, is given a real philosophical workout.

> *Socrates:* [I] can only ask again, what is the pious, and what is piety? Do you mean that they are a science of praying and sacrificing?
>
> *Euthyphro:* Yes, I do.
>
> *Socrates:* Then piety, Euthyphro, is an art which gods and men have of doing business with one another? . . . I wish, however, that you would tell me what benefit accrues to the gods from our gifts. . . . If they give everything and we give nothing, that must be an affair of business in which we have greatly the advantage of them.
>
> *Euthyphro:* And do you imagine, Socrates, that any benefit accrues to the gods from our gifts?
>
> *Socrates:* But if not, Euthyphro, what is the meaning of the gifts which are conferred by us upon the gods?
>
> *Euthyphro:* What else, but tributes of honor; and, as I was just now saying, what pleases them?
>
> *Socrates:* Piety, then, is pleasing to the gods, not beneficial or dear to them?
>
> *Euthyphro:* I should say nothing could be dearer. . . .

Socrates: Were we not saying that the holy or pious was not the same with that which is loved of the gods? . . . And are you not saying that what is loved of the gods is holy; and is not this the same as what is dear to them—do you see?

Euthyphro: True.

Socrates: Then we were either wrong in our former assertion; or, if we were right then, we are wrong now. (*The Dialogues of Plato.* "Euthyphro." Trans. Benjamin Jowett. Vol. 1. New York: Random House, 1937. 13a–16a.)

A focal point of the above discussion is a distinction that Socrates and Euthyphro make between what subjectively pleases the gods and what is holy, that is, what objectively makes an action worthy of being appreciated by the gods. The question is, where does piety fit? And this question suggests the larger one—which, in times of religious zealotry and repression, proved to be a very dangerous one—of why humans should bother to pray. The passage above illustrates my earlier remark that no topic is immune from philosophical investigation.

Here is a question for you: A letter recently appeared in my local newspaper supporting affirmative action. It included the claim that the founders of our country believed in equality but did not live up to their ideals. Thomas Jefferson was specifically mentioned. What the writer of the letter failed to mention is that, several times in the course of his life, Jefferson specifically stated his belief that blacks were by nature inferior to the white race. Now, Jefferson's assertion is not exactly the avowal of equality that the letter writer ascribed to our third president. Should I write a letter to the local paper pointing out this error? Should I even try to begin a public discussion of the question? Should I risk being misunderstood as someone who agrees with Jefferson? A philosopher is not deterred by fear. At least Socrates would say it is better to lose your life than block the path of inquiry.

Notice that Socrates and Euthyphro agree on at least one claim: the gods are not the sort of creatures who need human assistance. They could still have discussed piety without this agreement. But their difficulty in arriving at an answer to the question of the nature of piety partially depends on this agreement. After all, if the gods did need human assistance, then—as Socrates and Euthyphro obviously realize—the gods would not be the gods! You may not be able to settle on a particular definition of piety, but you can come to see that if you believe something about the nature of the gods, you will be committed to other specific views on issues such as the nature of piety, the existence of human free will, and the possibility of divine foreknowledge of our choices. Certain beliefs require you to hold other beliefs, which, in turn, saddle you with still others. The dialogue between Socrates and Euthyphro demonstrates that Wilfred Sellars was right when he defined philosophy as the study of the ways things in general hang together. How is that for a clear and concise definition of philosophy?

Socrates and his student Plato, who wrote the dialogues in which Socrates is the primary speaker, have their own concept of philosophic inquiry, called the Socratic method. You have just seen it in action in the above passage from the dialogue "Euthyphro": the Socratic method requires the philosopher or teacher to ask the other participant in the dialogue question after question, basing each new question on the participant's responses. Often a participant is required to offer a definition, as Euthyphro does above for piety, and then to answer questions about it. The questions are aimed at clarifying the reasoning behind the beliefs of the participant, who sometimes, in the course of the dialogue, discovers errors in his beliefs. Sometimes the Socratic method leads to no particular conclusion, as in the above discussion of piety. But that's all right. The point of the Socratic method is not to assert the superiority of the philospher's position at all costs, but to clarify positions and to reveal error in order to arrive, if possible, at truth.

So can we put all our attempts at definition together and come up with a coherent notion of what philosophy is? We might be able to do so, if we stayed within the Western philosophical tradition. But even then we would fall short by making very minimal claims. For instance, some people think that Socrates was not trying to get us to reach any philosophical truths. These people treat him as a skeptic who perhaps believed that happiness came from realizing that he knew nothing. Socrates himself supposedly remarked that he was the wisest of all men because others thought they knew something and he knew that he knew nothing. The inconsistency inherent in claiming that one knows that one knows nothing is just too obvious for it not to be another Socratic flourish.

But if I have to point to the core of philosophy I would have to say that it is a discipline in which one is always on the road to a conclusion. As Stanley Cavell said, philosophers are indeed the hoboes of thought, and we enjoy being travelers. We consider arguing with people to be a sign of respect. And we believe that the unexamined life is not worth living. Some philosophers even believe that philosophy is the only road to a happy life. I would like to think that any good philosopher appreciates the process of seeking answers to questions that cannot be answered finally, and that this appreciation translates into both rigorous investigation and also a sense of humor informed by the human condition.

I.4   WHAT DOES PHILOSOPHY ACCOMPLISH?

Some philosophers, like Descartes, might tell you that philosophy's job is to provide the foundations of the natural and social sciences. Others might say that it tries to dissolve what we call philosophical questions by showing that they are based in category mistakes or outworn metaphors. Perhaps philosophy is just an attack on traditional religious and political beliefs. Or it may be the natural development of religious thought that moves from a narrative phase appropriate to a popular uneducated audience to a reasoned one appropriate for the more sophisticated elite. And there are even philosophers who would hold that philosophy has established some truths.

But perhaps the one goal of philosophy most often agreed upon is to help people lead a better life. Socrates understood this goal. His attachment to philosophy had made him a thoughtful person who would not embark upon a rash course of action. He was also a person who was interested in important issues and not trivial gossip or worldly success. I will not be rash enough to claim that a wider appreciation of philosophy would lead to a better society. But it does seem that philosophical inquiry allows you to form your own opinions about crucial issues in a manner appropriate to a free adult. Maybe philosophy is about growing up.

This goal of helping people live better has always been important in philosophy. Ancient philosophers worked to arrive at a concept of wisdom that would serve them in the effective pursuit of a truly happy life, and philosophers today pursue the same goal with growing interest, whether they are concerned with the philosophy of technology, professional ethics, or even the theory of knowledge. The notion that philosophy is concerned with human happiness is important to both Western and non-Western philosophic traditions, though with certain differences of approach. These differences are worth looking at briefly.

As they invented Western philosophic thought, the Greeks generated a wide variety of rational constructions of the good life. By "rational," I mean that Western philosophers have always sought to answer these questions on the basis of evidence that has withstood reasoned criticism. This is the response of Western philosophy to the narrative, often mystical answers given by the great religious traditions: the Western philosopher responds to creation stories with the question *who made God?* In the dialogue on piety sampled above, both Socrates and Euthyphro are concerned with the nature of the deity and the way humans should regard the divine.

Now, by using the word *rational* in conjunction with Western thought, I do not mean to withhold it in its honorific sense from non-Western thought. Non-Western philosophy, however, often gives more credence to narratives and appeals to emotions and intuitions than Western philosophy does. Non-Western philosophy also has a greater *tendency* to respect the mystical and see unanswerable questions as occasions for intellectual and spiritual insight and growth. Consider the style of argument in the following selection from Chuang-Tzu:

When an archer is shooting for nothing
He has all his skill.
If he shoots for a brass buckle
He is already nervous.
If he shoots for a prize of gold
He goes blind
Or sees two targets—
He is out of his mind!
His skill has not changed. But the prize
Divides him. He cares.

He thinks more of winning
Than of shooting—
And the need to win
Drains him of his power.
(*The Way of Chuang Tzu.* Trans. Thomas Merton. New York: New Directions Press, 1965. 107.)

What conclusion does Chuang-Tzu want you to accept? What evidence does he offer? Is his argument a good one? Why or why not?

For a final example of philosophy's dedication to the pursuit of the good life, let's look back at ancient philosophy. The skeptic Sextus Empiricus (c. 200) tells us that he began the study of philosophy in order to arrive at knowledge so that he could lead a good life. And, like the painter who wanted to depict foam at the mouth of a horse and only succeeded when he became frustrated and threw a sponge at the painting, Sextus arrived at happiness by accident. By coming to the view that he did not know if knowledge were even possible, he fell into a condition he calls ataraxia, which he tells us is freedom from belief—and in that freedom, he found happiness. So, in the case of Sextus, even a skepticism that suspects that knowledge is not possible for humans led to a vision of the good life.

Perhaps I should remind you here that, today, for you, there is an immediate reason why philosophy may hold a key to the good life. Remember that philosophy majors score significantly higher than majors from other liberal arts, the social sciences, and most sciences on all standardized tests for professional schools. Philosophy also provides the critical thinking skills valued by quality corporations who seek to hire flexible, creative employees. If you are going to live in a world where you will change careers three or five times, a little philosophy is going to go a long way.

I.5   MAJOR BRANCHES OF PHILOSOPHY

The branches or subdisciplines of philosophy identify different types of questions philosophers ask about the nature of being, the nature of learning. One of the most interesting things about the branches is that, the further you explore into them, the more intimately they seem to be interconnected, so that the questions one subdiscipline asks may eventually seem to be pretty much the same questions asked by another, only from a different perspective. I hope the following brief overview of subdisciplines gives you some notion of their interconnectedness.

I.5.1   Metaphysics

Metaphysics is concerned with the ultimate components of the universe and with the ultimate nature of the universe itself. If you think of the universe as a room, then metaphysics would be a study of what furniture is in the room and the nature of the room itself, including its origin. Typical metaphysical inquiries are devoted to discussing such topics as the proofs of the existence of a deity, the nature of human free choice, the existence of mental as well as physical objects and events, the interaction of mental and physical substances, and the existence of relations, such as causality, and universals, such as human nature. The name *metaphysics* comes from the title of one of Aristotle's treatises. Metaphysics might seem to be similar to science, except that the metaphysician would call into question many of the beliefs that a working scientist would take for granted. But having said that, I hasten to add that much of theoretical physics, which is done without empirical testing, is certainly akin to metaphysics. The tool of the metaphysician is more often reason than experiment.

I.5.2 Epistemology

Epistemology, or the theory of knowledge, is concerned with the nature and justification of knowledge, the nature of belief, and, more recently, with the relationship between philosophy and psychology. Many epistemologists today see epistemology as a part of psychology and neurobiology and are satisfied to describe how humans learn and process information, considering the question of the justification of scientific knowledge claims to be beyond reasonable dispute.

I.5.3 Ethics

Philosophers attempt, but do not always succeed, to use the terms *ethics* and *morals* in distinct senses. Most of us probably use use these terms interchangeably, with the exception of times when we talk about professional ethics. Rarely does anyone mention professional morality and mean a code of ethics. In any case, you should presume that when philosophers speak of morals they mean a habitual pattern of actions that perhaps has been instilled by membership in a social institution such as a church or profession. Morality refers to the ways you tend to act, including how you would respond to questions about what actions you take to be right or wrong.

Ethics is the philosophical study of morality. Ethicists seek for rational justifications for the claim that a certain way of living is right. The discussion of piety from Socrates and Euthyphro that we looked at above comes close to being an ethical discussion when it raises the issue of whether we owe service and praise to the gods. Ethical debates tend to focus on whether the right-making quality of actions are their consequences or their motives. However, there are philosophers who would reject both those alternatives and appeal instead to empathic understanding, stages of psychological growth, divine commands, or the nature of the virtues. Chapter 10 is devoted to basic ethical theories, since these play a major part in philosophy courses packaged for preprofessionals in many American colleges and universities.

I.5.4 Metaethics

Metaethics is the study of the language of ethics and, in particular, the meaning of ethical terms and the nature of moral assertions. Metaethicists sometimes discuss whether moral statements are more like descriptions of facts or like expressions of feelings.

I.5.5 Social and Political Philosophy

Social and political philosophy deals with issues such as freedom, equality, justice, and rights. It may be seen as a branch of ethics concerned with our obligations to the government, fellow citizens, recent immigrants, or humanity in general. Social and political philosophy deals with questions such as the nature of distributive, retributive, and compensatory justice; anarchism versus the state; the nature of rights; and the justification of revolution and war.

I.5.6 Aesthetics

Aesthetics attempts to provide a reasoned guide to the appreciation of art. It is an attempt to explain and justify human responses to both natural and artificial creations that could be considered to have an aesthetic component. Some would quarrel with my inclusion of natural objects as works of art. I am no theist, but I have seen the Lofoten Islands, and I see them as works of art, even if they are just the products of evolution. Aesthetics sometimes tries to provide definitions of high and low art.

I.5.7 Logic

Logic was once considered the study of the laws of thought. Now it is more common to think of it as the study of correct reasoning. You will probably take a course in informal logic in college where a great deal of attention will be paid to telling you what ways not to arrive at conclusions. In other words, most critical thinking courses focus on the common forms of incorrect reasoning that humans are tempted to adopt.

There are subcategories of logic. Informal logic addresses the differences between premises and conclusions, valid and invalid arguments, deductive and non-deductive reasoning. It may even introduce you to the construction of argumentative essays. Symbolic logic courses are often devoted to translating natural language arguments into a mathematical form that allows formal determination of an argument's validity.

This short list of the major areas of philosophy is far from exhaustive. A typical college catalog will show several courses in professional ethics, applied ethics or moral problems courses, courses in the philosophy of a special area such as religion or social science, and interdisciplinary courses that relate philosophy to other subjects such as literature or psychology. But the kinds of issues you will confront in these courses will be variations on questions addressed in the broader subdisciplines I have named. Philosophy of religion, for instance, primarily addresses questions of metaphysics, epistemology, and ethics.

I.6   PHILOSOPHY TODAY

The American Philosophical Association is the major professional organization of philosophers in the United States. There are three conventions held each year, and many smaller philosophical societies hold meetings in conjunction with the meetings of the APA. Although the majority of papers presented on the main program of the APA meetings are within the Anglo-American tradition of philosophy, there is quite a diverse collection of philosophical perspectives represented by the smaller societies on the supplemental program. One can easily find sessions devoted to pragmatism, Chinese philosophy, and the philosophy of war, to name just a few subtopics.

The major philosophical movement of the twentieth century in Great Britain and the United States is analytic philosophy, which at different times and stages of its development has gone by the names logical atomism, logical positivism, Anglo-American philosophy, and ordinary language philosophy. I would hazard the statement that most philosophy department faculty members in a majority of publicly funded graduate schools and four-year colleges in America were trained in analytic thought. These instructors will be inclined to place philosophy closer to mathematics and natural science than to other humanities. Analytic philosophers tend to place great emphasis on the use of logic and the clarification of philosophical problems through rigorous analysis of the language in which they are posed.

The wide variety of philosophical movements that have ebbed and flowed in Europe for the past hundred years is commonly referred to as Continental philosophy. Perhaps the most common element in these diverse philosophies is a reliance on special experiences as revelatory of the human condition. Continental philosophers are inclined to rely on literary works for insight into philosophical problems, believe in historical progression in philosophy, and at times present philosophy as a form of anthropology.

Finally, there has been increased dialogue between analytic and Continental philosophers since I was a graduate student in the seventies, when a term-paper reference to a Continental philosopher like Sartre might have cost me a letter grade. The decline of analytic orthodoxy in the United States has led to renewed interest in non-Western philosophy. And I think the political events of the last thirty years have provoked a return to philosophy's ancient concern with living a good and wise life. Many hospitals now have bioethicists on their permanent staff. I had one colleague who taught a course on death and dying to death row inmates at McAlester Prison in Oklahoma. I also had the great pleasure of teaching just-war theory at Oklahoma City's Tinker Air Force Base. Aristotle pointed out that the exercise of a faculty is more satisfying than its passive possession. And philosophers seem to have realized the great pleasure to be had in the exercise of their art in the public sphere.

PART ONE

A Handbook of Style
for Philosophy

1

Writing as Communication

I will not have in my writing any elegance or effect or originality to hang in the way between me and the rest like curtains. I will have nothing hang in the way, not the richest curtains. What I tell I tell for precisely what it is.

—Walt Whitman, *Leaves of Grass*, 1855

1.1 WRITING TO LEARN

Good writing is a way of ordering your experience. Think about it. No matter what you are writing—it may be a paper for your class, a short story, a limerick, a grocery list—you are putting pieces of your world together in new ways and making yourself freshly conscious of these pieces. This is one of the reasons writing is so hard. From the infinite welter of data that your mind continually processes, you are selecting only certain items significant to the task at hand, relating them to other items, and phrasing them in a new coherence. You are mapping a part of your universe that has hitherto been unknown territory. You are gaining a little more control over the processes by which you interact with the world around you.

This is why the act of writing, no matter what it leads to, is never insignificant. It is always communication, if not with another human being, then with yourself. You may, for example, have consulted your notes on the night before the big exam and wondered, "Now what could I have possibly meant by that?" Writing is an attempt to order your world creatively and critically. It can also be a way of entering the world of others, communicating your own views. And when you fail to communicate, when you cannot understand your own notes, writing can indicate the areas of your world that need to be reexamined.

In graduate school I had a professor who advised me to write philosophy as if I were writing for the travel section of a newspaper. His explanation was that if I wrote about a place I had seen for an audience who may never get to visit it in person I would be less likely to overlook needed details and would provide the transitions necessary for comprehension. Often students conceive their audience to be their instructor or other students in a class. You will do better to write for someone who has never visited the places you have been. A roommate or friend who has not taken the class or read the material can be a good test of whether you can communicate your ideas effectively or need to rework them in some way. And if you have a paper due it is important to write the first draft a few days ahead of time. Sometimes, as in the case where we take notes we later cannot comprehend, we think we understand what we mean. If we write a paper and allow it to sit for a week and then revisit it, our lack of comprehension of our own past thoughts can point us in the directions we need to go to improve our work.

Writing, therefore, is also one of the best ways to learn. This statement, at first, may sound odd. If you are an unpracticed writer, you may share a common notion that the only purpose writing can have is to express what you already know or think. According to this view, any learning that you as a writer might do has already been accomplished by the time your pen meets the paper; your task is to inform or even surprise the reader. But if you are a practiced writer, you know that at any moment as you write, you are capable of surprising yourself. And it is surprise that you look for: the shock of seeing what happens in your own mind when you drop an old, established opinion into a batch of new facts or bump into an unquestioned belief from a different angle. Writing synthesizes new understanding for the writer. E. M. Forster's famous question "How do I know what I think until I see what I say?" is one that all of us could ask. We make meaning as we write, jolting ourselves by little, surprising discoveries into a larger and more interesting universe. We think much better when we use our pencils or keyboards than we do when we use just our brains.

The help that writing gives us with learning and with controlling what we learn is one of the major reasons why your instructors will require a great deal of writing from you. To write is to believe in something, and to know what we believe in is the product of successful writing. One of the things that all Americans have in common is the belief that they have a right to believe anything they want. Our private beliefs are like our homes, supposedly immune from invasion.

Philosophy will require you to clarify and defend beliefs that you have felt were beyond questioning. Perhaps you will adapt easily and find yourself developing new and better arguments for your most cherished beliefs. Or perhaps you will be troubled and angered when confronted with opposing points of view that challenge you. But remember that the value of your critique is either to point you in the direction of the truth or remind you of the reasons that make your cherished beliefs true and thereby reinvigorate them for you. John Stuart Mill thought that if all of society except for one person were in agreement on an issue it would be wrong for society to silence the one dissenter. The dissenter can be of the greatest

---

LEARNING BY WRITING

Here is a way to test the notion that writing is a powerful learning tool: Rewrite the notes you have taken from a recent class lecture. It does not matter which class; it can be history, chemistry, advertising. Choose a difficult class, if possible, one in which you are feeling somewhat unsure of the material, and one for which you have taken copious notes.

As you rewrite, provide the transitional elements (the connecting phrases, like *in order to, because of, and, but, however*) that you were unable to supply in class because of the press of time. Furnish your own examples or illustrations of the ideas expressed in the lecture.

This experiment forces you to supply necessary coherence out of your own thought processes. See if the loss of time it takes you to rewrite the notes is not more than compensated for by a gain in your understanding of the lecture material.

---

value to society by correcting a false belief or engaging the society in producing better arguments for its views. You can make little progress in doing philosophy, in learning how to argue your point of view or an as yet unfixed new conclusion, unless you commit your ideas to dialogue with others. And one of the most effective ways of engaging in dialogue with others, and yourself, is by committing your views to paper, disk, or the online discussion group.

Learning to be a philosopher requires commitment to a variety of professions. If you are interested in the philosophy of science or law, then you will have to maintain an acquaintance with those fields also. You will also need to master enough of the history of philosophy to partake in the discussions that occur in your classes and with fellow students. There is also the technical side of philosophy, a field with its own specialized terms that, unfortunately, overlap with common expressions in a way that is not always illuminating. The term *metaphysics,* for example, means something different to your philosophy instructor than to the proprietor of an occult bookstore. And finally, you have to learn not to let the fear of looking foolish deter you from asking basic questions. Part of our acculturation process is learning to take some things for granted. Children have not learned to do this yet; they question everything without worrying if their questions make them seem ignorant. Paradoxically, to be a good philosopher you need to become a lot like a little child again.

Writing is the entryway into philosophy, and into public life as well. Virtually everything that happens in public life happens on paper first. Documents are wrestled into shape before their contents can affect the public. Great speeches are written before they are spoken. The last forty years have seen philosophers becoming increasingly involved in public life, at least indirectly. You will notice at your college or university that a great number of philosophy courses are applied courses. Philosophers are interested in the professional ethics of disciplines such as law and medicine. Feminist philosophers are major influences on your local and federal laws governing abortion and pornography. Philosophers participate in political life by writing and teaching on topics such as ethics in government, criminal justice, and nuclear war. No longer do philosophers feel they have to make their work incomprehensible in order to be professionally respected. Philosophers serve on ethics boards at your local hospital. Major cultural figures who were trained as philosophers include Steve Martin, T. Boone Pickens, and William Bennett.

The written word has helped bring slaves to freedom, end wars, and shape the values of nations. Take Frederick Douglas's 1852 speech "What to the Slave Is the Fourth of July?" in which Douglas attacked the conscience of northern whites and helped fuel the New England opposition to slavery:

> What, to the American slave, is your 4th of July? I answer; a day that reveals to him, more than all other days of the year, the gross injustice and cruelty to which he is the constant victim. To him, your celebration is a sham; your boasted liberty, an unholy license. (*The American Intellectual Tradition*. Vol. 2. Ed. David A. Hollinger and Charles Capper. New York: Oxford University Press, 1993. 405.)

After pointing out the inconsistency of a nation committed to equality and liberty that tolerates slaves while welcoming oppressed European immigrants to its shores, Douglas enlists the Constitution in advancing the cause of emancipation.

Often gaining recognition for ourselves and our ideas depends less upon what we say than upon how we say it, although there does seem to be more tolerance for lack of style in philosophy than in other disciplines. While accurate and persuasive writing is absolutely vital to the philosopher, honesty is the primary virtue. We do not hide our premises in order to become more persuasive. How often do you read a newspaper editorial and find the writer telling you right off the bat what premises are the basis of the argument you are about to encounter and how the argument will proceed from premises to the conclusion? This is typical procedure for a philosopher.

1.1.1   Challenge Yourself

There is no way around it: writing is a struggle. Did you think you were the only one to feel this way? Take heart! Writing is hard for everybody, great writers included. Bringing order to our thoughts about the world is never easy. One of the most significant twentieth-century philosophers, Wilfred Sellars, had an extremely difficult time placing his thoughts on paper. This must have been an exceedingly troublesome block for Sellars, since his father was a professional philosopher also.

The younger Sellars recounts his childhood memories of his father ascending the stairs each night to confront his typewriter; Sellars remembered the steady clicks he heard into the night. Eventually the young Sellars devised a pattern of writing borrowed from the Austrian philosopher Ludwig Wittgenstein and started arranging his thoughts in a logical progression and expressing them in numbered paragraphs.

The rewards of the writing struggle may include delight as well as understanding. The careful craftsmanship that went into the famous passage below, from Henry David Thoreau's *Walden,* is obvious. Notice how Thoreau first grasps his reader's attention with vivid images that reduce the life of labor to the ridiculous, then marshals the Bible to support his praise of idleness, and then finally brings his point home by comparing the life of the so-called free man to that of a slave. Also apparent in the energy of the passage and the charm of its images is the joy that all writers experience when they have connected with a subject that matters to them and are finding their way through it with confidence.

> I see young men, my townsmen, whose misfortune it is to have inherited farms, houses, barns, cattle, and farming tools; for these are more easily acquired than got rid of. Better if they had been born in the open pasture and suckled by a wolf, that they might have seen with clearer eyes what field they were called to labor in. Who made them serfs of the soil? Why should they eat their sixty acres, when man is condemned to eat only his peck of dirt? Why should they begin digging their graves as soon as they are born? They have got to live a man's life, pushing all these things before them, and get on as well as they can. How many a poor immortal soul have I met well nigh crushed and smothered under its load, creeping down the road of life, pushing before it a barn seventy-five feet by forty. . . . The portionless, who struggle with no such unnecessary inherited encumbrances, find it labor enough to subdue and cultivate a few cubic feet of flesh.
>
> But men labor under a mistake. The better part of the man is soon ploughed into the soil for compost. By a seeming fate, commonly called necessity, they are employed, as it says in an old book, laying up treasures which moth and rust will corrupt and thieves break through and steal. It is a fool's life, as they will find when they get to the end of it, if not before. . . .
>
> Most men, even in this comparatively free country, through mere ignorance and mistake, are so occupied with the factitious cares and superfluously coarse labors of life that its finer fruits cannot be plucked by them. . . .
>
> I sometimes wonder that we can be so frivolous, I may almost say, as to attend to the gross but somewhat foreign form of servitude called Negro Slavery, there are so many keen and subtle masters that enslave both north and south. It is hard to have a southern overseer; it is worse to have a northern one; but worst of all when you are the slave-driver of yourself. (*Walden, or Life in the Woods.* New York: Viking Press Library of America, 1985. 326–328.)

Even though we may not all have Thoreau's talents, the writing process makes use of skills we all have. The ability to write, in other words, is not some magical competence bestowed on the rare, fortunate individual. We are all capable of phrasing thoughts clearly and in a well-organized fashion. But learning how to do so takes practice. The one sure way to improve your writing is to write.

Remember this, too: One of the toughest but most important jobs in writing is to maintain enthusiasm for your writing project. Commitment may sometimes be hard to come by, given the difficulties inherent in composition, difficulties that can be made worse when the project assigned is unappealing at first glance. How, for example, can you be enthusiastic about having to write a paper analyzing Thomas Hobbes's theory of the social contract when you have never once thought about the justification of government and look upon the very process of providing such justification as the rationalizations of an oppressor?

One of the worst mistakes that unpracticed student writers sometimes make is to fail to assume responsibility for keeping themselves interested in their writing. No matter how hard it may seem at first to drum up interest in your topic, you have to do it—that is, if you want to write a paper you can be proud of, one that contributes useful material and a fresh point of view to the topic. One thing is guaranteed: If you are bored with your writing, your reader will be, too. So what can you do to keep your interest and energy level high? Challenge yourself. Think of the paper not as an assignment for a grade, but as a piece of writing that has a point to make. To get this point across persuasively is the real reason why you are writing, not the simple fact that a teacher has assigned you a project. If someone were to ask you why you are writing your paper, what would you answer? If your immediate, unthinking response is, "Because I've been given a writing assignment," or "Because I want a good grade," or some other nonanswer along these lines, your paper may be in trouble. If, on the other hand, your first impulse is to explain the challenge of your main point—"I'm writing to show that if the Bosnian Muslims and the Bosnian Croats have a right to political self-determination through secession, then so do the Bosnian Serbs"—then you are thinking usefully about your topic.

1.1.2   The Nature of the Writing Process

As you engage in the writing process, you are doing many different things at once. While planning, you are no doubt defining the audience for your paper at the same time that you are thinking about the paper's purpose. As you draft the paper, you may organize your next sentence while revising the one you have just written. Different parts of the writing process overlap, and much of the difficulty of writing is that so many things happen at once. Through practice—in other words, through writing—it is possible to learn how to control those parts of the process that can be controlled and to encourage those mysterious, less controllable activities.

No two people go about writing in exactly the same way. It is important for you to recognize routines, modes of thought as well as individual exercises, that help you negotiate the process successfully. When I write, I like to change my envi-

ronment, writing one day at home, the next day outside, sometimes in the auto repair shop's waiting room (that 1985 Peugeot is good for something), and especially
while traveling.

The Georgian poet Vladimir Mayakovsky was, for a time, a committed social-
ist. When another poet, Sergey Esenin, committed suicide, Mayakovsky saw Esenin's despair as an attack on the ideals of the Soviet system. Mayakovsky resolved
to defuse the force of Esenin's beautiful suicide poem by constructing a poem of
his own that would both speak to Esenin and replace the beauty of death with the
beauty of a committed social struggle. Ironically, Mayakovsky himself committed
suicide four years later, leaving behind perhaps the most beautiful suicide poem
ever written, "Past One O'Clock." Here is how Mayakovsky described the process of
writing "To Sergey Esenin."

> For about three months I came back day after day to my subject and could think
> of nothing sensible. . . . The same hotel rooms, the same water-pipes, the same
> enforced solitude.
>
> These surroundings wound me into themselves, they wouldn't let me es-
> cape, they refused me the feelings and words I needed in order to brand and
> negate, they gave me no material from which I could educe sane and healthy
> impulses.
>
> Whence comes what is almost a rule: to do anything poetic you positively
> need a change of place or of time. . . . In order to write about the tenderness of
> love, take bus No. 7 from Lubyansky Square to Nogin Square. The appalling
> jolting will serve to throw into relief for you, better than anything else, the
> charm of a life transformed. A shake-up is essential, for the purpose of compari-
> son. (*How Verses Are Made.* London: Grossman Publishers, 1970. 30–33.)

It is also important to give yourself as much time as possible to complete the
process. Procrastination is one of the writer's greatest enemies. It saps confidence,
undermines energy, destroys concentration. Working regularly, keeping as close as
possible to a well-thought-out schedule, often makes the difference between a successful paper and an embarrassment.

1.1.3   Maintaining Self-Confidence

Having a sense of confidence in your ability to write well about your topic is
essential for good writing. This does not mean that you will always know what the
end result of a particular writing activity will be. In fact, you have to cultivate your
ability to tolerate a high degree of uncertainty while weighing evidence, testing hy-
potheses, experimenting with organizational strategies and wording. Be ready for
temporary confusion, for seeming dead ends, and remember that every writer
faces them. It is from your struggle to combine fact with fact, to connect fact and
value judgments, to buttress conjecture with evidence, that order arises.

Do not be intimidated by the amount and quality of work already done in your field of inquiry. The array of opinion and evidence that confronts you in the published literature can be confusing. But remember that no important topic is ever exhausted. There are always gaps, questions that have not yet been satisfactorily explored either in the published research on a subject or in the prevailing popular opinion. For example, new technologies such as in vitro fertilization are causing us to re-examine our views on issues such as abortion. It is in these gaps that you establish your own authority, your own sense of control. And it is through confronting hard cases on the borderline of your established moral distinctions that you establish your own self and values.

Remember that the various stages of the writing process reinforce each other. Establishing a solid motivation strengthens your sense of confidence about the project, which in turn influences how successfully you organize and write. If you start out well, using good work habits, and give yourself ample time for the various activities to gel, you should produce a paper that will reflect your best work, one that your audience will find both readable and useful.

1.2   ORGANIZING YOUR WRITING

As in other disciplines, philosophy will require you to write specific types of papers, with structures that may seem governed as much by blind tradition as by the characteristics of the subject. When rigid external controls are placed on their writing, some writers tend to feel stifled, their creativity impeded by a "paint-by-numbers" approach to structure. It is vital to the success of your writing that you never allow yourself to be overwhelmed by the pattern rules of a particular type of paper. Remember that such controls are in place not to limit your creativity but to make the paper immediately and easily useful to its intended audience. It is as necessary to write clearly and confidently in a position paper or a policy analysis as in a term paper for English literature, a résumé, a short story, or a job application letter.

1.2.1   The Nature of the Process

Although the various parts of the writing process are interwoven, there is naturally a general order to the work of writing. You have to start somewhere! What follows is a description of the various stages of the writing process—planning, drafting, revising, editing, proofreading—along with suggestions on how to approach each most successfully. Planning includes all activities that lead up to the writing of the first draft. These activities differ from person to person. Some writers, for instance, prefer to compile a formal outline before writing that draft. Some writers perform brief writing exercises to jump-start their imaginations. Some draw diagrams; some doodle. Later on we'll look at a few individual starting strategies, and you can determine which may be of help to you. Right now, however, let us discuss some early choices that all writers must make about their writing during the planning stage.

1.2.2   Selecting a Topic

No matter how restrictive an assignment may seem to be, there is no reason to feel trapped by it. Within any assigned subject you can find a range of topics to explore. What you are looking for is a topic that engages your own interest. Let curiosity be your guide. If, for example, you have been assigned the subject of evaluating utilitarian and deontological theories (now is a good time to check the glossary), then find some issue common to both of these forms of ethical theory that will allow you to illustrate, refine, and compare them. Perhaps you are an aeronautical engineering major. The *Challenger* disaster may occur to you as the sort of incident appropriate to ethical analysis. How much risk is acceptable in aircraft design?

Any good topic comes with a set of questions; you may well find that your interest increases if you simply begin asking questions. One strong recommendation: Ask your questions on paper. Like most other mental activities, the process of exploring your way through a topic is transformed when you write down your thoughts as they come instead of letting them fly through your mind unrecorded. It is not egotistical to keep a notebook. Remember the old adage from Louis Agassiz, "A pen is often the best of eyes" (*A Scientist of Two Worlds: Louis Agassiz.* Ed. Catherine Owens Pearce. Philadelphia: Lippincott, 1958. 106).

While it is vital to be interested in your topic, you do not have to know much about it at the outset of your investigation. In fact, having too heartfelt a commitment to a topic can be an impediment to writing about it; emotions can get in the way of objectivity. Better often to choose a topic that has piqued your interest yet remained something of a mystery to you, a topic discussed in one of your classes, perhaps, or mentioned on television or in a conversation with friends.

1.2.3   Narrowing Your Topic

The task of narrowing your topic offers you a tremendous opportunity to establish a measure of control over the writing project. It is up to you to hone your topic to just the right shape and size to suit both your own interests and the requirements of the assignment. Do a good job of it, and you will go a long way toward guaranteeing yourself sufficient motivation and confidence for the tasks ahead of you. Do it wrong, and somewhere along the way you may find yourself without direction and out of energy.

Generally, the first topics that come to your mind will be too large to handle in your research paper. Beginning philosophy students often submit topic proposals such as "Nature or Nurture?" or my favorite, "Humans: Good or Evil?" Both top-

EXERCISE: Narrowing Topics

The following general topics were assigned to undergraduate students in a course on political philosophy. Their task was to write an essay of 2,500 words on one of the topics. Following each general topic is an example of a way in which students narrowed it to make manageable paper topics.

General Topic   Paper Topic

General Topic	Paper Topic
Plato	Plato's philosophy of the role of women in politics
Freedom	A comparison of Rousseau's concept of freedom with John Locke's
Revolution	Arguments for the legitimacy of revolution used by Thomas Paine
Thomas Hobbes	Hobbes's definition of the state in Leviathan

Without taking time to research them, see what kinds of viable narrowed topics you can make from the following general topics: capital punishment, police use of deadly force, minorities and the death penalty, affirmative action, human rights, the right to secede, living wills, the moral responsibilities of talk show hosts. (For example, do television station owners have a moral right or obligation to intervene and remove shows that they believe have gone astray morally from the air?)

ics, in addition to being, perhaps, false dilemmas, are obviously too large for a lifetime, let alone a five-page paper. But even advanced students attempt to evaluate all of Western philosophy or maybe just Plato in ten pages. Instead of trying to find an answer for an overwhelming dilemma, it would be more practical for you to address only a part of the question. Rather than trying to determine if abortion is always bad or always good, you might compare accepted practices of disposing of frozen embryos; rather than attempting to determine the nature of truth, how about discussing some aspects of Descartes's and Sextus Empiricus's handling of the problem of finding a criterion of truth?

The problem with most topics is not that they are too narrow or too completely explored; it is that they are too rich. There are so many useful ways to address the topic that choosing the best focus is often difficult. Take some time on the job of narrowing the topic. Think through the possibilities that occur to you, and, as always, jot down your thoughts. Remember that it is all right to say explicitly that you cannot handle aspects of a topic in the space and time provided. For instance, you may wish to postpone for another time the question of whether disposing of embryos is moral and concentrate your paper on a comparison of two practices. Just make sure you let your reader know early on what the scope and focus of your paper are.

Often it can be helpful to jot down your immediate ideas and associations for a particular topic. This should tell you what, if anything, you have to say about the issue. For instance, I find that many students, given a choice of essay topics, select the one they want to write about. But that topic is often the one that they know the least about or possess the strongest feelings about. Either situation can lead to problems. The former can lead to a poorly substantiated thesis if sufficient extra research is not conducted. The latter can lead to an inefficient reasoning process that blinds us to the worth of arguments on the other side. When confronted with alternative topics for a paper or an exam, do a quick outline, and then chose the one you are best prepared to handle in the time available, whether or not it is the topic you most wish to explore.

1.2.4   Defining a Purpose

There are many ways to classify the purposes of writing, but in general, most writing is undertaken either to inform or to persuade an audience. The goal of informative or expository writing is, simply, to impart information about a particular subject, while the aim of persuasive writing is to convince your reader of your point of view on an issue. The distinction between expository and persuasive writing is not hard and fast. Most writing has elements of both exposition and persuasion. Most effective writing, however, has a clearly chosen focus of either exposition or persuasion.

It is common for instructors to assign expository papers, especially for beginning students. These papers can vary in length. Some teachers assign frequent short expository papers to reinforce learning; others assign less frequent, more extensive papers to provide an opportunity for comparing and contrasting positions. Some assign both. Obviously, the extent of depth in your essay will depend upon the space allowed to you.

But philosophy instructors generally desire to move you at some point in the course to persuasive papers. That is where the real fun is. The views of free will advocated by Spinoza and William James are interesting in themselves, but your involvement in the processes of philosophy deepens not just when you make them argue with each other in an expository paper but when you have to arrive at a tentative position of your own in response to their arguments. In my Criminal Justice Ethics class I am happy if students recognize on the first exam the ethical values behind various positions on whistle-blowing in the police force (pun intended). By the final exam, however, I want them to write policy statements on deadly force or prisoners' rights, using major ethical theories as the explicit foundation of their views.

EXERCISE: To Explain or to Persuade

Can you tell from the titles of these two papers, both written on the same topic, which is an expository and which a persuasive paper?

1) Roe v. Wade and the New Reproductive Technology
2) Roe v. Wade: A Bad Decision

Let us take the first and less controversial topic above. This title probably led most of you to say that it is an expository paper. Your task in such a paper would be to describe the Roe v. Wade decision, and in particular the role of reproductive technology in that decision, in as coherent and impartial a manner as possible. If you feel strongly about this issue it may be very difficult to refrain from evaluative comments on the decision. But that would be acceptable as long as your feelings do not produce static that interferes with your rendering of the details of the decision relevant to your topic. As you develop your topic you will come to the question of the role of new technologies in moving our concept of the point of viability (the moment when independently viable life begins) earlier than the six-month cutoff accepted by the Supreme Court. In an expository paper you would ordinarily stop at that point. But I am sure you perceive the moral relevance of an earlier point of viability established by medical technology to a decision made when that technology was not available. Expository papers can and should, as long as facts are relevant to moral decision-making, lead into moral discussions.

So if you are writing an expository paper, your task could be to describe in as coherent and impartial way the Roe v. Wade decision, the state of medical technology at the time of the decision, and recent relevant improvements that bear on the question of viability. If you are trying to persuade your reader that there should be more stringent regulation of the time when abortions may be performed, your strategy may be different because you are now writing to influence the opinions of the audience toward the subject. And this strategy should show up in your opening paragraphs, where you tell your reader how you are going to use both facts and values to arrive at an evaluative decision. But in philosophy we like to encourage persuasive writers to use only rationally sound and not emotive or fallacious reasoning to establish a position, no matter how much more effective nonrational means are. If argument is wrestling or war, it does not follow that we should fight without rules. Using rational means of persuasion theoretically widens the audience you may reach and ethically shows respect for other persons. It also prevents you from gaining agreement without proper reasons. It makes you convince yourself fairly as you seek to convince others.

Writing assignments break down the distinction between expository and persuasive writing in a number of ways. You may be called upon to analyze sociopolitical situations such as the police action in Bosnia, or to evaluate government programs such as Aid to Families with Dependent Children or Affirmative Action. You may have to speculate on directions in social policy such as regulating police use of force, or to identify or define problems within a field or range of fields. In any of these papers, your instructor may expect you to suggest solutions and make predictions. It is very important to spend planning time sharpening your sense of purpose.

Know what you want to say. By the time of your final draft, you must have a very sound notion of the point you wish to argue or the position you wish to support. If, during the writing of that final draft, someone were to ask you to state your thesis, you should be able to give a satisfactory answer with a minimum of delay and no prompting. If, on the other hand, you have to hedge your answer because you cannot easily form a notion of your thesis in your own mind, you may not yet have arrived at a final draft.

Two writers have been asked what point they wish to make in their papers. Which of the writers has a better grip on her writing task?

> Writer 1: "My paper is about whether someone in the reserves should be called to serve in a police action in another country."
>
> Writer 2: "My paper argues that although we have a volunteer military it is unfair to call these volunteers to fight in areas where the United States lacks a well-defined interest, a just cause, and the ability to protect its own troops without violating the international rules of engagement."

The first writer knows what her general area of concern is: whether volunteering for the military transfers to the government the absolute right to decide where and whether you will keep the peace. But the second writer has a more developed sense of how she is going to approach this issue. Note that the second writer has narrowed the field of information she is going to consult to establish her point. Her topic statement, for instance, does not require her to look at the details of the enlistment contract but does require her to make reference to international law and the moral notion of just cause. It may be that you will have to write a draft or two or engage in one or two of the prewriting activities described below in order to arrive at a secure understanding of your task.

Watch out for bias! There is no such thing as pure objectivity. You are not a machine. No matter how hard you may try to produce an objective paper, the fact is that every choice you make as you write is influenced to some extent by your personal beliefs and opinions. What you tell your readers is colored—sometimes without your knowing—by a multitude of factors: your environment, upbringing, and education; your attitude toward your audience; your political affiliation; your race and gender; your career goals and your ambitions for the paper you are writing. The influence such factors produce can be very subtle, and it is something you must work to identify in your own writing as well as in the writing of others in order not to mislead or be misled. Remember that one of the reasons why you write is self-discovery. The writing you will do in classes—as well as the writing you will do for the rest of your life—will give you a chance to discover and confront honestly your own views on your subjects. Responsible writers keep an eye on their own biases and are honest with their readers about them. One of the most responsible things you can do for your readers is to speak clearly on those matters that you have strong beliefs about and let them have a chance to correct for bias. Also, remember that it is one thing to admit that your race or gender may influence your beliefs and quite another to claim that someone else's background makes his or her views false or irrelevant.

1.2.5   Finding a Thesis

No matter what type of paper you are assigned, you will be expected to produce a clearly labeled and appropriately narrowed thesis statement. It should occur at the outset of your paper. And, of course, any thesis you assert will require the support of reasons. You can easily see, however, that if every assertion requires a reason, you will never finish the paper. When have you given enough support to a claim? One answer is when your reasons are uncontested or generally accepted. But the most reliable gauge is the extent of support required for assertions by your instructor in class and the readings for the course.

As you plan, be on the lookout for an idea that would serve as your major thesis. I say *major* because any thesis worth arguing about will be the result of a great number of subsidiary arguments that you will produce and evaluate along the way to your major conclusion. A thesis is not a statement that can be immediately proven by recourse to recorded information; it is, instead, a hypothesis worth discussing. Your thesis sentence should reveal to your reader not only the argument you have chosen but also your orientation toward it, the conclusion that your paper will attempt to prove, and how you will go about establishing it.

Here is an excerpt from a short article by Dino Corbin, general manager of television station KHSL in Chico, California. See if you can find his major thesis, and develop a narrowed thesis of your own that you would use to respond to his argument.

> On October 20 [1995], I canceled talk show Jenny Jones from KHSL-TV. I canceled the program and breached the contract because the show seriously stepped outside of the guidelines of decency that KHSL has stood for in this community since 1953. . . . America has rejected the idea that these shows are representative of this country. They are representatives of the worst of this country. Your response has also caused our industry to stop and take note of its impact and obligations to our society. In short, it is obvious that the American people expect and demand more from the greatest medium on earth.
>
> As broadcasting grew it became quickly apparent it possessed a unique power and impact on society. Because of this unique dynamic and in an effort

to insure the spirit of the First Amendment the government issued a license to broadcast, which is ultimately granted by the people of the community served by the broadcast license.

The owner or general manager became obligated as the gatekeeper; someone held locally responsible for the proper operation of the station. It is set forth in law, a broadcaster shall operate in the best interest of his or her community. A simple straight forward approach that has worked for over 45 years. Unfortunately, a dictate so simple it is easily forgotten by those of us in the day to day battle for ratings and dollars.

I have heard the excuse that the media just reflects society. That is true to some extent. It does not have to be the norm however. Today our society is not as healthy as in the past. Unfortunately a cycle develops that continues to feed upon itself. From our movies to the video games our children play, violence and unacceptable behavior begin to take on the image of normalcy. Add to this equation the corrosion of the American family, throw in a dose of government and you have a recipe for disaster.

It is apparent that the most powerful factor here is the media. Then, can not the media take a position toward correcting the problem? People in my position need to accept the notion that we have an obligation first and foremost to the communities we serve. (Editorial, *Chico Enterprise-Record*, 3 December 1995.)

In looking for a thesis, you are doing four jobs at once:

1. You are limiting the amount and kind of material that you must cover, making it manageable.
2. You are also increasing your own interest in the narrowing field of study.
3. You are working to establish your paper's purpose, the reason why you are writing about your topic. (If the only reason you can see for writing is to earn a good grade, then you probably won't.)
4. You are establishing your notion of who your audience is and what sort of approach to the subject might best catch their interest.

In short, you are gaining control over your writing context. For this reason, it is a good idea to come up with a thesis early on, a working thesis, which will very probably change as your thinking deepens but which will allow you establish a measure of order in the planning stage.

1.2.6   The Thesis Sentence

The introduction of your paper will contain a sentence that expresses in a nutshell the task that your paper intends to accomplish. This thesis sentence communicates your main idea, the one you are going to prove or defend or illustrate. The thesis sets up an expectation in the reader's mind that is your job to satisfy. But a thesis sentence is more than just the statement that informs your reader of your goal. In the planning stage, the thesis is a valuable tool to help you narrow your focus and confirm in your own mind your paper's purpose.

Imagine that you are taking a course on the philosophy of war and your initial topic is sovereignty and secession. You may be drawn to discuss the NATO action to rescue the sovereignty of the Bosnian State. So your thesis might be "NATO has a duty to protect sovereign governments in Europe constituted by democratic means." Some investigation into NATO's charter, however, will make it more difficult to include protecting the sovereignty of non-NATO members with NATO's mission. And investigation of the establishment of Bosnia via secession will uncover the fact that the Serbian population boycotted the elections to express their desire to keep their territory associated with the former Yugoslavia. So your eventual thesis might focus on the question of whether majority vote is sufficient to justify a central government established through secession and whether NATO is chartered to interfere in civil wars.

Note that your thesis develops in two ways. First, in your research you go beyond the assumptions presented as fact in the media to determine what NATO's charter is. Of course, the charter is open to interpretation, but you need to read the relevant documents in order to find the source of the interpretations and weigh their plausibility. The second way you develop your thesis is by asking questions of value. What is the relative value of the traditional association of a minority with the self-determination of a majority? Does a majority that secedes have the right to take a minority with it? What is the relevance of fears based on past human rights violations versus the duty to punish more current ones? You have just begun to untangle the thesis by consulting past fact and clashing values. And the process can go on further, as it will in the real world. Your basic duty is to refine the thesis into a manageable proposition that confronts the real aspects of a real problem and not an imagined scenario.

At some time during your preliminary thinking on a topic, you should consult the library to see how much published work has already been done. This search is beneficial in at least two ways:

1. It acquaints you with a body of writing that will become very important in the research phase of the paper.
2. It gives you a sense of how your topic is generally addressed by the community of scholars you are joining.

Is the topic as important as you think it is? Has there already been so much research on the topic as to make your inquiry, in its present formulation, irrelevant? These questions can be answered by turning to the literature. Unfortunately, many libraries have fallen behind the march of scholarship and current events. If the items in your bibliography (and your syllabus) are all from a previous decade or your parents' college years, you may want to consult the latest electronic research tools such as CD-ROM indexes or the internet to find more recent sources.

As you go about determining your topic, remember that one goal of writing philosophy is to enhance your reasoning abilities. Do not be afraid of the conclusions your reasoning leads you to accept on paper. You need not act on your conclusions at this moment in time. You can always postpone action to consider more argument. But allow yourself to participate in what Plato called the healing power of the argument. Your philosophy papers are just first, tentative steps toward forming your own views on the important issues of your life, and your philosophy instructors will not be sending copies of your papers home to your parents to evaluate.

1.2.7   Defining Your Audience

In any class that requires writing from you, it may sometimes be difficult to remember that the point of your writing is not simply to jump through the technical hoops imposed by the assignment. The point is communication, the transmission of your knowledge, your conclusions, to the reader in a way that suits you. Your task is to pass to your reader the spark of your own enthusiasm for your topic. Readers who were indifferent to your topic should look at it in a new way after reading your paper. This is the great challenge of writing: to enter into your reader's mind and leave behind new knowledge, new questions.

© Tribune Media Services. All Rights Reserved. Reprinted with permission.

It is tempting to think that most writing problems would be solved if the writer could view his or her writing as if it had been produced by another person. The ego barrier between writer and audience is the single greatest impediment to accurate communication. In order to reduce the discrepancy between your understanding and that of your audience, you must learn to consider the audience's needs. By the time you begin drafting, most, if not all, of your ideas have begun to attain coherent shape in your mind, so that virtually any words in which you try to phrase those ideas will reflect your thought accurately—to you. Your readers, however, do not already have in mind the conclusions that you have so painstakingly achieved. If you leave out of your writing material that is necessary to complete your readers' understanding of your argument, they may well not be able to supply that information themselves.

The potential for misunderstanding is present for any audience, whether it is made up of general readers, experts in the field, or your professor, who is reading, in part, to see how well you have mastered the constraints that govern the relationship between writer and reader. Consider a humorous example of miscommunication. The first British visitors to Australia asked the Aborigines the name of a curious-looking animal. They replied, "Kangaroo." Only on a subsequent visit, after the animal and its name had been introduced into the English language, did the British discover that "kangaroo" was an Aboriginal term meaning "What did you say?" Knowing your audience and communicating clearly can sometimes be more difficult than it first appears.

In view of the dangers of miscommunication, make your presentation as complete as possible, writing always as if to an audience whose previous knowledge of your topic is limited to information easily available to the general public. Do not write for your professor. Suppose you find yourself wondering whether you should include something and conclude you do not need to because "the professor knows that already." Include it. The professor wants to know what you have mastered, not what you think the professor already knows. It also helps to remember that your paper may not be read by the professor, but by a teaching assistant.

1.3   INVENTION STRATEGIES

In this chapter we have discussed methods of selecting and narrowing the topic of a paper. As your focus on a specific topic sharpens, you naturally begin to think about the kinds of information that will go into the paper. In the case of papers that do not require formal research, material comes largely from your own recollections. Indeed, one of the reasons instructors assign such papers is to convince you of the incredible richness of your memory, the vastness and variety of the "database" that you have accumulated and that, moment by moment, you continue to build.

So vast is your horde of information that it can sometimes be difficult to find within it the material that would best suit your paper. In other words, finding out what you already know about a topic is not always easy. Invention, a term borrowed from classical rhetoric, refers to the task of discovering, or recovering from memory, information about your topic. As we write, all of us go through some sort of invention procedure that helps us explore our topic. Some writers seem to have little problem coming up with material; others need more help. Over the centuries writers have devised different exercises that can help locate useful material housed in memory. We shall look at a few of these briefly.

1.3.1   Freewriting

Freewriting is an activity that forces you to get something down on paper. There is no waiting around for inspiration. Instead, you set yourself a time limit—three minutes, five minutes—and write for that length of time without stopping, not even to lift the pen from the paper or your hands from the keyboard. You can freewrite on a typewriter or a computer. Focus on the topic, and don't let the difficulty of finding relevant material stop you from writing. If necessary, you may begin by writing, over and over, some seemingly useless phrase, like, "I cannot think of anything to write about," or, perhaps, the name of your topic. Eventually, something else will occur to you. (It is surprising how long a three-minute freewriting can seem to take!)

At the end of the freewriting, look over what you have produced for anything of use. Granted, much of the writing will be unusable, but there may be an insight or two that you did not know you possessed.

In addition to its ability to recover usable material for your paper, freewriting has a couple of other benefits attached to it. First, it takes little time to do, which means you may repeat the exercise as often as you like within a relatively short span of time. Second, it breaks down some of the resistance that stands between you and the act of writing. There is no initial struggle to find something to say; you just write.

EXERCISE: Freewriting

Here are some sample topics from various philosophy classes. Surely you are in a class where at least one of these topics is relevant. Try freewriting on a topic or two and then apply it later when you are working on a paper assignment. It would be especially helpful to have a classmate perform the exercise also and exchange papers for comments. When you comment, do not be overly kind but avoid hurtful expressions. In other words, do not write comments such as "great idea" or "this is stupid." Ideally, a third classmate should then comment on the original freewriting and on the other reader's comments.

Is God's knowledge of the future compatible with human free will?

Should citizens serve as members of police review boards that investigate police use of force?

Should a non–family member have the power to veto a living will?

Do real estate brokers have a moral responsibility to tell clients that they are obliged to represent the interests of the seller, not the buyer?

Should the engineers in the *Challenger* disaster have gone public with their doubts about the O-ring?

Should agricultural conglomerates be allowed to patent genetically engineered strains of wheat?

1.3.2   **Brainstorming**

Brainstorming is, simply, making a list of ideas about a topic. It can be done quickly and, at first, without any need to order items into a coherent pattern. The point is to write down everything that occurs to you quickly and as briefly as possible, in individual words or short phrases. Once you have a good-sized list of items, you can then group the items according to relationships that you see among them. Brainstorming, then, allows you to uncover both ideas stored in your memory and useful associations among those ideas.

EXERCISE: Brainstorming

In my Criminal Justice Ethics class I asked students to brainstorm on police use of deadly force. Here is one student's list of responses.

Los Angeles
Rodney King
flight danger to the community
cops get shot too
body mass
the death penalty
my career
my family
due process
punishment
fellow officers

The student quickly realized that some of his associations fell into natural categories:

- The role of the police: apprehend offenders, protect the community, due process, apprehend but do not punish
- Conflicting personal duties: to the community, to my family and partner, to the suspect
- Questions of justice: whether deadly force is disproportionately applied to minorities; whether it should be applied to people fleeing crimes that would not result in the death penalty

This student decided to write on the third topic: whether there is reason to believe that police forces apply deadly force in a racially biased manner. Which of the remaining items in the original list would be helpful in developing this paper? Why?

1.3.3 Asking Questions

It is always possible to ask most or all of the following questions about any topic: Who? What? When? Where? Why? How? These questions force you to approach the topic in something like the way a journalist does, setting the topic within different perspectives that can then be compared to discover resonances within the material.

EXERCISE: Asking Questions

For a class in bioethics, a professor asked her class to write a paper describing the impact of living wills on the medical process. Here are some questions that a student in the class might logically ask to begin thinking toward a thesis.

Who are the candidates for mercy killing? (May parents write such wills for children?)

What are the qualifications for monitoring and overseeing the carrying out of a living will?

What, exactly, will be allowed in such a will? (Will doctors merely order the removal of life-sustaining technology, or will they also terminate feeding or administer terminal doses of drugs to end suffering?)

When during the course of an illness is a patient no longer competent to write such a will?

Where will living wills be carried out? (Is there a good reason not to allow such practices in a hospital, the home, or a nursing home?)

How are the wills to be written, filed, and stored?

Why do some people have living wills? Why would someone need to terminate life-supporting treatment?

When does the state or another social institution such as a religious hospital have a right to interfere in the application of a living will?

Can you think of other questions that would make for useful inquiry?

As you engage in invention strategies you are also doing other work. You are still narrowing your topic, for example, as well as making decisions that will affect your choice of tone or audience. You move forward on all fronts, each decision you make affecting the others. This means you must be flexible enough in your understanding of the paper's development to allow for slight course adjustments, alterations in your understanding of your goal. Never be so determined to prove a particular theory that you fail to notice when your own understanding of it changes. Seek out people who disagree with you. They are actually your best guides to refining your own views and attempting to approach something like objectivity.

1.3.4 Outlining

A paper that has all the facts but gives them to the reader in an ineffective order will confuse rather than inform or persuade. While there are various methods of grouping ideas, none is potentially more effective than outlining. Unfortunately, no organizing process is more often misunderstood.

1.3.4.1 Outlining for Yourself

There are really two jobs that outlining can do. First, it can serve as a means of forcing you, the writer, to gain a better understanding of your ideas by arranging them according to their interrelationships. There is one primary rule of outlining: Ideas of equal weight are placed on the same level within the outline. This rule requires you to determine the relative importance of your ideas. You have to decide which ideas are of the same type or order and into which subtopic each idea best fits.

If, in the planning stage, you arrange your ideas with care in a coherent outline, your grasp of your topic will be greatly enhanced. You will have linked your ideas logically together and given a skeleton to the body of the paper. This sort of subordinating and coordinating activity is difficult, however, and as a result, inexperienced writers sometimes fail to pay the necessary attention to the outline and begin to write their first draft without an effective outline, hoping for the best. That hope is usually disappointed, especially in complex papers involving research.

1.3.4.2 Outlining for Your Reader

The second job that an outline does is aimed not at the writer's understanding, but at the reader's. An outline accompanying your paper can serve the reader as a blueprint to the paper, a summary of the paper's points and their interrelationships. A busy policy maker, for example, can quickly get a sense of your paper's goal and the argument you have used to promote it by consulting your outline. This accompanying outline, then, is very important, since its clarity and coherence help to determine how much attention your audience will give to your ideas.

1.3.4.3 Formal Outline Pattern

Following the pattern below during the planning stage of your paper helps to guarantee that your ideas are placed logically.

Thesis sentence (prefaces the organized outline)
  I. First main idea
    A. First subordinate idea
      1. Reason, example, or illustration
      2. Reason, example, or illustration

a. Detail supporting reason #2
b. Detail supporting reason #2
B. Second subordinate idea
II. Second main idea

Notice that each level of the paper must have more than one entry; for every A there must be at least a B (and, if required, a C, D, and so on), for every 1 there must be a 2. This arrangement forces you to compare ideas, looking carefully at each one to determine its place among the others. The insistence on assigning relative values to your ideas is what makes your outline an effective organizing tool.

1.3.5 Organizing Your Thoughts

Kareem, a student in a bioethics class, researched the treatment of newborn Down syndrome children who are also born with intestinal blockage. Typically, hospitals allow parents of such children to refuse a medical procedure to remove the blockage, allowing their child to die by starvation. Kareem was initially intrigued by the idea that it would be more humane to give the child a lethal injection. He also noticed the inconsistency of allowing some Down children to die just because they conveniently had another easily corrected medical condition. Kareem knew the real reason these children were euthanized was that they had Down syndrome.

Kareem understood that he had to consider several different issues in coming to terms with this social practice. He knew that there were cases of euthanasia that were voluntary, involuntary, and nonvoluntary. And his initial idea was that the difference between involuntary and nonvoluntary had to do with whether the patient was in a state in which to give consent. So an unconscious person would only be a candidate for nonvoluntary euthanasia, unless he or she had filed a living will.

As Kareem outlined his paper, another distinction arose between actively terminating someone or merely letting that person die. He decided to label these alternatives active and passive euthanasia. Kareem was unsure whether removing life support systems was active or passive, because that action did involve doing something to the patient, but eventually he classified the action as passive since it did not seek directly to bring about death.

Do you think that Kareem made the correct logical groupings? How many types of euthanasia are there if we agree that Kareem's categories are mutually exclusive and exhaustive? In which category should Kareem place the practice described above for children with intestinal blockage?

EXERCISE: Formulate a Thesis

As an exercise, formulate a thesis about the morality of the form of euthanasia described in the case of Kareem above. Can you fill in the outline sketch above with your own ideas? Can you produce a more extensive outline? It might help you to freewrite before attempting the outline.

1.4   THE ROUGH DRAFT

Sometime toward the end of the planning comes the writing of the first draft. Using your thesis and outline as direction markers, you must now weave your amalgam of ideas, data, and persuasion strategies into logically ordered sentences and paragraphs. Though adequate prewriting may make the drafting easier than it might have been, still it will not be easy. Writers establish their own individual methods of encouraging themselves to forge ahead with the draft, but here are some tips to bear in mind.

1. Remember that this first effort at writing is a *rough draft,* not the final draft. At this stage, it is not necessary that every word you write be the best possible word. Do not put that sort of pressure on yourself; you must not allow anything to slow you down now. Writing is not like sculpting, where every chip is permanent; you can always go back to your draft later and add, delete, reword, rearrange. No matter how much effort you have put into planning, you cannot be sure how much of this first draft you will eventually keep. It may take several drafts to get one that you find satisfactory.

2. Give yourself sufficient time to write. Don't delay the first draft by telling yourself there is still more research to do. You cannot uncover all the material there is to know on a particular subject, so don't fool yourself into trying. Remember that writing is a process of discovery. You may have to begin writing before you can see exactly what sort of final research you need to do. Remember that there are other tasks waiting for you after the first draft is finished, so allow for them as you determine your writing schedule.

This matter of giving yourself time is very important for another reason. The more time that passes after you write a draft, the better your ability to view it with greater objectivity. It is very difficult to evaluate your writing accurately soon after you complete it. You need to cool down, to recover from the effort of putting all those words together. The "colder" you get on your writing, the better able you are to read it as if it were written by someone else. Thus the better able you will be to acknowledge the changes you will need to make to strengthen the paper.

3. Stay sharp. Keep in mind the plan you created for yourself as you narrowed your topic, composed a thesis sentence, and outlined the material. But if as you write you feel a strong need to change the plan a bit, do not be afraid to do so. Be ready for surprises dealt you by your own growing understanding of your topic. Your goal is to render your best thinking on the subject as accurately as possible.

1.4.1   Language Choices

To be convincing, your writing has to be authoritative. That is, you have to sound as if you have complete confidence in your ability to convey your ideas in words. Sentences that sound stilted, that suffer from weak phrasing or the use of clichés, are not going to win supporters for the aims that you express in your paper. So a major question becomes: How can I sound confident? Here are some points to consider as you work to convey to your readers that necessary sense of authority.

Level of Formality

Tone is one of the primary methods by which you signal to your readers who you are and what your attitude is toward them and toward your topic. The major choice you make has to do with the level of language formality that you feel is most appropriate to your audience. The informal tone you would use in a letter to a friend might well be out of place in a paper on "The Argument from Design as a Proof of the Existence of God." Remember that tone is only part of the overall decision that you make about how to present your information. Formality is, to some extent, a function of individual word choices and phrasing. Is it appropriate to use contractions like "isn't" or "they'll"? Would the strategic use of a sentence fragment for effect be out of place? The use of informal language, the personal "I," and the second person "you" is traditionally forbidden—for better or worse—in certain kinds of writing. Often part of the challenge of writing a formal paper is, simply, how to give your prose bite while staying within the conventions.

1.4.2   Descriptive Language

Language that appeals to the reader's senses will always engage his interest more fully than language that is abstract. This is especially important for writing in disciplines that tend to deal in abstracts, such as philosophy. The typical paper, with its discussions of abstract principles, is usually in danger of floating off on a cloud of abstractions, drifting further away in each paragraph from the felt life of the reader. Whenever appropriate, appeal to your reader's sense of sight, hearing, taste, touch, or smell.

1.4.2.1 Jargon

One way to lose readers quickly is to overwhelm them with jargon—phrases that have a special, usually technical meaning within your discipline but are unfamiliar to the average reader. The very occasional use of jargon may add an effective touch of atmosphere, but anything more than that will severely dampen a reader's enthusiasm for the paper. Often a reason for jargon is the writer's desire to impress the reader by sounding lofty or knowledgeable. Unfortunately, all jargon usually does is make for confusion. In fact the use of jargon is often an index of the writer's lack of connection to the audience.

Philosophical writing is a mine field of jargon. For better or worse, philosophers have borrowed many technical terms from ordinary usage, such as "utilitarian" and "idealism," and given them special technical meanings. Be careful: You may think you understand a philosophical term when you do not. How do you know when to check a glossary like the one at the back of this book? You could scan it now and see which terms are familiar. Read those terms and see if they have meaning different from what you associate with them. (What *is* metaphysics anyway?) Or use the rule that if a term recurs several times in a philosopher's work you had better check it.

Jargon also occurs when writers do not commonly address nonspecialists and believe their readers are all completely attuned to their terminology. It may be that these writers occasionally hope to obscure damaging information or potentially unpopular ideas in confusing language. Or the problem could simply be fuzzy thinking on the writer's part. Unfortunately, not all the great philosophers were great writers. Whatever the reason, do not imitate the style of writers, no matter how great they are as philosophers, if they engage in jargon and obfuscation.

Students may feel that, in order to be accepted as philosophers, their papers should conform to the practices of their published peers. This is a mistake. Remember that it is never better to write a cluttered or confusing sentence than a clear one and that burying your ideas in jargon defeats the effort that you went through to form them.

EXERCISE: Spot the Jargon

Here are some words that are part of philosophical jargon. You will run into a good number of them. Some of them appear deceptively simple, some are difficult to penetrate since they appear in ordinary language with firm associations, and some are even more impenetrable after years of studying and teaching. See if you can write a sentence or two about some of them, saying what you think they mean: freedom, free will, idealism, pragmatism, rationality, human rights, natural rights, utilitarian, the right to life, a woman's right to choose, epistemology, being, becoming, dread.

1.4.2.2   Clichés

In the heat of composition, as you are looking for words to help you form your ideas, it is sometimes easy to plug in a cliché—a phrase that has attained universal recognition by overuse. (Clichés differ from jargon in that clichés are part of the general public's everyday language, while jargon is specific to the language of experts in a particular field.) Our vocabularies are brimming with clichés:

It's raining cats and dogs.

That issue is dead as a doornail.

It's time for the governor to face the music.

Angry voters made a beeline for the ballot box.

Unless you have some very special reason for using a cliché, *don't.* They can sap energy out of your prose.

1.4.2.3   Avoid Weasel Words

Weasel words get their name from the practice weasels have of removing eggs from a nest, sucking out the good stuff inside, and replacing the empty shell in the nest. Whether out of politeness or an attempt to avoid criticism, philosophers often fall into the habit of using weasel words. Some examples are "it appears that," "it seems to me to follow that," and "this supports the conclusion that." These and many similar phrases essentially say that something might be the case and that the writer believes it is the case. Weasel words are devices for hiding the fact that you have little or no evidence for a conclusion but advocate a view nonetheless. By using them you also free yourself from having to offer evidence, since you make only a modest claim and yet leave the impression that you have said something substantial. Besides being intellectually dishonest, weasel words are redundant; a string of them makes for awkward reading. You should not have to tell your audience what seems to be the appropriate conclusion. Just state it. It is your paper. They will know it is your conclusion.

1.4.2.4   Sexist Language

Language can be a very powerful method of either reinforcing or destroying cultural stereotypes. By treating the sexes in subtly different ways in your language, you may unknowingly be committing an act of discrimination. A common example is the use of the pronoun *he* to refer to a person whose gender has not been identified. But there are many other writing situations in which sexist bias may appear. For example:

SEXIST: A lawyer should always treat his client with respect.

CORRECTED: A lawyer should always treat his or her client with respect.

CORRECTED: Lawyers should always treat their clients with respect.

SEXIST: Man is a political animal.

CORRECTED: People are political animals.

There are other methods of avoiding sexual bias in your writing. Some writers, faced with the pronoun dilemma illustrated above, alternate the use of male and female personal pronouns (a strategy used for examples in this manual).

In its more obvious forms, sexist language denies role models to a large number of your readers and so hampers communication. Make sure your writing is not guilty of this subtle form of discrimination. Remember, language is more than the mere vehicle of your thought. Your words shape perceptions for your reader. How well you say something will profoundly affect your reader's response to it.

1.5   REVISING YOUR WRITING

Revising is one of the most important steps in assuring that your essay is a success. While unpracticed writers often think of revision as little more than making sure all the i's are dotted and t's are crossed, it is much more than that. Revising is *reseeing* the essay, looking at it from other perspectives, trying always to align your view with the view that will be held by your audience. Research in composition indicates that we are actually revising all the time, in every phase of the writing process, as we reread phrases, rethink the placement of an item in an outline, or test a new topic sentence for a paragraph. Subjecting your entire hard-fought draft to cold, objective scrutiny is one of the hardest activities to master in the writing process, but it is absolutely necessary. You have to make sure that you have said everything that needs to be said clearly and in logical order. One confusing passage and the reader's attention is deflected from where you want it to be. Suddenly the reader has to become a detective, trying to figure out why you wrote what you did and what you meant by it. You don't want to throw such obstacles in the path of meaning.

Here are some tips to help you with revision.

1. *Give yourself adequate time to revise.* As discussed above, you need time to become "cold" on your paper in order to analyze it objectively. After you have written your draft, spend some time away from it. Try to come back to it as if it had been written by someone other than yourself.

2. *Read the paper carefully.* This is tougher than it sounds. One good strategy is to read it aloud or to have a friend read it aloud while you listen. (Note, however, that friends do not usually make the best critics. They are rarely trained in revision techniques and are often unwilling to risk disappointing you by giving your paper a really thorough examination.)

3. *Have a list of specific items to check.* It is important to revise in an orderly fashion, in stages, looking first at large concerns, such as the overall structure, then rereading the paper for problems with smaller elements such as paragraph organization or sentence structure.

4. *Check for unity*—the clear and logical relation of all parts of the essay to its thesis. Make sure that every paragraph relates well to the whole of the paper and is in the right place.

5. *Check for coherence.* Make sure there are no gaps between the different parts of the argument. Look to see that you have adequate transition everywhere it is needed. Transitional elements are markers indicating places where the paper's focus or attitude changes. Transitional elements can be one word long—*however, although, unfortunately, luckily*—or as long as a sentence or a paragraph. Transitional elements rarely introduce new material. Instead, they are direction pointers, either indicating a shift to new subject matter or signaling how the writer wishes certain material to be interpreted by the reader. Because you, the writer, already know where and why your paper changes direction and how you want particular passages to be received, it can be very difficult for you to catch those places in your paper where transition is needed. One place where transitional elements are particularly important, and where they do introduce new material, is in persuasive papers. When you switch from exposition to evaluation and persuasion you introduce new material and should formulate another paragraph in which you explain how you are about to relate fact to a value decision. Here is an example of this sort of transitional paragraph:

> The major responsibility of the media is to educate viewers. Talk shows are the only place on television where the various ethnic minorities that make up America speak to each other honestly as equals. They also provide a uniquely honest discussion of two crucial areas of contemporary life: sex and drugs. I will argue that Mr. Corbin shirks responsibility by limiting this discussion.

6. *Avoid unnecessary repetition.* There are two types of repetition that can annoy a reader: repetition of content and repetition of wording.

Repetition of content occurs when you return to a subject that you have already discussed. Ideally, you want to say what you have to say about a topic once, memorably, and then move on to your next topic. Organizing a paper is a difficult task, however, that usually occurs through a process of enlightenment as to purposes and strategies. It is possible for an early draft to circle back to a subject that you have already dealt with and to begin to treat the same material over again. This sort of repetition can happen even if you have made use of prewriting strategies. What is worse, it can be difficult for you, the writer, to acknowledge the repetition to yourself—to admit to yourself that the material you have worked so hard to shape on page two returns on page five in much the same shape.

As you write and revise, bear this in mind: Any unnecessary repetition of content that you allow into your final draft is potentially annoying to your reader, who is working to make sense of the argument she is reading and does not want to be distracted by a passage repeating material already encountered. You must train yourself, through practice, to read through your draft, looking for material that you have repeated unnecessarily.

Repetition of wording occurs when you overuse certain phrases or words. This sort of repetition can make your prose sound choppy and uninspired, as the following examples indicate:

- The subcommittee's report on education reform will surprise a number of people. A number of people will want copies of the report.
- The chairman said at a press conference that he is happy with the report. He will circulate it to the local news agencies in the morning. He will also make sure that the city council has copies.
- I became upset when I heard how the committee had voted. I called the chairman and expressed my reservations about the committee's decision. I told him I felt that he had let the teachers and students of the state down. I also issued a press statement.

Avoid a condition known by composition teachers as the I-syndrome, a version of which occurs in the last passage above. The most characteristic manifestation of the I-syndrome in philosophy papers is the use of the expressions "I think," "I feel," and "I believe." Their use is, of course, redundant. But they also signal to the critical reader that you have just offered a claim that, given the use of these expressions in ordinary language, is probably unsupported. So the occurrence of these expressions in your drafts can be a handy guide for where revision is appropriate.

Not all repetition is bad. You may wish to repeat a phrase for rhetorical effect or special emphasis: *I came. I saw. I conquered.* Just make sure that any repetition in your paper is intentional, placed there to produce a specific effect.

1.5.1 Editing

Editing is sometimes confused with the more involved process of revising. But editing happens later, after you have wrestled through your first draft—and maybe your second and third—and arrived at the final draft. Even though your draft now contains all the information you want to impart and has arranged the information to your satisfaction, there are still many factors to check, such as sentence structure, spelling, and punctuation.

It is at this point that an unpracticed writer might let down his guard. After all, most of the work on the paper is finished; the big jobs of discovering material and organizing and drafting it have been completed. But watch out! Editing is as important as any other job in the writing process. Any error you allow in the final draft will count against you in the mind of the reader. It may not seem fair, but a minor error—a misspelling or the confusing placement of a comma—will make a much greater impression on your reader than perhaps it should. Remember: Everything about your paper is your responsibility. That includes getting even the supposedly little jobs right. Careless editing undermines the effectiveness of your paper. It would be a shame if all the hard work you put into prewriting, drafting, and revising were to be damaged because you carelessly allowed a comma splice.

Most of the tips given above for revising hold for editing as well. It is best to edit in stages, looking for only one or two kinds of errors each time you reread the paper. Focus especially on errors that you remember committing in the past. If, for instance, you know you have a tendency to misplace commas, go through your paper looking at each comma carefully. If you have a weakness for writing unintentional sentence fragments, read each sentence aloud to make sure that it is, indeed, a complete sentence. Have you accidentally shifted verb tenses anywhere, moving from past to present tense for no reason? Do all the subjects in your sentences agree in number with their verbs? Now is the time to find out.

1.5.2 Catching Mistakes

One tactic for catching mistakes in sentence structure is to read the sentences aloud, starting with the last one in the paper and then moving to the next-to-last, then the previous sentence, thus going backward through the paper (reading each sentence in the normal, left-to-right manner, of course) until you reach the first sentence of the introduction. This backward progression strips each sentence of its rhetorical context and helps you to focus on its internal structure.

1.5.3 Miscues

Watch out for miscues—problems with a sentence that the writer simply does not see. Remember that your search for errors is hampered in two ways:

1. As the writer, you hope not to find any errors with your writing. This desire not to find mistakes can lead you to miss sighting them when they occur.
2. Since you know your material so well, it is easy to supply missing material unconsciously as you read—a word, a piece of punctuation—as if it were present.

EXERCISE: Miscues

How difficult is it to see that something is missing in the following sentence?

Unfortunately, legislators often have too little regard their constituents.

We can even guess that the missing word is probably *for,* which should be inserted after *regard.* It is quite possible, however, that the writer of the sentence, as he reads it, will supply the missing word automatically, as if he has seen it on the page. This is a miscue, and miscues can be hard for writers to spot because they are so close to their material.

Editing is the stage where you finally answer those minor questions that you put off earlier when you were wrestling with wording and organization. Any ambiguities regarding the use of abbreviations, italics, numerals, capital letters, titles (when do you capitalize the title *president,* for example?), hyphens, dashes (usually created on a typewriter or computer by striking the hyphen key twice), apostrophes, and quotation marks have to be cleared up now. You must check to see that you have used the required formats for footnotes, endnotes, margins, and page numbers.

Guessing is not allowed. Sometimes unpracticed writers who realize that they don't quite understand a particular rule of grammar, punctuation, or format often do nothing to fill that knowledge gap. Instead they rely on guesswork and their own logic—which is not always up to the task of dealing with so contrary a language as English—to get them through problems that they could solve if only they referred to a writing manual. Remember this: It does not matter to the reader why or how an error shows up in your writing. It only matters that, in this instance, you as the writer have dropped your guard. You must not allow a careless error to undo the good work that you have done.

1.5.4   Proofreading

Before you hand in your final version of the paper, it is vital that you check it over one more time to make sure there are no errors of any sort. This job is called proofreading or proofing. In essence, you are looking for many of the same things you checked for during editing, but now you are doing it on the last draft, which has been typed and is about to be submitted to your audience. Proofreading is as important as editing; you may have missed an error that you still have time to find, or an error may have been introduced when the draft was recopied or typed for the last time. Like every other stage of the writing process, proofreading is your responsibility.

At this stage, it is essential that you check for typing mistakes: letters transposed or left out of words, missing words, phrases, or punctuation. If you have had the paper professionally typed, you still must check it carefully. Do not rely solely on the typist's proofreading. If you are creating your paper on a computer or a word processor, you may have unintentionally inserted a command that alters a passage of your document drastically—either slicing out or doubling a word or a line or a sentence at the touch of a key. Make sure such accidental mistakes have not occurred. Even if you use the computer's spellcheck, it is still important to proofread your paper, since the program, which will catch only those words that are spelled incorrectly, may not find words that are correctly spelled but are wrong in context (such as typing "three" when "there" is meant).

Above all else, remember that your paper represents you. It is a product of your best thought, your most energetic and imaginative response to a writing challenge. If you have maintained your enthusiasm for the project and worked through the different stages of the writing process honestly and carefully, you should produce a paper you can be proud of, one that will serve its readers well.

2

Writing Competently

Properly written texts are like spiders' webs: tight, concentric, transparent, well-spun and firm. They draw into themselves all the creatures of the air. Metaphors flitting hastily through them become their nourishing prey. Subject matter comes winging towards them. The soundness of a conception can be judged by whether it causes one quotation to summon another. Where thought has opened up one cell of reality, it should, without violence by the subject, penetrate the next. It proves its relation to the object as soon as other objects crystallize around it. In the light that it casts on its chosen substance, others begin to glow.

—Theodor Adorno

2.1 GENERAL RULES OF GRAMMAR AND STYLE

2.1.1 Competent Writing

Good writing places your thoughts in your readers' minds in exactly the way you want them to be there. Good writing tells your readers just what you want them to know without telling them anything you do not wish to say. That may sound odd, but the fact is, writers have to be careful not to let unwanted messages slip into their writing. Look, for example, at the passage below, taken from a paper analyzing the impact of a worker-retraining program in the writer's state. Hidden within the prose is a message that jeopardizes the paper's success. Can you detect the message? What's wrong here?

Recent articles written on the subject of police use of deadly force have had little to say about the particular problems dealt with in this paper. Since few of these articles focus on the role of race in the application of deadly force.

Chances are, when you reached the end of the second "sentence," you sensed something missing, a gap in logic or coherence, and your eye ran back through both sentences to find the place where things went wrong. The second sentence is actually not a sentence at all. It does have certain features of a sentence—a subject, for example ("few"), and a verb ("focus")—but its first word ("Since") subordinates the entire clause that follows, taking away its ability to stand on its own as a complete idea. The second "sentence," which is properly called a subordinate clause, merely fills in some information about the first sentence, telling us why recent articles about dislocated workers fail to deal with problems discussed in the present paper.

The sort of error represented by the second "sentence" is commonly called a sentence fragment, and it conveys to the reader a message that no writer wants to send: that the writer either is careless or, worse, has not mastered the language. Language errors such as fragments, misplaced commas, or shifts in verb tense send up little red flags in readers' minds. The result is that readers lose a little of their concentration on the issue being discussed. They become distracted and begin to wonder about the language competency of the writer. The writing loses effectiveness.

Remember, whatever goal you set for your paper, whether you want it to persuade, describe, analyze, or speculate, you must also set another goal: to display language competence. Without it, your paper will not completely achieve its other aims. Language errors spread doubt like a virus; they jeopardize all the hard work you have done on your paper.

Credibility for the majority of your audience still depends upon language competence. Anyone who doubts this should remember the beating that Dan Quayle took in the press when he was Vice President of the United States for misspelling the word "potato" at a Trenton, New Jersey, spelling bee on 15 June 1992. His error caused a storm of humiliating publicity for the hapless Quayle, adding to an impression of his general incompetence.

Correctness Is Relative

Although they may seem minor, the fact is that the sort of language errors we are discussing—often called surface errors—can be extremely damaging in certain kinds of writing. Surface errors come in a variety of types, including misspellings, punctuation problems, grammar errors, and the inconsistent use of abbreviations, capitalization, or numerals. These errors are an affront to your reader's notion of correctness, and therein lies one of the biggest problems with surface errors. Different audiences tolerate different levels of correctness. You already know that you can get away with surface errors in, say, a letter to a friend, who will not judge you harshly for them, while those same errors in a job application letter might eliminate you from consideration for the job. Correctness depends to an extent upon context.

Another problem with correctness is that the rules governing correctness shift over time. What would have been an error to your grandparent's generation—the splitting of an infinitive, for example, or the ending of a sentence with a preposition—is taken in stride today by most readers. So how do you write correctly when the rules shift from person to person and over time? Here are some tips.

2.1.2   Consider Your Audience

One of the great risks of writing is that even the simplest of choices you make regarding wording or punctuation can sometimes prejudice your audience against you in ways that may seem unfair.

For example, look again at the old grammar "rule" forbidding the splitting of infinitives. After decades of counseling students to *never* split an infinitive (something this sentence has just done), composition experts now concede that a split infinitive is not a grammar crime. But suppose you have written a position paper trying to convince your city council of the need to hire security personnel for the library, and half of the council members—the people you wish to convince—remember their eighth-grade grammar teacher's outdated warning about splitting infinitives. How will they respond when you tell them, in your introduction, that librarians are ordered "to always accompany" visitors to the rare book room because of the threat of vandalism? How much of their attention have you suddenly lost because of their automatic recollection of a nonrule? It is possible, in other words, to write correctly and still offend your readers' notions of language competence.

Make sure that you tailor the surface features of your writing to the level of competency that your readers require. When in doubt, take a conservative approach. The same goes for the level of formality you should assume. Your audience might be just as distracted by contractions as by a split infinitive.

2.1.3   Aim for Consistency

When dealing with a language question for which there are different answers—such as whether or not to place a comma after the second item in a series of three ("In his discourse the young philosopher addressed freedom of religion, the inequities of the slave system, and the question of who holds earthly authority in a frontier community")—always use the same strategy. If, for example, you avoid splitting one infinitive, avoid splitting *all* infinitives.

2.1.4   Have Confidence in What You Know

It is easy for unpracticed writers to allow their occasional mistakes to depress them about their writing ability. The fact is, most of what we know about writing is right. We are all capable, for example, of phrasing utterances that are grammatically sound, even if we cannot list the grammar rules by which we achieve coherence. Most writers who worry about their chronic errors have fewer than they think. Becoming distressed about errors makes writing more difficult.

Grammar

As various composition theorists have pointed out, the word *grammar* has several definitions. One meaning is "the formal patterns in which words must be arranged in order to convey meaning." We learn these patterns very early in life and use them spontaneously, without thinking. Our understanding of grammatical patterns is extremely sophisticated, despite the fact that few of us can actually cite the rules by which the patterns work. Patrick Hartwell tested grammar learning by asking native English speakers of different ages and levels of education, including high school teachers, to arrange these words in natural order:

French   the   young   girls   four

Everyone he asked could produce the natural order for this phrase: "the four young French girls." Yet none of Hartwell's respondents said they knew the rule that governs the order of the words. (Patrick Hartwell. "Grammar, Grammars, and the Teaching of Grammar." *College English* 47 (1985), 111.)

2.1.5   Eliminate Chronic Errors

All right, then, the question arises: If just thinking about our errors has a negative effect on our writing, then how do we learn to write more correctly? Perhaps the best answer is simply to write as often as possible. Give yourself practice in putting your thoughts into written shape, and get lots of practice in revising and proofing your work. And as you write and revise, be honest with yourself, and patient. Chronic errors are like bad habits; getting rid of them takes time.

You probably know of one or two problem areas in your writing that you could have eliminated but have not done so. Instead, you have "fudged" your writing at the critical points, relying upon half-remembered formulas from past English classes or trying to come up with logical solutions to your writing problems. (Warning: The English language does not always work in a way that seems logical.) You may have simply decided that comma rules are unlearnable or that you will never understand the difference between the verbs *lay* and *lie*. And so you guess, and get the rule wrong a good part of the time. What a shame, when just a little extra work would give you mastery over those few gaps in your understanding and boost your confidence as well.

Instead of continuing with this sort of guesswork, instead of living with the gaps, why not face the problem areas now and learn the rules that have heretofore escaped you? What follows is a discussion of those surface features of a paper where errors most commonly occur. You will probably be familiar with most if not all of the rules discussed, but there may well be a few you have not yet mastered. Now is the time to do so.

2.2   SENTENCE STRUCTURE

2.2.1   Fused Sentences

A fused sentence is one in which two or more independent clauses (passages that can stand as complete sentences) have been run together without the aid of any suitable connecting word, phrase, or punctuation. There are several ways to correct a fused sentence:

INCORRECT: The philosophers were exhausted they had debated for two hours.

CORRECTED: The philosophers were exhausted. They had debated for two hours. [The linked independent clauses have been separated into two sentences.]

CORRECTED: The philosophers were exhausted; they had debated for two hours. [A semicolon marks the break between the two clauses.]

CORRECTED: The philosophers were exhausted, having debated for two hours. [The second independent clause has been rephrased as a dependent clause.]

INCORRECT: Our policy analysis impressed the committee it also convinced them to reconsider their action.

CORRECTED: Our policy analysis impressed the committee and also convinced them to reconsider their action. [The second clause has been rephrased as part of the first clause.]

CORRECTED: Our policy analysis impressed the committee, and it also convinced them to reconsider their action. [The two clauses have been separated by a comma and a coordinating word.]

While a fused sentence is easily noticeable to the reader, it can be maddeningly difficult for the writer to catch in proofreading. Unpracticed writers tend to read through the fused spots, sometimes supplying the break that is usually heard when sentences are spoken. To check for fused sentences, read the independent clauses in your paper carefully, making sure that there are adequate breaks among all of them.

2.2.2   Sentence Fragments

A fragment is an incomplete part of a sentence that is punctuated and capitalized as if it were an entire sentence. It is an especially disruptive error, because it obscures the connections that the words of a sentence must make in order to complete the reader's understanding.

Students sometimes write fragments because they are concerned that a particular sentence is growing too long and needs to be shortened. Remember that cutting the length of a sentence merely by adding a period somewhere along its length often creates a fragment. When checking your writing for fragments, it is essential that you read each sentence carefully to determine whether it has: (1) a complete subject and a verb, and (2) a subordinating word before the subject and verb, which makes the construction a subordinate clause rather than a complete sentence.

2.2.2.1   *Types of Sentence Fragments*

Some fragments lack a verb:

INCORRECT: The chairperson of our department, having received a letter from the newspaper editor. [Note: The word *having*, which resembles a verb, is here being used as a gerund introducing a participial phrase. Watch out for words that look like verbs but are being used in another way.]

CORRECTED: The chairperson of our department received a letter from the newspaper editor.

Some fragments lack a subject. They are simply continuations of a sentence:

INCORRECT: Our study shows that there is broad support for improvement in the health care system. And in the unemployment system.

CORRECTED: Our study shows that there is broad support for improvement in the health care system and in the unemployment system.

Some fragments are subordinate clauses:

INCORRECT: After the latest edition of the newspaper came out. [This clause has the two major components of a complete sentence:

a subject (*edition*) and a verb (*came*). Indeed, if the first word (*After*) were deleted, the clause would be a complete sentence. But that first word is a *subordinating word,* which acts to prevent the following clause from standing on its own as a complete sentence. Watch out for this kind of construction. It is called a *subordinate clause,* and it is not a sentence.]

CORRECTED: After the latest edition of the newspaper came out, the chancellor's press secretary was overwhelmed with phone calls. [A common method of correcting a subordinate clause that has been punctuated as a complete sentence is to connect it to the complete sentence to which its meaning is most closely connected.]

INCORRECT: Several congressmen asked for copies of the feminist philosopher's position paper. Because it called for the banning of pornography. [The clause beginning after the first period is a subordinate clause written as if it were a complete sentence.]

CORRECTED: Several congressmen asked for copies of the feminist philosopher's position paper because it called for the banning of pornography.

2.2.3   Dangling Modifiers

A *modifier* is a word or group of words used to describe—to *modify* our understanding of—another word in the sentence. A *dangling modifier* appears either at the beginning or ending of a sentence and seems to be describing some word other than the one the writer obviously intended. The modifier therefore "dangles," disconnected from its intended meaning. It is often hard for the writer to spot a dangling modifier, but readers can—and will—find them, and the result can be disastrous for the sentence, as the following examples demonstrate:

INCORRECT: Flying low over Washington, the White House was seen.
CORRECTED: Flying low over Washington, we saw the White House.

INCORRECT: Worried at the cost of the program, sections of the bill were trimmed in committee.

CORRECTED: Worried at the cost of the program, the committee trimmed sections of the bill.

CORRECTED: The committee trimmed sections of the bill because they were worried at the cost of the program.

INCORRECT: To lobby for prison reform, a lot of effort went into the TV ads.

CORRECTED: The lobby group put a lot of effort into the TV ads advocating prison reform.

INCORRECT: Stunned, the television broadcast the defeated senator's concession speech.

CORRECTED: The television broadcast the stunned senator's concession speech.

Note that in the first two incorrect sentences above, the confusion is largely due to the use of passive-voice verbs: ". . . the White House *was seen*," ". . . sections of the bill *were trimmed*." Often, though not always, the cause of a dangling modifier is the fact that the actor in the sentence—*we* in the first sentence, *the committee* in the second—is either distanced from the modifier or obliterated by the passive voice verb. It is a good idea to avoid passive voice unless you have a specific reason for using it.

One way to check for dangling modifiers is to examine all modifiers at the beginnings or endings of your sentences. Look especially for *to be* phrases (*to lobby*) or for words ending in *-ing* or *-ed* at the start of the modifier. Then check to see if the modified word is close enough to the phrase to be properly connected.

2.2.4   Parallelism

Series of two or more words, phrases, or clauses within a sentence should be structured in the same grammatical way. Parallel structures can add power and balance to your writing by creating a strong rhetorical rhythm. Here is a famous example of parallelism from the U.S. Constitution. (The capitalization, preserved from the original document, follows eighteenth-century custom. Parallel structures have been italicized.)

Preamble to the Constitution
We the People of the United States, in Order *to form a more perfect Union, Establish Justice, insure Domestic Tranquility, provide for the common defence, promote the general Welfare, and secure the Blessings of Liberty to ourselves and our Posterity,* do *ordain* and *establish* this Constitution for the United States of America.

There are actually two series in this sentence, the first composed of six phrases that each complete the infinitive phrase beginning with the word *to* (*to form*, [*to*] *Establish*, [*to*] *insure*, [*to*] *provide*, [*to*] *promote*, [*to*] *secure*), the second consisting of two verbs (*ordain* and *establish*). These parallel series appeal to our love of balance, of pattern, and give an authoritative tone to the sentence. The writer, we feel, has thought long and carefully about the matter at hand and has taken firm control of it.

Because we find a special satisfaction in balanced structures, we are more likely to remember ideas phrased in parallelisms than in less highly ordered language. For this reason, as well as for the sense of authority and control that they suggest, parallel structures are common in political and philosophical utterances:

> We hold these truths to be self-evident, that all men are created equal, that they are endowed by their Creator with certain unalienable Rights, that among these are Life, Liberty, and the pursuit of Happiness. (Declaration of Independence)

> But, in a larger sense, we can not dedicate—we can not consecrate—we can not hallow—this ground. The brave men, living and dead, who struggled here, have consecrated it, far above our poor power to add or detract. The world will little note, nor long remember what we say here, but it can never forget what they did here. (Abraham Lincoln, Gettysburg Address)

> A little song, a little dance, a little seltzer down your pants. (Chuckles the Clown on the meaning of life, the Mary Tyler Moore television show)

> Life in the state of nature is "solitary, poore, nasty, brutish, and short." (Thomas Hobbes, *Leviathan*)

Faulty Parallelism

If the parallelism of a passage is not carefully maintained, the writing can seem sloppy and out of balance. Scan your writing to make sure that all series and lists have parallel structure. The following examples show how to correct faulty parallelism:

INCORRECT: The mayor promises not only *to reform* the police department, but also *the giving of raises* to all city employees. [Note: Connective structures such as *not only . . . but also,* and *both . . . and* introduce elements that should be parallel.]

CORRECTED: The mayor promises not only *to reform* the police department, but also *to give* raises to all city employees.

INCORRECT: The cost *of doing* nothing is greater than the cost *to renovate* the apartment block.

CORRECTED: The cost *of doing* nothing is greater than the cost *of renovating* the apartment block.

INCORRECT: Here are the items on the committee's agenda: 1) *to discuss* the new property tax, 2) *to revise* the wording of the city charter, 3) *a vote* on the city manager's request for an assistant.

CORRECTED: Here are the items on the committee's agenda: 1) *to discuss* the new property tax, 2) *to revise* the wording of the city charter, 3) *to vote* on the city manager's request for an assistant.

2.3   PRONOUN ERRORS

2.3.1   *Its* versus *It's*

Do not make the mistake of trying to form the possessive of *it* in the same way that you form the possessive of most nouns. The pronoun *it* shows possession by simply adding an *s*:

The prosecuting attorney argued the case on its merits.

The word *it's* is a contraction, meaning *it is*:

It's the most expensive program ever launched by the council.

What makes the *its/it's* rule so confusing is that most nouns form the singular possessive by adding an apostrophe and an *s*:

The jury's verdict startled the crowd.

When proofreading, any time you come to the word *it's*, substitute the phrase *it is* while you read. If the phrase makes sense, you have used the correct form.

2.3.2   Vague Pronoun References

Pronouns are words that stand in place of nouns or other pronouns that have already been mentioned in your writing. The most common pronouns include *he, she, it, they, them, those, which, who.* You must make sure that each pronoun reference is clear, in other words, that there is no confusion about the reference. Following are two examples of clear pronoun references:

- Socrates' last words were that *he* owed Asclepius a cock.
- The argument *that* drew the most criticism from the evolutionists was the argument from design.

The word that the pronoun replaces is called its *antecedent*. To check the accuracy of your pronoun references, ask yourself, *To what does the pronoun refer?* Then answer the question carefully, making sure that there is not more than one possible antecedent.

Consider the following example:

Several special interest groups decided to defeat the new regulation governing the forwarding of electronic mail. *This* became the turning point of the
government's reform campaign.

In the sentence above, to what does the word *This* refer? The immediate answer seems to be the words *new regulation* at the end of the previous sentence. It is
more likely the writer was referring to the attempt of the special interest groups to
defeat the bill, but there is no word in the first sentence that refers specifically to
this action. The reference is unclear. One way to clarify the reference is to change
the beginning of the second sentence:

Several special interest groups decided to defeat the new regulation governing the forwarding of electronic mail. *Their attack on the bill* became the turning point of the government's reform campaign.

Consider another example:

When Plato appointed Isocrates his successor as head of the Academy, *he* had
little idea that Aristotle would leave to found his own school.

To whom does the word *he* refer? It is unclear whether the writer is referring to
Plato or to Isocrates. One way to clarify the reference is simply to repeat the antecedent instead of using a pronoun:

When Plato appointed Isocrates his successor as head of the Academy, *Plato*
had little idea that Aristotle would leave to found his own school.

2.3.3   Pronoun Agreement

Remember that a pronoun must agree with its antecedent in both gender
and number, as the following examples demonstrate:

* Crito said that *he* appreciated Socrates' willingness to explain *his* decision not
  to flee from Athens.
* One student asked the philosopher what *she* would do if the Athenian people
  charged *her* with impiety.
* Having listened to our case, the judge decided to rule on *it* within the week.
* Engineers working on the housing project said *they* were pleased with the ren-
  ovation so far.

The following words, however, can become troublesome antecedents. They may
look like plural pronouns but are actually singular: *everybody, nobody, everyone, no one,*

somebody, each, someone, either, anyone. A pronoun referring to one of these words in a sentence must be singular, too:

INCORRECT: *Each* of the women in the support group brought *their* children.

CORRECT: *Each* of the women in the support group brought *her* children.

INCORRECT: Has *everybody* received *their* ballot?

CORRECT: Has *everybody* received *his or her* ballot? [The two gender-specific pronouns are used to avoid sexist language.]

CORRECT: Have all the delegates received *their* ballots? [The singular antecedent has been changed to a plural one.]

2.3.4   Shift in Person

It is important to avoid shifting unnecessarily among first person (*I, we*), second person (*you*), and third person (*she, he, it, they*). Such shifts can cause confusion.

INCORRECT: *Most people* [third person] who read philosophy find that if *you* [second person] read only a few pages at a time, *you* [second person] will comprehend more than if *you* [second person] read one hundred pages the night before a test.

CORRECT: *Most people* who read philosophy find that if *they* read only a few pages at a time, *they* will comprehend more than if *they* read one hundred pages the night before a test.

INCORRECT: *One* [first person singular] cannot tell whether *they* [third person plural] are cut out for a career as a philosopher until *they* [third person plural] rationally confront *their* [third person] own most cherished beliefs.

CORRECT: *One* cannot tell whether *one* is cut out for a career as a philosopher without rationally confronting *one's* most cherished beliefs.

2.4   PUNCTUATION

2.4.1   Apostrophes

An apostrophe is used to show possession; when you wish to say that something belongs to someone or to another thing, you add either an apostrophe and an *s* or an apostrophe alone to the word that represents the owner. When the owner is singular (a single person or thing), the apostrophe precedes an added *s*:

- According to Vice President Moore's memo, the faculty are not allowed to speak to the media.
- The union's lawyers challenged the government's policy in court.
- Somebody's briefcase was left in the auditorium.

The same rule applies if the word showing possession is a plural that does not end in *s*:

- The women's club sponsored several debates during the last presidential campaign.
- Governor Smith has proven himself a tireless worker for children's rights.

When the word expressing ownership is a plural ending in *s*, the apostrophe follows the *s*:

- The new regulation was discussed at the chairs' conference.

When a word that is singular ends in *s*, form its possessive in one of two ways:

1. By adding an apostrophe and an *s:* Adams's policy.
2. By adding only an apostrophe: Adams' policy.

Remember to *be consistent* with the style you choose.

There are two ways to form the possessive for two or more nouns:

1. To show joint possession (both nouns owning the same thing or things), the last noun in the series is possessive:
    - The president and first lady's invitations were sent out yesterday.
2. To indicate that each noun owns an item or items individually, each noun must show possession:
    - Mayor Scott's and Mayor MacKay's speeches took different approaches to the same problem.

The importance of the apostrophe is obvious when you consider the difference in meaning between the following two sentences:

- Be sure to pick up the dean's mail on your way to the airport.
- Be sure to pick up the deans' mail on your way to the airport.

In the first of these sentences, you have only one dean to worry about, while in the second, you have at least two!

2.4.2 Capitalization

2.4.2.1 When to Capitalize

Here is a brief summary of some hard-to-remember capitalization rules.

RULE 1. You may, if you choose, capitalize the first letter of the first word in a full sentence following a colon. (But remember to use whichever style you choose consistently.)

> CORRECT: Our instructions are explicit: *D*o not allow anyone into the reception without an identification badge.
>
> ALSO CORRECT: Our instructions are explicit: *d*o not allow anyone into the reception without an identification badge.

RULE 2. Capitalize proper nouns (nouns naming specific people, places, or things) and proper adjectives (adjectives made from proper nouns). A common noun following the proper adjective is usually not capitalized, nor is a common adjective preceding the proper adjective (such as *a, an,* or *the*):

Proper nouns	Proper adjectives
Methodist	Methodist officials
Iraq	the Iraqi ambassador
Shakespeare	a Shakespearean tragedy

Proper nouns include:

- *Names of famous monuments and buildings:* the Washington Monument, the Empire State Building, Graceland
- *Historical events, certain eras, and certain terms concerning calendar dates:* the Civil War, the Roaring Twenties (but: the sixties), Monday, December, Martin Luther King Day
- *Parts of the country:* North, Southwest, Eastern Seaboard, the West Coast, New England. [Note: When words like *north, south, east, west, northwest* are used to designate direction rather than geographical region, they are not capitalized: "We drove *east* to Boston and then made a tour of the *East Coast.*"]
- *Words referring to race, religion or nationality:* Islam, Muslim, Caucasian, White (or white), Oriental, Negro, Black (or black), Slavic, Arab, Jewish, Hebrew, Buddhism, Buddhists, Southern Baptists, the Bible, the Koran, American, Latino
- *Names of languages:* English, Chinese, Latin, Sanskrit

- *Titles of corporations, institutions, businesses, universities, organizations:* Dow Chemical, General Motors, the National Endowment for the Humanities, University of Tennessee, Fordham University, Kiwanis Club, American Association of Retired Persons, the Oklahoma State Senate [Note: Some words once considered proper nouns or adjectives have, over time, become common: *french fries, pasteurized milk, arabic numerals, italics, panama hat.*]

RULE 3. Titles of individuals are capitalized if they precede a proper name; otherwise, titles are usually not capitalized:

- The committee honored Professor Levin.
- The committee honored the professor from New York.

- A story on Queen Elizabeth's health appeared in today's paper.
- A story on the queen's health appeared in today's paper.

2.4.2.2 *When Not to Capitalize*

In general, you do not capitalize nouns when your reference is nonspecific. For example, you would not capitalize the phrase *the senator,* but you would capitalize *Senator Smith.* The second reference is as much a title as it is a term of identification, while the first reference is a mere identifier. Likewise, there is a difference in degree of specificity between the phrase *the state treasury* and *the Texas State Treasury.*

The meaning of a term may change somewhat depending on capitalization. What, for example, might be the difference between a *Democrat* and a *democrat?* (When capitalized, the word refers to a member of a specific political party; when not capitalized, the word refers to someone who believes in the democratic form of government.)

Capitalization depends to some extent on the context of your writing. For example, if you are writing a policy analysis for a specific corporation, you may capitalize words and phrases—*Board of Directors, Chairman of the Board, the Institute*—that would not be capitalized in a paper written for a more general audience. Likewise, in some contexts it is not unusual to see titles of certain powerful officials capitalized even when not accompanying a proper noun: The *President* took few members of his staff to Camp David with him.

Another way that context affects capitalization is when someone capitalizes, or does not capitalize, to make a political or cultural statement. The African American feminist whose name is bell hooks chooses not to capitalize her name. You should respect her wishes.

2.4.3   Colons

We all know certain uses for the colon. A colon can, for example, separate the parts of a statement of time (4:25 A.M.), separate chapter and verse in a Biblical quotation (Psalms 3:16), and close the salutation of a business letter (Dear Mr. Limbaugh:). But there are other uses for the colon that writers sometimes don't quite learn, yet that can add an extra degree of flexibility to sentence structure.

The colon can introduce into a sentence certain kinds of material, such as a list, a quotation, or a restatement or description of material mentioned earlier:

- *List*

  The committee's research proposal promised to do three things: (1) establish the extent of the problem, (2) examine several possible solutions, and (3) estimate the cost of each solution.

- *Quotation*

  In his speech, the chair challenged us with these words: "How will your research make a difference in the life of our culture?"

- *Restatement or description*

  Ahead of us, according to the provost, lay the biggest job of all: convincing our students and their parents of the benefits of general education.

2.4.4   Commas

The comma is perhaps the most troublesome of all marks of punctuation, no doubt because so many variables govern its use, such as sentence length, rhetorical emphasis, or changing notions of style. The most common problems are outlined below.

2.4.4.1   *The Comma Splice*

A *comma* splice is the joining of two complete sentences by only a comma:

- An impeachment is merely an indictment of a government official, actual removal usually requires a vote by a legislative body.
- An unemployed worker who has been effectively retrained is no longer an economic problem for the community, he has become an asset.
- It might be possible for the city to assess fees on the sale of real estate, however, such a move would be criticized by the community of real estate developers.

In each of these passages, two complete sentences (also called *independent clauses*) have been spliced together by a comma, which is an inadequate break between sentences.

One foolproof way to check your paper for comma splices is to read carefully the structures on both sides of each comma. If you find a complete sentence on each side, and if the sentence following the comma does not begin with a coordinating conjunction (*and, but, for, nor, or, so, yet*), then you have found a comma splice.

Simply reading the draft through to try to "hear" the comma splices may not work, since the rhetorical features of your prose—its "movement"—may make it hard to detect this kind of sentence completeness error. There are five commonly used ways to correct comma splices.

1. Place a period between the two independent clauses:

    INCORRECT: A political candidate receives many benefits from his or her af-
    filiation with a political party, there are liabilities as well.

    CORRECT: A political candidate receives many benefits from his or her af-
    filiation with a political party. There are liabilities as well.

2. Place a comma and a coordinating connective (*and, but, for, or, nor, so, yet*) be-
    tween the sentences:

    INCORRECT: The councilman's speech described the major differences of
    opinion over the economic situation, it also suggested a possi-
    ble course of action.

    CORRECT: The councilman's speech described the major differences of
    opinion over the economic situation, and it also suggested a
    possible course of action.

3. Place a semicolon between the independent clauses:

    INCORRECT: Some people feel that the federal government should play a
    large role in establishing a housing policy for the homeless,
    many others disagree.

    CORRECT: Some people feel that the federal government should play a
    large role in establishing a housing policy for the homeless;
    many others disagree.

4. Rewrite the two clauses of the comma splice as one independent clause:

    INCORRECT: Television ads played a big part in the campaign, however they
    were not the deciding factor in the challenger's victory over the
    incumbent.

    CORRECT: Television ads played a large but not a decisive role in the chal-
    lenger's victory over the incumbent.

5. Change one of the two independent clauses into a dependent clause by be-
    ginning it with a *subordinating word* (for example, *although, after, as, because, be-
    fore, if, though, unless, when, which, where*), which prevents the clause from
    being able to stand on its own as a complete sentence.

    INCORRECT: The election was held last Tuesday, there was a poor voter
    turnout.

    CORRECT: When the election was held last Tuesday, there was a poor voter
    turnout.

2.4.4.2   *Commas in a Compound Sentence*

A *compound sentence* is comprised of two or more independent clauses—two complete sentences. When these two clauses are joined by a coordinating conjunction, the conjunction should be preceded by a comma to signal the reader that another independent clause follows. (This is method number two for fixing a comma splice described above.) When the comma is missing, the reader does not expect to find the second half of a compound sentence and may be distracted from the text.

As the following examples indicate, the missing comma is especially a problem in longer sentences or in sentences in which other coordinating conjunctions appear. Notice how the comma sorts out the two main parts of the compound sentence, eliminating confusion:

INCORRECT: The president promised to visit the hospital and investigate the problem and then he called the press conference to a close.

CORRECT: The president promised to visit the hospital and investigate the problem, and then he called the press conference to a close.

INCORRECT: The water board can neither make policy nor enforce it nor can its members serve on auxiliary water committees.

CORRECT: The water board can neither make policy nor enforce it, nor can its members serve on auxiliary water committees.

An exception to this rule arises in shorter sentences, where the comma may not be necessary to make the meaning clear:

The mayor phoned and we thanked him for his support.

However, it is never wrong to place a comma between the independent clauses and before the conjunction. If you are the least bit unsure of your audience's notions about what makes for "proper" grammar, it is a good idea to take the conservative approach and use the comma:

The mayor phoned, and we thanked him for his support.

2.4.4.3   *Commas in a Series*

A series is any two or more items of a similar nature that appear consecutively in a sentence. The items may be individual words, phrases, or clauses. In a series of three or more items, the items are separated by commas:

The *philosopher, the mayor,* and *the police chief* all attended the ceremony.

Because of the new zoning regulations, *all trailer parks must be moved out of the neighborhood, all small businesses must apply for recertification and tax status,* and *the two local churches must repave their parking lots.*

The final comma, the one before the *and,* is sometimes left out, especially in newspaper writing. This practice, however, can make for confusion, especially in longer, complicated sentences like the second example above. Here is the way that sentence would read without the final comma:

Because of the new zoning regulations, all trailer parks must be moved out of the neighborhood, all small businesses must apply for recertification and tax status and the two local churches must repave their parking lots.

Notice that without a comma the division between the second and third items in the series is not clear. This is the sort of ambiguous structure that can cause a reader to backtrack and lose concentration. You can avoid such confusion by always using that final comma. Remember, however, to follow your chosen style consistently; make sure it appears in every series in your paper or, alternatively, in none of them.

2.4.4.4   *Commas with Restrictive and Nonrestrictive Elements*

A nonrestrictive element is part of a sentence—a word, phrase, or clause—that adds information about another element in the sentence without restricting or limiting the meaning of that element. While the information it carries may be useful, the nonrestrictive element is not needed in order for the sentence to make sense. To signal the inessential nature of the nonrestrictive element, we set it off from the rest of the sentence with commas.

Failure to use commas to indicate the nonrestrictive nature of an element can cause confusion. See, for example, how the presence or absence of commas affects our understanding of the following sentence:

- The mayor was talking with the policeman, who won the outstanding service award last year.
- The mayor was talking with the policeman who won the outstanding service award last year.

Can you see that the comma changes the meaning of the sentence? In the first version of the sentence, the comma makes the information that follows it incidental: *The mayor was talking with the policeman, who happens to have won the service award last year.* In the second version of the sentence, the information following the word *policeman* is important to the sense of the sentence; it tells us, specifically, *which* policeman—presumably there are more than one—the mayor was addressing. Here the lack of a comma has transformed the material following the word *po-*

liceman into a *restrictive element,* meaning an element necessary to our understanding of the sentence.

Be sure that in your paper you make a clear distinction between nonrestrictive and restrictive elements by setting off the nonrestrictive elements with commas.

2.4.5   Quotation Marks

It can be difficult to remember when to use quotation marks and where they go in relation to other marks of punctuation. When faced with a gap in their knowledge of the rules, unpracticed writers often try to rely on logic rather than referring to a rule book. But the rules governing quotation marks do not always seem logical. The only way to make sure of your use of quotation marks is to memorize the rules. There are not many.

2.4.5.1   *When to Use Quotation Marks*

Use quotation marks to enclose direct quotations that are not longer than four typed lines:

> Near the end of the dialogue *Euthyphro,* Socrates tells Euthyphro, "If you had not certainly known the nature of piety and impiety, I am confident that you would never, on behalf of a servant, have charged your aged father with murder."

Longer quotes are placed in a block of double-spaced indented prose—*without* quotation marks:

> Most of us are acculturated to accept a dichotomy between high and low art. Richard Shusterman attacks this distinction for many reasons. But his most persuasive argument is the following:

>> The strongest and most urgent reason for defending popular art is that it provides us (even us intellectuals) with too much aesthetic satisfaction to accept its wholesale denunciation as debased, dehumanizing, and aesthetically illegitimate. To condemn it as fit only for the barbaric taste and dull wit of the unenlightened, manipulated masses is to divide us not only against the rest of our community but against ourselves. We are made to disdain the things that give us pleasure and to feel ashamed of the pleasure they give.

Use single quotation marks to set off quotations within quotations:

"I intend," said the philosopher, "to use in my article a line from Hamsun's poem 'Island Off the Coast.'" [Note: When the interior quote occurs at the end of the sentence, both single and double quotation marks are placed outside the period.]

Use quotation marks to set off the following kinds of titles:

- Titles of short poems (those not printed as a separate volume): "The Second Coming," by William Butler Yeats (short poem); *The Dark Sister,* by Winfield Townley Scott (long poem published as a book)
- Titles of short stories
- Titles of articles or essays
- Titles of songs
- Episodes of television or radio shows

Use quotation marks to convey irony:

The "neutral" Clinton administration has armed the Croatian government.

Use quotation marks to set off a technical term:

To "equivocate" is to use a term, consciously or unconsciously, with at least two different meanings that are essential to the persuasive power of an argument. [Note: Once the term is defined, it is not placed in quotation marks again.]

2.4.5.2 *Quotation Marks in Relation to Other Punctuation*

Always place commas and periods inside closing quotation marks:

"My fellow Americans," said the president, "we are on a peace mission in Somalia."

Place colons and semicolons outside closing quotation marks:

- In his speech on Bosnia, the president warned against "mission creep"; he was referring to policing the hostile populations.
- There are several victims of the government's campaign to "Turn Back the Clock": the homeless, the elderly, the mentally impaired.

Place question marks, exclamation points, and dashes inside or outside closing quotation marks depending upon context. If the punctuation is part of the quotation, it goes inside the quotation mark:

- "When will Congress recognize the rights of the unborn?" asked the pro-lifer.
- The demonstrators shouted, "More philosophy courses!" and "No more physical education requirements at the university!"

If the punctuation is not part of the quotation, it goes outside the quotation mark:

> Which philosopher said, "Always act so that the maxim of your action can become a universal law"? [Note: Although the quote was a complete sentence, you do not place a period after it. There can only be one piece of "terminal" punctuation (punctuation that ends a sentence).]

2.4.6 Semicolons

The semicolon is another little used punctuation mark that is worth incorporating into your writing strategy because of its many potential applications. A semicolon can be used to correct a comma splice:

INCORRECT:	Socrates faced death with equanimity, his arguments had convinced his disciples.
CORRECTED:	Socrates faced death with equanimity; his arguments had convinced his disciples.
INCORRECT:	Several guests at the fundraiser had lost their invitations, however, we were able to seat them, anyway.
CORRECTED:	Several guests at the fundraiser had lost their invitations; however, we were able to seat them, anyway.

Conjunctive adverbs like *however, therefore,* and *thus* are not coordinating words (such as *and, but, or, for, so, yet*) and cannot be used with a comma to link independent clauses. If the second independent clause begins with a *however,* it must be preceded by either a period or a semicolon.

As you can see from the second example above, connecting the two independent clauses with a semicolon instead of a period strengthens the relationship between the clauses.

Semicolons can separate items in a series when the series items themselves contain commas:

> The newspaper account of the rally stressed the march, which drew the biggest crowd; the mayor's speech, which drew tremendous applause; and the party afterwards in the park, which left behind a lot of garbage.

Avoid misusing semicolons. For example, use a comma, not a semicolon, to separate an independent clause from a dependent clause:

INCORRECT: Students from the college volunteered to answer phones dur-
              ing the pledge drive; which was set up to generate money for
              the new philosophy library.

CORRECTED: Students from the college volunteered to answer phones dur-
              ing the pledge drive, which was set up to generate money for
              the new philosophy library.

Do not overuse semicolons. Although they are useful, too many semicolons
in your writing can distract your reader's attention. Avoid monotony by using semicolons sparingly.

2.5   SPELLING

All of us have problems spelling certain words that we have not yet committed to memory. But most writers are not as bad at spelling as they believe themselves to be. An individual usually finds only a handful of words troubling. It is important to be as sensitive as possible to your own particular spelling problems—and
to keep a dictionary handy. There is no excuse for failing to check spelling.

The following lists present commonly confused words and commonly mis-
spelled words. Read through the lists, looking for those words that tend to give you
trouble. If you have any questions, *consult your dictionary*.

2.5.1   Commonly Confused Words

accept/except	conscience/conscious	forth/fourth
advice/advise	corps/corpse	hear/here
affect/effect	council/counsel	heard/herd
aisle/isle	dairy/diary	hole/whole
allusion/illusion	descent/dissent	human/humane
an/and	desert/dessert	its/it's
angel/angle	device/devise	know/no
ascent/assent	die/dye	later/latter
bare/bear	dominant/dominate	lay/lie
brake/break	elicit/illicit	lead/led
breath/breathe	eminent/immanent/	lessen/lesson
buy/by	imminent	loose/lose
capital/capitol	envelop/envelope	may be/maybe
choose/chose	every day/everyday	miner/minor
cite/sight/site	fair/fare	moral/morale
complement/compliment	formally/formerly	of/off

passed/past
patience/patients
peace/piece
personal/personnel
plain/plane
precede/proceed
presence/presents
principal/principle
quiet/quite
rain/reign/rein
raise/raze
reality/realty

respectfully/respectively
reverend/reverent
right/rite/write
road/rode
scene/seen
sense/since
stationary/stationery
straight/strait
taught/taut
than/then
their/there/they're
threw/through

too/to/two
track/tract
waist/waste
waive/wave
weak/week
weather/whether
were/where
which/witch
whose/who's
your/you're

2.5.2   Commonly Misspelled Words

a lot
acceptable
accessible
accommodate
accompany
accustomed
acquire
against
annihilate
apparent
arguing
argument
authentic
before
begin
beginning
believe
benefited
bulletin
business
cannot
category

committee
condemn
courteous
definitely
dependent
desperate
develop
different
disappear
disappoint
easily
efficient
environment
equipped
exceed
exercise
existence
experience
fascinate
finally
foresee
forty

fulfill
gauge
guaranteed
guard
harass
hero
heroes
humorous
hurried
hurriedly
hypocrite
ideally
immediately
immense
incredible
innocuous
intercede
interrupt
irrelevant
irresistible
irritate
knowledge

license
likelihood
maintenance
manageable
meanness
mischievous
missile
necessary
nevertheless
no one
noticeable
noticing
nuisance
occasion
occasionally
occurred
occurrences
omission
omit
opinion
opponent
parallel
parole
peaceable
performance
pertain
practical
preparation
probably
process
professor

prominent
pronunciation
psychology
publicly
pursue
pursuing
questionnaire
realize
receipt
received
recession
recommend
referring
religious
remembrance
reminisce
repetition
representative
rhythm
ridiculous
roommate
satellite
scarcity
scenery
science
secede
secession
secretary
senseless
separate
sergeant

shining
significant
sincerely
skiing
stubbornness
studying
succeed
success
successfully
susceptible
suspicious
technical
temporary
tendency
therefore
tragedy
truly
tyranny
unanimous
unconscious
undoubtedly
until
vacuum
valuable
various
vegetable
visible
without
women
writing

2.6   TECHNICAL AND ORDINARY USAGE OF PHILOSOPHICAL TERMS

All of us have had the experience of arguing an issue with someone only to realize after a while that we are arguing about different issues. Sometimes our arguments are rooted in the fact that we do not attach the same meaning to a key phrase. Certain words are particularly troublesome in philosophy because they have meanings in ordinary usage that only approximate their established philosophical meanings. Unlike scientists, philosophers tend to adopt words from ordinary language to express technical meanings rather than introduce new terminology.

A glossary of important philosophical terms is provided in the back of the text. Following is a list of the most problematic terms. Pay special attention to the ways in which philosophers use them.

absolute	humanism	paradigm
analytic	idea	pragmatic
argument	idealism	pragmatism
authenticity	instrumentalism	rationalism
determinism	intuition	reduction
dilemma	materialism	synthetic
double effect	metaphysics	utilitarian
egoism	naturalism	
explanation	objectivism	

PART TWO

Conducting Research in Philosophy

3

Organizing the Research Process

The unexamined life is not worth living.

—Socrates

The examined life is no picnic.

—Robert Fulghum

3.1 GAINING CONTROL OF THE RESEARCH PROCESS

The research paper is where all your skills as an interpreter of details, an organizer of facts and theories, and a writer of clear prose come together. If you are a philosophy major your research paper may serve as the basis of an honors project, a graduate paper, or a thesis later in graduate school. But even if you are taking a philosophy course as an elective or as fulfillment of a general education requirement, the skills you acquire in writing your research paper will probably serve you well in your career.

Some disciplines are more inclined to assign traditional research papers than philosophy. The type of research paper your philosophy instructor is likely to assign you might be a short expository paper, a compare-and-contrast paper, a case study of an emerging ethical issue, a historical paper, or the traditional research paper with a full bibliography and footnotes. Plenty of guidance on the preparation of these papers will be provided in subsequent chapters. But there are some guidelines for research that will be helpful to you regardless of the nature of your assignment. And that is where I will begin.

Students new to the writing of research papers sometimes find themselves intimidated by the job ahead of them. After all, the research paper adds what seems to be an extra set of complexities to the writing process. Like any other expository or persuasive paper, a research paper should present an original thesis using a carefully organized and logical argument. But a research paper investigates a topic that is outside the writer's own expertise. This means that writers must locate and evaluate information that is new to them, in effect educating themselves as they explore their topics. A beginning researcher sometimes feels overwhelmed by the basic requirements of the assignment or by the authority of the source material being investigated.

In my first year of graduate school I took a course devoted to philosophy of religion. The central historical figures we studied were Immanuel Kant and Georg Wilhelm Hegel. Toward the end of the semester our instructor announced we would have a visiting lecturer, an expert on Hegel who had recently joined the faculty. Professor Blue (not his real name) gave a fine presentation on Hegel's early philosophy of religion. During the discussion our instructor complimented Professor Blue and then asked why he had restricted his comments to Hegel's early thought and not commented on his lectures on the philosophy of religion. (There is a three-volume collection of Hegel's later lectures on the philosophy of religion available in an English translation.) Professor Blue responded, "I have never read Hegel's lectures on the philosophy of religion." There was silence. I know what I thought: "Here is an honest person." Now, whenever a student asks me for an opinion about something I have not read, I confess my ignorance.

One other thing I learned from Professor Blue that day is that even the experts have not read everything. And if they have not read everything, then they may not have thought everything, either. Even a beginning student in a subject as remote and specialized as Hegel's philosophy of religion may have information to contribute or opinions to offer that have been overlooked by experts.

You also should be skeptical of experts, especially when they are commenting on each other's views about a historical figure. Currently there is a great deal of interest in the French philosopher Michael Foucault. Foucault borrowed some of his ideas from British philosopher Jeremy Bentham's nineteenth-century proposals calling for social reform through the extension of a social institution Bentham called the Panopticon. You should be suspicious of any opinion expressed by experts on Foucault concerning Bentham's view of the Panopticon, since their views of Bentham will be affected by their focus on Foucault. If you are interested in Bentham's ideas, go to the original source.

As you begin a research project, it may be difficult to establish a sense of control over the different tasks you are undertaking. You may have little notion of which direction to search for a thesis, or even where the most helpful sources of information might be located. If you do not carefully monitor your own work habits, you may find yourself unwittingly abdicating responsibility for the paper's argument by borrowing it wholesale from one or more of your sources.

Who is in control of your paper? The answer must be *you*—not the instructor who assigned you the paper, and certainly not the published writers and interviewees whose opinions you investigate. If all your paper does is paste together the opinions of others, it has little use. It is up to you to synthesize an original idea from a judicious evaluation of your source material. While there are, of course, many elements of your paper about which you are unsure at the beginning of your research project—you will probably not yet have a definitive thesis sentence, for example, or even much understanding of the shape of your argument—you can establish a measure of control over the process you will go through to complete the paper. And if you work regularly and systematically, keeping yourself open to new ideas as they present themselves, your sense of control will grow. Here are some suggestions to help you establish and maintain control of your paper.

1. *Understand your assignment.* It is possible for a research assignment to go bad simply because the writer did not read the assignment carefully. Considering how much time and effort you are about to put into your project, it is a very good idea to make sure you have a clear understanding of what it is your instructor wants you to do. *Be sure to ask your instructor about any aspect of the assignment that is unclear to you—but only after you have read it carefully.* Recopying the assignment in your own handwriting is a good way to start, even though your instructor may have given the assignment to you in writing. (I wish it were not necessary to note this, but it is. You are entitled to be given a written copy of all assignments. And your syllabus and written assignments are treated as legal contracts by the administration at your university.) Before you dive into the project, make sure that you have considered the questions in the paragraphs that follow.

2. *What is your topic?* The assignment may give you a great deal of specific information about your topic, or you may be allowed considerable freedom in establishing one for yourself. In a history of modern philosophy class in which you are studying metaphysical or epistemological issues (issues dealing with the ultimate nature of reality and with our ability to acquire knowledge), your professor might give you a very specific assignment—a paper, for example, examining the views of freedom or truth found in the works you are reading by Kant and Spinoza. Or the instructor may allow you to choose for yourself the issue that your paper will address. You need to understand the terms, set up in the assignment, within which you may design your project. Otherwise you may do a perfectly respectable paper on a topic in political philosophy, such as Hobbes's and Spinoza's views of the social contract, only to be told its focus is inappropriate.

3. *What is your purpose?* Whatever the degree of latitude you are given in the matter of your topic, pay close attention to the way in which your instructor has phrased the assignment. Is your primary job to *describe* a current ethical dilemma or to *take a stand* on it? Are you to *compare* several arguments for their views about a particular ethical question and, if so, to what end? Are you to *classify, persuade, sur-*

vey, analyze? Look for such descriptive terms in the assignment in order to determine the purpose of the project.

Some philosophy instructors do not assign argumentative papers in their beginning classes. Instead, they decide to concentrate on developing analytical abilities. So you might be given the assignment of explaining Kant's and Mill's views of justice but not asked to develop a thesis about their relative merits.

I have never met a philosophy instructor who objected to hearing an opinion after the analytical work had been done. If you are the sort of person who feels a strong need to evaluate the authors you are studying, then you might ask your instructor if it would be acceptable to include your own opinion in your paper. But do not confuse the acceptability of doing extra work with absolution from doing the work assigned. You cannot express a reasonable view of Kant's notion of justice without telling the reader what Kant's concept of justice is.

4. *Who is your audience?* Your own orientation to the paper is profoundly affected by your conception of the audience for whom you are writing. Granted, your number one reader is your instructor, but who else would be interested in your paper? Imagining your audience can help you gain an understanding of many elements of your paper. Are you writing about an issue of interest to the voters of a community? You might use your paper as the occasion to formulate a letter to the editor of your local newspaper. A paper that describes a proposal for revising the process for filing a living will may justifiably contain much more technical jargon for an audience of hospital administrators than for a hospital advisory group that includes members of the local community. Your research may serve several audiences, but you will have to rewrite for each audience to communicate effectively.

5. *What kind of research are you doing?* You will be doing one if not both of the following kinds of research:

a. *Primary research* requires you either to work on original published and unpublished texts or to produce your own information through surveys, polls, or interviews. In philosophy, most primary research is of the first type: firsthand work on important texts. For instance, in a course in the history of philosophy you will probably read Descartes's *Meditations on First Philosophy*. Many editions of this classic work contain six sets of objections from philosophers and theologians who were Descartes's contemporaries. Your instructor is sure to point out to you that the fifth set of objections was formulated by another significant philosopher of the modern period, Thomas Hobbes. You might decide to do your paper on Hobbes's criticism of Descartes's proof of his own existence. And, as part of understanding Hobbes, you will probably want to read the section of his *Leviathan* devoted to his views of knowledge. Here you will be doing primary research, since both Descartes's *Meditations* and Hobbes's *Leviathan* are considered primary sources. Other examples of primary sources are such things as manuscripts and notebooks, the dialogues of Plato, or a newly published but original perspective on an ethical issue in a professional journal.

Another sort of primary research students sometimes pursue is looking behind the published works at an author's unpublished material. This type of research can be difficult since it often requires travel to special collections. But you may be surprised by the holdings your library has available on microfilm. My library, for example, has thirty-three reels of the unpublished writings of the American philosopher Charles Peirce.

Finally, you may do primary research that takes you outside the field of philosophy when you venture into interdisciplinary courses or courses on professional ethics. In most professional ethics courses you will survey existing codes of professional ethics. You might be required to contact the public relations office of a local firm to ask what considerations went into the formulation of the firm's code of ethics and personnel procedures. Or you might want to write your paper in criminal justice ethics on the question of whether civilians should sit on police review boards. It would be a good idea to interview the local police chief and some patrol officers. Conducting such surveys and interviews is a kind of primary research.

b. *Secondary research* makes use of secondary sources, that is, published accounts of primary materials. Unfortunately, many American university courses center on secondary material embodied in textbooks. On the other hand, some material that is considered secondary makes an original contribution to scholarship and understanding. Genevieve Lloyd's *Man of Reason,* for example, brings feminist scholarship to bear on the so-called "dead white males" that make up the canon of Western thought. Secondary sources include such items as Gerald Myers's book on the thought of William James, articles in *The Encyclopedia of Philosophy,* articles in journals devoted to historical figures such as Descartes, or an interpretative paper explaining the reactions of patrol officers to the proposed inclusion of civilians on review boards.

The most important thing to remember when reading secondary sources is that their authors have their own philosophical allegiances. If possible, select secondary sources from different schools of philosophy. If you are enrolled in a course on Kant's *Critique of Pure Reason,* try to read commentaries from both analytic philosophers such as Strawson and Continental philosophers such as Heidegger.

Alfred North Whitehead remarked that all philosophy is just a footnote to Plato. If you have not already guessed, today's secondary sources may be judged primary sources by posterity. Still, we can make the rough-and-ready distinctions to guide you in selecting sources for your bibliography.

Some sources are difficult to classify as either primary or secondary. Consider, for example, that Wilfred Sellars's *Science and Metaphysics* is not only a study of Kant but a significant philosophical work on its own. Another example is Heidegger's encyclopedia article on phenomenology, which is often cited as an original source.

6. *Keep your perspective.* Whichever type of research you perform, you must keep your results in perspective. There is no way in which you, as a primary re-

searcher, can be completely objective and exhaustive in your research. And your instructor does not expect you to be. She realizes that the state of your library, the availability of materials, the length of the assignment, and even the difficulty of the material all effect how much research you can accomplish. Just choose your sources wisely, consult your instructor, stay on the topic, and select sources with a variety of philosophical perspectives. You need not exhaust the field of alternatives.

Likewise, if you are conducting secondary research, you must remember that the articles and journals you are reading are shaped by the aims of their writers, who are interpreting primary materials for their own ends. The further you get from a primary source, the greater the possibility for distortion. Your job as a researcher is to be as accurate as possible, and that means keeping in view the limitations of your methods and their ends. And a good primary source may not be a good secondary source. Giles Deleuze is a prominent contemporary French philosopher who published a book on Spinoza. The book is a good source for understanding Deleuze, but not Spinoza.

3.2   EFFECTIVE RESEARCH METHODS

In any research project there will be moments of confusion, but you can prevent this confusion from overwhelming you by establishing an effective research procedure. You need to design a schedule for the project that is as systematic as possible, yet flexible enough so that you do not feel trapped by it. A schedule will help keep you from running into dead ends by always showing you what to do next. At the same time, the schedule helps you to retain the presence of mind necessary to spot new ideas and new strategies as you work.

Allow Plenty of Time

You may feel like delaying your research for many reasons: unfamiliarity with the library, the press of other tasks, a deadline that seems comfortably far away. But do not allow such factors to deter you. Research takes time. Working in a library seems to speed up the clock, so that the hour you expected it to take you to find a certain source becomes two hours. You must allow yourself the time it takes not only to find material but to read it, assimilate it, set it in context with your own thoughts. If you delay starting, you may eventually find yourself distracted by the deadline, having to keep an eye on the clock while trying to make sense of a writer's complicated argument.

The following schedule lists the steps of a research project in the order in which they are generally accomplished. Remember that each step is dependent upon the others, and that it is quite possible to revise earlier decisions in the light of later discoveries. After some background reading, for example, your notion of the paper's purpose may change, a fact that may in turn alter other steps. One of the strengths of a good schedule is its flexibility. Note that this schedule lists tasks for both primary and secondary research; you should use only those steps that are relevant to your project.

RESEARCH SCHEDULE

Task	Date of completion
Determine topic, purpose, and audience	
Do background reading in reference books, such as *The Encyclopedia of Philosophy* and *The Encyclopedia of Bioethics*	
Narrow your topic; establish a tentative conclusion	
Develop a working bibliography	
Write for needed information, such as codes of ethics	
Read and evaluate written sources, taking notes	
Determine whether to conduct interviews	
Draft a thesis and outline	
Write a first draft	
Obtain feedback (show draft to instructor, if possible)	
Do more research, if necessary	
Revise draft	
Correct bibliographical format of paper	
Prepare final draft	
Run spelling check program	
Proofread	
Proofread *again*, looking for characteristic errors	
Deadline for final draft	

Do Background Reading

Whether you are doing primary or secondary research, you need to know what kinds of work have already been done in your field of study. A good way to start is by consulting general reference works, though you do not want to overdo it.

Warning: Be very careful not to rely too exclusively on material taken from general encyclopaedias, such as *Encyclopaedia Britannica* or *Colliers Encyclopedia*. You may wish to consult one for an overview of a topic with which you are unfamiliar, but students new to research are often tempted to import large sections, if not entire articles, from such volumes, and this practice is not good scholarship. One major reason why your instructor has assigned a research paper is to let you experience the kinds of books and journals in which the discourse of philosophy is conducted. General reference encyclopedias are good places for instant introductions to subjects; some even include bibliographies of reference works at the ends of their articles. But to write a useful paper you will need much more detailed information about your subject. Once you have learned what you can from a general encyclopedia, move on to other sources.

Narrow Your Topic and Establish a Working Thesis

Before beginning to explore outside sources, it would be a good idea for you to find out what you already know or think about your topic, a job that can only be accomplished well through writing. You might wish to investigate your own attitude toward your topic and your beliefs concerning it, using one or more of the prewriting strategies described in Chapter 1. You might also be surprised by what you know—or don't know—about the topic. This kind of self-questioning can help you discover a profitable direction for your research.

For a research paper in a course in Business Ethics, for example, Karen Eliot was given the general topic of studying the environmental impact of energy providers. She chose to focus on nuclear power plants. Here is the course her thinking took as she looked for ways to limit the topic effectively and find a thesis:

GENERAL TOPIC:	Environmental impact of nuclear power
POTENTIAL TOPICS:	How is nuclear waste stored?
	Are there alternate energy sources?
	Are government and industry publications reliable sources of information about energy?
WORKING THESIS:	Since no one knows how to store nuclear waste safely, nuclear power should not be our major source of information about energy.

Specific methods for discovering a thesis are discussed in Chapter 1. It is unlikely that you will come up with a satisfactory thesis at the beginning of your project. You need a way to guide yourself through the early stages of research toward a main idea that is both useful and manageable. Having in mind a *working thesis*—a preliminary statement of your purpose—can help you select material that is of greatest interest to you as you examine potential sources. The working thesis will probably evolve as your research progresses, and you should be ready to accept such change. You must not fix on a thesis too early in the research process, or you may miss opportunities to refine it.

Develop a Working Bibliography

As you begin your research, you will look for published sources—essays, books, encyclopedia articles by experts in the field—that may help you with your project. This list of potentially useful sources is your *working bibliography*. There are many ways to discover items for the bibliography. The cataloging system in your library will give you titles, as will specialized published bibliographies in your field. (Some of these bibliographies are listed in Chapter 4.) The general reference works in which you did your background reading may also list such sources, and each specialized book or essay you find will itself have a bibliography of sources that may be useful to you. The American Philosophical Society (APA) home page has links to bibliographies as well as discussion lines devoted to philosophical issues and historical figures, everyone from Ayn Rand to Charles Peirce.

It is from your working bibliography that you will select the items for the bibliography that will appear in the final draft of your paper. Early in your research you do not know which of your sources will be of help to you and which will not, but it is important to keep an accurate description of each entry in your working bibliography so that you will be able to tell clearly which items you have investigated and which you will need to consult again. Establishing the working bibliography also allows you to practice using the bibliographical format you are required to follow in your final draft. As you make your list of potential sources, be sure to include all the information about each one in the proper format, using the proper punctuation. (Chapter 7 describes in detail the bibliographical format most often required for philosophy papers.)

Evaluate Written Sources, Taking Notes

Few research experiences are more frustrating than trying to recall information found in a source that you can no longer identify. You must establish an efficient method of examining and evaluating the sources in your working bibliography. Suggestions for compiling an accurate record of your written sources are described below.

Determine Quickly the Potential Usefulness of a Source

For books, you can read through the prefatory material (the introduction, foreword, and preface) looking for the author's thesis; you can also examine chapter headings, dust jackets, and indexes. The footnotes of the author you are studying can be particularly fruitful areas to investigate. Often we assume that if an author footnotes someone else there is no profit to be gained from studying the cited source. We are charitable and assume that our author has correctly understood the source and conveyed to us all that is worthwhile in the source. We assume that any further research we do should be on material written about our author. Do not make this assumption.

A journal article should announce its intention in its introduction, which in most cases will be a page or less in length. *The Philosopher's Index* publishes abstracts of articles from leading philosophy journals within a few months of their appearance in print. It also is a good source for references to reviews of recent philosophy books. And the journal *Philosophical Investigations* is entirely devoted to book reviews.

I always look at the index of a potential source first. If I were working on the topic of repeat-offender programs, I would look in the back of the book for entries on due process and repeat offenders. I would hope to find several references, one of which would be at least a couple of pages long. I would then read the longest reference, which usually determines whether I decide to spend more time investigating a potential source. *Whatever you decide about the source, copy its title page,* making sure that all important publication information (including title, date, author, volume number, and page numbers) is included. Write on the photocopied page any necessary information that is not printed there. Without such a record, later on in your research you may forget that you have consulted a text, in which case you may find yourself repeating your work.

When you have determined that a potential source is worth closer inspection, explore it carefully. If it is a book, you must determine whether you should invest the time it will take to read it in its entirety. Whatever the source, make sure you understand not only its overall thesis, but also each part of the argument that the writer sets up to illustrate or prove the thesis. You need to get a feel for the writer's argument—how the subtopics form (or do *not* form) a logical defense of the main point. What do you think of the writer's logic and the examples used? Coming to an accurate appraisal may take more than one reading.

As you read, try to get a feel for the larger argument in which this source takes its place. Its references to the works of other writers will show you where to look for additional material and indicate the general shape of scholarly opinion concerning your subject. If you can see the article you are reading as only one element of an ongoing dialogue instead of an attempt to have the last word on the subject, then you can place the argument of the paper in perspective.

Use Photocopies

Periodicals and most reference works cannot be checked out of the library. Before the widespread placement of photocopy machines, students could use these materials only by sitting in the library, reading sources, and jotting down information on note cards. While there are advantages to using the old note-card method (see below), photocopying saves you time in the library and allows you to take the source information in its original shape home with you, where you can decide how to use it at your convenience.

If you do decide to copy source material, you should do the following:

- Be sure to follow all copyright laws.
- Have the exact change for the photocopy machines. Do not trust the change machines at the library. They are usually battle-scarred and cantankerous.
- Record all necessary bibliographical information on the photocopy. If you forget to do this, you may find yourself making an extra trip to the library just to get an accurate date of publication or a set of page numbers.

Remember that photocopying a source is not the same thing as examining it. You will still have to spend time going over the material, assimilating it in order to use it accurately. It is not enough merely to have the information close at hand, or even to have read it once or twice. You must *understand* it thoroughly. Be sure to give yourself time for this kind of evaluation.

The Note Card: A Thing of the Past?

In many ways note cards are an old-fashioned method of recording source material, and for unpracticed researchers they may seem unwieldy and unnecessary, since the information jotted on them—one fact per card—will eventually have to be transmitted again into the research paper. However, before you decide to bury the note-card system once and for all, consider its advantages:

- Using note cards is a way of forcing you to think productively as you read. In translating the language of the source material into the language of your notes, you are assimilating the material more completely than you would by merely reading it.
- Note cards give you a handy way to arrange and rearrange your facts, looking for the best possible organization for your paper. Not even a computer gives you the flexibility of a pack of cards as you try to order your paper.

Draft a Thesis and Outline

No matter how thoroughly you may hunt for data or how fast you read, you will not be able to find and assimilate every source pertaining to your subject, especially if it is a popular or controversial one, and you should not prolong your research unduly. You must bring the research phase of the project to an end—with the option of resuming it later if the need arises—and begin to shape both the material you have gathered and your thoughts about it into a paper. During the research phase of your project, you have been thinking about your working thesis, revising it in accordance with the material you have discovered and considering ways to improve it. Eventually you must formulate a thesis that sets out an interesting and useful task, one that can be satisfactorily managed within the limits of your assignment and that effectively employs much, if not all, of the source material you have gathered.

Instructors increasingly require students to make oral presentations in class. An in-class presentation can be a good form for trying out your thesis and the major ideas of your paper. Think of your oral presentation as a first draft and the classroom feedback as an opportunity to revise your work before finalizing it. Oral presentations can be nerve-wracking, however. When asked to give my first presentation in graduate school, I choked and fled the room. Fortunately, I had professors who were understanding and encouraged me to resume my studies. If you can choose when to make your first oral presentation, pick a class in which you feel some degree of comfort.

Once you have formulated your thesis, it is a good idea to make an outline of the paper. In helping you to determine a structure for your paper, the outline is also testing the thesis, prompting you to discover the kinds of work your paper will have to do in order to complete the task set out by the thesis. Chapter 1 discusses the structural requirements of the formal and the informal outline. (If you have used note cards, you may want to start the outlining process by first organizing your cards according to the headings you have given them and looking for logical connections among the different groups of cards. Experimenting with structure in this way may lead you to discoveries that will further improve your thesis.)

No thesis or outline is written in stone. There is still time to improve the structure or purpose of your paper even after you have begun to write your first draft, or, for that matter, your final draft. Some writers actually prefer to write a first draft of the paper before outlining, then study the draft's structure in order to determine what revisions need to be made. *Stay flexible,* always looking for a better connection, a sharper wording of your thesis. All the time you are writing, the testing of your ideas goes on.

Write a First Draft

Despite all the preliminary work you have done on your paper, you may feel a resistance to beginning the writing of your first draft. Integrating all your material, your ideas, into a smoothly flowing argument is a complicated task. It may help to think of your first attempt as only a *rough draft,* which can be changed as necessary. Another strategy for reducing the resistance to starting is to begin with the part of the draft that you feel most confident about instead of with the introduction. You may write sections of the draft in any order, piecing the parts together later. But however you decide to start writing—*start.*

Obtain Feedback

It is not enough that *you* understand your argument; others have to understand it, too. If your instructor is willing to look at your rough draft, you should take advantage of the opportunity and pay careful attention to any suggestions for improvement. Other readers may be of help, although having a friend or a relative read your draft may not be as helpful as having it read by someone who is knowledgeable in your field. In any event, be sure to evaluate carefully any suggestions you receive for improvement. Remember, the final responsibility for the paper rests with you.

3.3   ETHICAL USE OF SOURCE MATERIAL

You want to make as effective use of your source material as possible. This will sometimes mean that you should quote from a source directly, while at other times you will recast source information in your own words. At all times, you should work to integrate the source material skillfully into the flow of your written argument.

When to Quote

You should quote directly from a source when the original language is distinctive enough to enhance your argument, or when rewording the passage would lessen its impact. In the interest of fairness, you should also quote a passage to which you will take exception. Rarely, however, should you quote a source at great length (longer than two or three paragraphs). Nor should your paper, or any lengthy section of it, be merely a string of quoted passages. The more language you take from the writings of others, the more the quotations will disrupt the rhetorical flow of your own language. Too much quoting creates a "scissors-paste" paper, a choppy patchwork of varying styles and borrowed purposes in which your sense of your own control over your material is lost.

Quotations in Relation to Your Own Writing

When you do use a quotation, make sure that you insert it skillfully. Chapter 2 offers examples of the ways in which to integrate quotations of various length into your paper. Remember that quotes of four lines or fewer should be integrated into your text and set off with quotation marks. Quotations longer than four lines should begin on a new line and be indented five spaces from the left-hand margin.

Also, see how skillfully you can place the name of your source within the sentence. Papers and articles that contain too many author tags, such as "Heidegger says, '. . .,'" can become tedious. Students tend to write like this whenever they fall in love with a new writer.

Acknowledge Quotations Carefully

Failing to signal the presence of a quotation skillfully can lead to confusion or choppiness:

> The U.S. Secretary of Labor believes that worker retraining programs have
> failed because of a lack of trust within the American business culture. "The

American business community does not visualize the need to invest in its workers" (Winn 1992, 11).

The phrasing of the first sentence in the above passage seems to suggest that the
following quote comes from the Secretary of Labor. Note how this revision clarifies
the attribution:

> According to reporter Fred Winn, the U.S. Secretary of Labor believes that
> worker retraining programs have failed because of a lack of trust within the
> American business culture. Summarizing the secretary's view, Winn writes, "The
> American business community does not visualize the need to invest in its work-
> ers" (11).

The origin of each quote must be indicated within your text at the point
where the quote occurs as well as in the list of works cited, which follows the text.

Quote Accurately

If your transcription of a quotation introduces careless variants of any kind,
you are misrepresenting your source. Proofread your quotations very carefully, paying close attention to such surface features as spelling, capitalization, italics, and
the use of numerals.

Occasionally, in order either to make a quotation fit smoothly into a passage,
to clarify a reference, or to delete unnecessary material, you may need to change
the original wording slightly. You must, however, signal any such change to your
reader. Some alterations may be noted by brackets:

> "Several times during his oration, the philosopher said that his stand [on capital
> punishment] remains unchanged" (McAffrey 23).

Ellipses indicate that words have been left out of a quote:

> "The last time the Athenians chose to endorse one of the tyrant's policies . . .
> they created a disaster for themselves and their city" (Williams 132).

When you integrate quoted material with your own prose, it is unnecessary to
begin the quote with ellipses:

> Benton raised eyebrows with his claim that "nobody in the mayor's office knows
> how to tie a shoe, let alone work out a compromise" (Barnes 9).

Paraphrasing

Your writing has its own rhetorical attributes, its own rhythms and structural
coherence. Inserting several quotations into a section of your paper can disrupt

the patterns you establish in your prose and diminish the effectiveness of your own language. Paraphrasing, or recasting source material in your own words, is one way to avoid the choppiness that can result from a series of quotations.

Remember that a paraphrase is to be written in *your* language; it is not a near copy of the source writer's language. Merely changing a few words of the original does justice to no one's prose and frequently produces stilted passages. This sort of borrowing is actually a form of plagiarism. In order to fully integrate the material you wish to use into your writing, use your own language.

Paraphrasing may actually increase your comprehension of source material, because in recasting a passage you will have to think very carefully about its meaning, more carefully, perhaps, than you might if you merely copied it word for word.

Avoiding Plagiarism

Paraphrases require the same sort of documentation as direct quotes do. The words of a paraphrase may be yours, but the idea is someone else's. Failure to give that person credit, in the form of references within the text and in the bibliography, may make you vulnerable to a charge of plagiarism.

Plagiarism is the use of someone else's words or ideas without giving proper credit. While some plagiarism is deliberate, produced by writers who understand that they are guilty of a kind of academic thievery, much of it is unconscious, committed by writers who are not aware of the varieties of plagiarism or who are careless in recording their borrowings from sources. Sometimes plagiarism happens simply because of the passage of time. You read something when you are twenty, and when you think of it again when you are forty you think you are having an original thought. Plagiarism includes:

- Quoting directly without acknowledging the source
- Paraphrasing without acknowledging the source
- Constructing a paraphrase that closely resembles the original in language and syntax

One way to guard against plagiarism is to keep careful notes of when you have quoted source material directly and when you have paraphrased—making sure that the wording of the paraphrases is yours. Make sure that all direct quotes in your final draft are properly set off from your own prose, either with quotation marks or in indented blocks.

What kind of paraphrased material must be acknowledged? Basic material that you find in several sources need not be acknowledged by a reference. For example, it is unnecessary to cite a source for the information that Aristotle was a Greek philosopher and the tutor of Alexander the Great, because these are commonly known facts. Any information that is not widely known, however, whether factual or open to dispute, should be documented.

4

Information in Your Library and Similar Places

Come, and take choice of all my library. And so beguile thy sorrow.

—William Shakespeare, *Titus Andronicus*

As a student of philosophy, you will find much valuable information on the library shelves. Topics in philosophy, however, can also offer unusual opportunities to discover information sources outside the library, such as research institutes and political action groups. This chapter describes a variety of research sources in philosophy and in other fields of study that connect with philosophy in interdisciplinary courses. Please note that the point of this discussion is not to keep you from going to the library but to encourage you to use other sources of information.

4.1   INFORMATION RESOURCES IN YOUR COLLEGE LIBRARY

4.1.1   Directories

Adams, Charles J., et al., eds. *The Encyclopedia of Religion.* New York: Macmillan, 1987.

Alexander, Dey, ed. *Philosophy in Cyberspace.* Bowling Green, Ohio: Philosophy Documentation Center, 1995. A compilation and description of mailing lists and newsgroups dedicated to philosophy and allied fields, this collection has an international scope. It also contains information on web and fetch sites, gopher sites, and philosophy department home pages.

Bahm, Archie, ed. *The Directory of American Philosophers, 1996–1997.* Bowling Green, Ohio: Philosophy Documentation Center, 1996. This directory lists philosophy programs at all institutions of higher learning in the United States and Canada. It also lists philosophers associated with these institutions along with their areas of specialization. The directory contains a useful section on financial assistance available to graduate students, a description of major philosophical societies, e-mail addresses, web sites, and information about the major professional journals in philosophy.

Becker, Lawrence C., ed. *Encyclopedia of Ethics.* 2 vols. New York: Garland, 1992.

Cormier, Ramona, and Richard H. Lineback, eds. *International Directory of Philosophers, 1995–1996.* Bowling Green, Ohio: Philosophy Documentation Center, 1995. This directory attempts to cover the international scene in a manner similar to the American Directory. It lists philosophy programs and faculty at international institutions of higher learning.

DeConde, Alexander, ed. *Encyclopedia of American Foreign Policy.* 3 vols. New York: Scribners, 1978. The essays in these volumes discuss concepts, themes, events, and doctrines in the history of U.S. foreign relations. Contents are organized alphabetically by subject. Volume 3 includes a subject index.

Edwards, Paul, ed. *Encyclopedia of Philosophy.* 8 vols. New York: Macmillan, 1967. This encyclopedia contains over 1,500 articles on major figures, theories, movements, concepts, and controversies in the history of philosophy. The bibliographies are a little dated, but these volumes are still the best place to begin becoming familiar with philosophical concepts that have shaped Western thought.

Elliott, Stephen P., ed. *A Reference Guide to the United States Supreme Court.* New York: Facts on File, 1986. This volume publishes essays on various topics related to the Supreme Court, including the origin and development of the Court, major issues confronted by the Court, notable jurists, and the Court's relation to other branches of government. There are also summaries of historic cases. A general index is included.

Encyclopedia of Indian Philosophy. 5 vols. Princeton: Princeton University Press, 1977.

Fargis, Paul, and Sheree Bykofsky, eds. *The New York Public Library Desk Reference.* New York: Stonesong Press, 1989. This reference book includes "elemental and frequently sought material" on a vast range of topics, some of interest to political science studies, such as addresses for national, state, county, and city government consumer protection agencies; spoken and written forms of address for government officials and military personnel; brief accounts of events in world history; and descriptions of international organizations. There is an index.

Ferguson, John. *Encyclopedia of Mysticism and Mystery Religion.* New York: Crossroad, 1982.

Hastings, James, ed. *Encyclopedia of Religion and Ethics.* 13 volumes. New York: Scribners, n.d.

Hetherington, Norriss S., ed. *Encyclopedia of Cosmology.* New York: Garland, 1993.

Hoffman, Eric, ed. *Guidebook to Publishing in Philosophy.* Bowling Green, Ohio: Philosophy Documentation Center, 1996. Designed to provide information for both new and established writers, this guidebook contains information on journal publishing, book publishing, electronic publishing, and conference presentations in philosophy.

Humana, Charles, comp. *World Human Rights Guide.* 2d ed. New York: Facts on File, 1986. This volume uses charts and graphs to profile human rights in a variety of countries. Information comes from the responses of individuals, watch-groups, organizations, and embassy officials to questionnaires based on United Nations instruments. Included are comparative ratings of human rights progress. There is no index.

The Index and Abstract Directory: An International Guide to Services and Serials Coverage, 2d ed. Birmingham, AL: Ebsco, 1990. The directory gives information on the over 35,000 serial publications represented in Ebsco's publishing database. Entries are arranged alphabetically by subject. Included are twenty pages of listings for national and international political science periodicals. There are two indexes, one for titles and one for subjects.

Kay, Ernest. *Dictionary of International Biography.* Cambridge: Melrose Press. This annual volume publishes brief biographical citations of individuals of interest in several fields. There is no index.

Kennedy Institute of Ethics. *Bibliography of Bioethics.* Washington, DC, 1978–96. This ongoing bibliography contains abstracts of articles, legal decisions, and case studies of interest to bioethicists. There is a topical index.

Kurian, George. *Encyclopedia of the Third World,* 4th ed. 3 vols. New York: Facts on File, 1992. For each country surveyed, Kurian's book compiles data on various factors, including energy, labor, education, law enforcement, history, government, human rights, and foreign policy. Volume 3 includes appendixes, a bibliography of references, and a general index.

Lawson, Edward. *Encyclopedia of Human Rights.* New York: Taylor & Francis, 1991. Various topics concerning international human rights activities from 1945 to 1990 are discussed, and significant government documents reprinted, such as the text of the Convention Relating to the Status of Refugees (1951). The appendixes include a chronological list of international human rights documents and a list of worldwide human rights institutions. There is a subject index.

Lyons, Jerry L. *Encyclopedia of Values.* New York: Van Nostrand Reinhold, 1975.

McGraw-Hill Encyclopedia of World Biography. 12 vols. New York: McGraw-Hill, 1973. This series publishes biographical summaries on notable individuals from different time periods and fields. Each entry includes a list of references.

Malone, Dumas, ed. *Dictionary of American Biography.* 20 vols. New York: Scribners, 1936. This venerable work offers biographical essays on distinguished Americans no longer living. Eight supplementary volumes bring the series up to 1970. A separate volume contains a name index.

Montney, Charles, ed. *Directories in Print.* Detroit: Gale Research. According to the introduction of the two-volume 1994 edition, volume 1 of this annual set "describes 15,900 directories, rosters, guides, and other print and nonprint address lists published in the United States and worldwide" (vii). Each entry includes address, fax number, the price of the directory, and a description of its contents. Arrangement is by subject. Chapter 19 covers "Law, Military, and Government" directories. Volume 2 contains subject and title/keyword indexes.

National Historical Publications and Records Commission. *Directory of Archives and Manuscript Repositories in the United States.* Washington, DC: National Archives and Records Service, 1978. This volume lists and describes 2,675 manuscript repositories in the United States and U.S. holdings. The entries are arranged alphabetically by state, then by city. The types of holdings are characterized for each entry and indexed. There is also an index of repository names.

Reich, Warren T., ed. *Encyclopedia of Bioethics.* 4 vols. New York: Free Press, 1978.

Sheehy, Eugene P. *Guide to Reference Books,* 10th ed. Chicago: American Library Association, 1986. The reference works listed and described in this guide are grouped in chapters according to focus. Chapter titles include "General Reference Works," "The Humanities," "Social and Behavioral Sciences," and "History and Area Studies." The guide lists reference books that cover newspapers and government publications. There is a subject index.

Wiener, Philip P., ed. *Dictionary of the History of Ideas.* 5 vols. New York: Scribners, 1973. The essays in these volumes discuss ideas that have helped to shape and continue to shape human culture. The essays are arranged alphabetically by topic, within a series of broad subheadings. One subheading covers politics and includes sixty essays on such topics as "Authority," "Democracy," "Legal Concept of Freedom," "Liberalism," and "Social Attitudes Towards Women." Volume 5 consists of a subject and name index.

4.1.2   Dictionaries

There is a brief glossary of terms in the appendix of this book, and many introductory textbooks contain glossaries. But if you are a major or minor in philosophy, or are taking an advanced course, you will profit from purchasing an inexpensive dictionary. I recommend the following:

> Martin, Robert M. *The Philosopher's Dictionary,* 2d ed. Peterborough, Ontario: Broadview Press, 1994.

Another interesting dictionary with its own peculiarities is:

> Nisbet, Robert A. *Prejudices.* Oxford: Oxford University Press, 1982.

4.1.3   Periodicals

I have placed an asterisk next to those journals appropriate for introductory students. I do not mean to suggest that all the articles in these sources are readily understandable by beginning philosophy students. But they do contain a significant number of such articles. I have relied heavily for my references on Archie Bahm, ed., *The Directory of American Philosophers 1996–1997.*

> *Acta Analyteca*   This is the journal of the Slovenian Philosophical Association.
> *Agriculture and Human Values*
> *American Philosophical Quarterly*   This journal irregularly runs review articles of current research in areas of philosophy such as relativism and foundationalism.
> *Analysis*
> *Ancient Philosophy*
> *Apeiron: A Journal for Ancient Philosophy and Science*
> **Auslegung*   The Philosophy Graduate Student Association at the University of Kansas is the sponsor of this journal, which publishes the work of new Ph.D.s and graduate students.
> *Behavioral and Brain Sciences*   This is an interdisciplinary journal that includes peer commentary.
> *Behavior and Philosophy*
> *Between the Species: A Journal of Ethics*
> *Biology and Philosophy*
> *British Journal for the Philosophy of Science*
> **Business and Professional Ethics*
> **Business Ethics*
> **Business Ethics Quarterly*
> **Canadian Journal of Philosophy*
> **Carelton University Student Journal of Philosophy*

Chinese Studies in Philosophy

Clio: A Journal of Literature, History, and the Philosophy of History

Criminal Justice Ethics

Critical Inquiry

Dialogue   This journal publishes articles in French and English.

Economics and Philosophy

Eidos: The Canadian Graduate Student Journal of Philosophy

*Environmental Ethics

Erkenntnis   This journal focuses on epistemology and philosophy of science.

*Ethics

Ethics and Advocacy

Faith and Philosophy

Feminist Philosophy

Film and Philosophy

*Foreign Affairs   Primarily a political science journal, this publication contains cogent discussions of current foreign policy issues and can be especially helpful to students of just-war theory and international politics. It is a good source for case studies.

*Foreign Policy

*Free Inquiry

*Hastings Center Report   This is an excellent source for case studies in ethics and the professions.

History of Philosophy Quarterly

Humanist

Human Rights Quarterly

Hume Studies

Hypatia: A Journal of Feminist Philosophy

Idealistic Studies

*Informal Logic

Inquiry   This journal deals with epistemology and philosophy of science.

International Journal for Philosophy of Religion

*International Journal of Applied Philosophy

International Philosophical Quarterly

International Studies in Philosophy

*Interpretation: A Journal of Political Philosophy

*Journal for Aesthetics and Art Criticism

Journal for the Theory of Social Behaviour

Journal of Agricultural and Environmental Ethics

Journal of Business Ethics

Journal of Chinese Philosophy

Journal of Chinese Studies

Journal of Indian Philosophy

Journal of Medical Humanities

Journal of Medicine and Philosophy

Journal of Mind and Behavior

Journal of Neoplatonic Studies

Journal of Phenomenological Psychology

Journal of Philosophical Logic

Journal of Philosophical Research

Journal of Philosophy

Journal of Religious Ethics

*Journal of Social Philosophy

Journal of Speculative Philosophy   This journal concentrates on American and Continental philosophy.

Journal of Symbolic Logic

Journal of the American Academy of Religion

*Journal of the History of Ideas

Journal of the History of Philosophy

Journal of the History of Sport

*Journal of Value Inquiry   This journal covers ethics, social and political philosophy, and aesthetics.

*Kennedy Institute of Ethics Journal

*Kinesis: Graduate Journal in Philosophy   This journal publishes papers by graduate students.

Law and Philosophy

Linguistics and Philosophy

Man and World   This journal covers mostly existential and Continental philosophy.

Mediaeval Studies

*Medical Humanities Newsletter

Metaphilosophy

Midwest Studies in Philosophy   This journal, published annually, devotes each issue to one specific philosophical topic.

Mind   This journal focuses on epistemology, metaphysics, and philosophy of psychology.

*Monist   Published quarterly, this journal arranges each issue around a specific topic.

Nous

Pacific Philosophical Quarterly

Philosophia

Philosophia Mathematica

Philosophical Books   This is a journal of book reviews.

*Philosophical Forum

Philosophical Psychology

Philosophical Review

Philosophical Studies   The focus of this journal is analytical philosophy.

Philosophic Exchange

*Philosophy and Literature

Philosophy and Phenomenological Research

*Philosophy and Public Affairs

Philosophy and Rhetoric

*Philosophy and Social Criticism

Philosophy and Theology

Philosophy East and West   This journal focuses on Asian and comparative philosophy.

Philosophy in Science

Philosophy of Science

*Philosophy of the Social Sciences

*Philosophy Today   The dual focus of this journal is on existentialism and Continental philosophy.

Phoenix   This journal publishes articles in English and French.

Process Studies

*Professional Ethics

*Public Affairs Quarterly

*Reason Papers   This journal focuses on social and political philosophy.

Research in Phenomenology

Research in Philosophy and Technology

*Review of Metaphysics   The September issue of this journal prints a list of recently accepted Ph.D. dissertations. The list is arranged by school and includes statistics on each university's graduate program. The director and committee for each degree are generally listed also. The journal also runs an annual dissertation competition.

Russell: The Journal of the Bertrand Russell Archives

Science, Technology, and Human Values

Social Epistemology

Social Philosophy and Policy

Social Theory and Practice

Southern Journal of Philosophy

Synthese

Technology and Culture

Telos   The emphasis in this journal is on radical social and political theory.

Thinking: The Journal for Philosophy for Children

Thomist

Topoi   This journal focuses on analytic philosophy and philosophy of science.

Transactions of the Charles S. Peirce Society   Peirce is often the focus, but essays on all the classical American philosophers are included. Sometimes the editor also prints essays on contemporary philosophy.

Ultimate Reality and Meaning: Studies in the Philosophy of Understanding   This journal talks about virtually everything.

Zygon

This is just a selection from a much larger number of philosophy journals, the ones consulted most often by professional philosophers. Do not hesitate to ask your instructor for further references or consult Bahm's directory, the international directory, or *The Philosopher's Index*, cited below.

4.1.4   Periodical Indexes

Bibliographic Index

Biography Index

Book Review Index

Humanities Index

An Index to Book Reviews in the Humanities

Lineback, Richard H., ed. *The Philosopher's Index.* Vol. 30. Bowling Green, Ohio: Philosophy Documentation Center, 1996. This is "a subject and author index to philosophy articles, books, anthologies, and contributions to anthologies." Begun in 1967 as an index of journal articles, the index began listing anthologies and books in 1978. There are two retrospective indices covering articles in U.S. publications and in non-U.S. English-language publications between 1940 and 1978. The book review index is especially helpful in finding material that may help you formulate a critical review of a recent book. The subject index can also point you to a wide variety of articles on a pressing paper topic.

Reader's Guide to Periodical Literature

Social Sciences Index

4.2   OTHER SOURCES OF INFORMATION

4.2.1   Research Institutes

You will find it difficult if not impossible to find a topic on which nothing has been written. In fact, for any paper topic you can find, it is highly likely that substantial original research has already been done. Suppose that you could talk to someone who could tell you how to find information, easily and quickly, that might otherwise take you weeks of time to develop. Suppose further that you could take this information and evaluate its importance in view of information on the same topic that you have received from other sources. Your paper would certainly be superior to one for which this information was not available. Private research institutes may provide you with just such an opportunity. From private think tanks like the Brookings Institution to public agencies such as the National Institutes of Health, organizations are continuously conducting research on many topics of interest to students of philosophy. You may want to contact a few of them, tell them what you are doing, and inquire about resources that they may be able to make available to you. In order to find them, look up appropriate organizations for your topic in:

Dresser, Peter D., and Karen Hill, eds. *Research Centers Directory*. Detroit: Gale Research. Over 11,700 university-related and other nonprofit research organizations are briefly profiled in this annual two-volume publication. The entries are listed in sections by topics. There is a subject index and a master index as well as a supplemental volume.

4.2.2   Interest Groups

Many sources of information are not objective, in the sense that they are openly advocating a particular social or political cause. Despite their bias, these sources may still have substantial amounts of valuable information to contribute to your philosophy paper. After defining your topic as clearly as possible, you will find appropriate organizations described in the following volumes:

Daniels, Peggy Kneffel, and Carol A. Schwartz, eds. *Encyclopedia of Associations*. Detroit: Gale Research. This annually published guide lists entries for approximately 23,000 national and international organizations, arranged by subjects such as "Environmental and Agricultural Organizations," and "Legal, Governmental, Public Administration, and Military Organizations." Each entry includes a brief description of the organization's function and available publications. There are several indexes.

Minority Organizations: A National Directory, 4th ed. Garrett Park, MD: Garrett Park Press, 1992. This directory lists names and addresses of 7,700 organizations dedicated to the needs of minority groups. It also lists 2,800 "lost organizations," for which no current address was found. There are five indexes.

Scott, Mark W., ed. *National Directory of Non-Profit Organizations.* 2 vols. Rockville MD: Taft Group, 1993. This guide gives brief listings of over 167,000 non-profit organizations, citing addresses, phone numbers, and IRS filing status. Volume 1 covers organizations with annual revenues of $100,000 or over; volume 2 deals with organizations with revenues of $25,000 to $99,000. Included are an activity index and a geographic index.

Wasserman, Paul, ed. *Ethnic Information Sources of the United States,* 3d ed. Detroit: Gale Research, 1995. This volume lists names and addresses of such information sources as embassies, fraternal organizations, professional organizations, foundations, and periodical publications for a wide variety of ethnic groups and includes an index of organization names.

Wilson, Robert, ed. *American Lobbyists Directory.* Detroit: Gale Research, 1990. Over 65,000 registered federal and state lobbyists, along with the businesses they represent, are listed in this guide. Included are indexes for lobbyists, their organizations, and general subjects/specialties.

Zuckerman, Edward. *Almanac of Federal PACs.* Washington, DC: Amward. This annual directory profiles the campaign contributions of every political action committee (PAC) that gave $50,000 or more to candidates for the U.S. Senate or House of Representatives. PACs are arranged alphabetically within chapters devoted to different target groups. Each entry includes a brief description of the goals and yearly activities of the PAC. There is a name index.

5
Philosophy on the World Wide Web

Out flew the web and floated wide
The mirror cracked from side to side
'The curse is come upon me'
cried the Lady of Shalott.

—Alfred, Lord Tennyson

Oh what a tangled web we perceive
when first we practice to retrieve

—Shakespeare Scott

5.1 A WHIRLWIND INTRODUCTORY TOUR OF THE INTERNET

To understand the internet and how to use it, we need to begin with the basics. Follow along on our whirlwind tour of the internet. Let's let this symbol represent a computer: 🖥 Two or more computers linked together by a telephone line, fiber optic line, radio wave, or satellite beam compose a network:

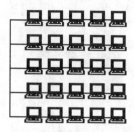

109

Let's call this dot [.] a symbol for a network composed of ten thousand computers, and place a dot on a map of the world for every ten thousand computers.

The map would look something like the one above. This map represents, very imperfectly, the internet. The *internet* is a network of thousands of computer networks that use a common computer language to communicate with each other, linked together by communications lines. The internet was conceived in the late 1960s when the Advanced Research Projects Agency of the U.S. Department of Defense began to develop a military communications system that would be capable of surviving a nuclear war. They produced a network of computers called the ARPANET, which at first included military research labs and universities, but which later added many more related computer systems.

Two decades later the National Science Foundation initiated a project called NSFNET, the purpose of which was to connect American supercomputer centers. Throughout the world similar networks were being established, and by the late 1980s, connections among these networks came to be known as the internet, which is now growing at a phenomenal rate. In 1991 there were only about 700,000 people using the internet. By 1996 that number was approaching 40 million, with 160,000 new users each month.

The World Wide Web (WWW) is an organized system for accessing the information on the internet. Tim Berners-Lee of CERN, the European Laboratory for Particle Physics in Geneva, Switzerland, launched the WWW when he successfully created a method for using a single means of access to the networks on the internet. The WWW is now the primary vehicle for access to information on the internet.

5.2   HOW DO I ACCESS THE INTERNET AND THE WORLD WIDE WEB?

The best way to access the internet is to obtain access to a new computer with the latest communications software and follow the directions included in the software. Before long you will be "surfing the net" to your heart's content. In the pages that follow we will examine briefly each stage of the process by which you may gain access to the internet. To access the WWW on the internet, you need four things:

- a computer
- a modem
- a service provider
- a browser

First, you need two pieces of "hardware": a computer (🖥) and a modem (🖲). We will assume that you know what a computer is, but you may not be aware that your local magazine stand or bookstore carries a wide variety of periodicals that review and rate computers. When the time comes for you to purchase one, you will make a much more informed choice if you read the articles in such magazines as *Consumer Reports* and the *Computer Shopper*. It is very important to buy a computer with the largest memory and hard drive disk capacity that you can afford. The internet is getting more sophisticated every day, and many of the materials that you will want to download (electronically transmit) from the internet to your computer will require substantial space on your computer's hard drive.

A *modem* is a device that connects your computer to a telephone line or other line of communication. Because it can take time to download files, and because many internet access programs charge their customers for the time they spend hooked up to the internet, it is important that your modem be capable of running at a fast rate of speed. Both computers and modems require software containing operations instructions.

Next, you will need an internet service, a commercial business that connects you to the internet and charges you a monthly fee that varies with the service and the amount of time you spend using it. Some of the most popular internet services, with telephone numbers you can use to contact them, are:

- America Online, 1-800-827-3338
- Compuserve, 1-800-848-8990
- Earthlink Network, 1-213-644-9500
- Global Network Navigator (GNN), 1-800-819-6112
- Microsoft Network (MSN), 1-800-386-5550
- Prodigy, 1-800-776-3449

Many smaller companies also provide internet service, and you may be able to get rates more suited to your own pattern of internet use from them. You will find these services listed in the yellow pages of your phone book. If you buy a new computer from a major manufacturer, you may find internet service product brochures and software included with your computer. In addition to connecting you to the World Wide Web, some services also provide you with news, communications, and other services.

Finally, you need a *browser,* which is a software program that allows you to search for information on the internet. In 1993 the National Center for Supercomputing Applications (NCSA) introduced Mosaic, a browser that greatly facilitated searching for information on the WWW and encouraged many people to gain access to the internet, but since that time other commercial browsers have become more popular. At the moment this book is being written, *Netscape Navigator* is the most popular browser, but Microsoft's *Internet Explorer* is challenging Navigator's dominance with some success. If you contract with MSN for internet service, you will be able to download MSN's browser, *Internet Explorer,* for free, and from time to time Netscape makes a special offer of its *Navigator* for free.

You will experience a browser as a window, or *dialog box,* on your computer screen that assists you in finding information on the internet.

Once you have opened the *home page* (the starting page for a web site) of your browser you will notice that it offers you a number of *search engines,* which are programs that allow you to search the internet using key words or phrases. Your browser will also provide a space in which you can type internet addresses to access search engines and other internet sites. Some of the most commonly used search engines, and their internet addresses, are the following:

- YAHOO: http://www.yahoo.com
- AltaVista: http://altavista.digital.com
- Webcrawler: http://webcrawler.com
- LYCOS: http://www.lycos.com
- EXCITE: http://www.excite.com

Let's suppose you use the Yahoo search engine. In the search engine's dialog box you type in the word "philosophy." The search engine will then make several clickable links appear on the screen. A *clickable link* is an icon or line of text that is highlighted and programmed so that when you click your mouse button on it, you immediately go to a new internet address. One of the clickable links that your Yahoo search engine will provide for you when you search under the topic of philosophy is "Organizations." Here you will find more clickable links, one of which will be entitled "APA," for American Philosophical Association. This is a good place to begin your search for information in philosophy.

The link entitled "Departments" provides links to home pages of philosophy departments at universities around the country and the world. But this is only the beginning. If you click on the "back" key on your browser, you can return to the Yahoo menu that lists sources of philosophy information. There you will encounter a wide variety of other resources, including many philosophy home pages that are wonderful resources for finding further information, like *Philosophy in Cyberspace,* and *Philosophy on the Web.*

Among the items that will appear on your screen during your search, you will find gophers. The original *Gopher* is an information system that allows you to browse information sources throughout the world by going through a series of menus. It was developed and is still operated by the University of Minnesota. Since the original Gopher, other gophers have been developed for a variety of purposes, and some of them offer links to a vast assortment of philosophy resources, all of which you can locate through your browser. For example, the University of California at Irvine's Department of Philosophy hosts a *Directory of Philosophy Gophers.* Through your browser or this directory you will find many other gophers, such as:

- North Carolina State University Library Gopher
- The Pipeline Gopher (United States and United Kingdom)
- University of Michigan Library Gopher
- University of Southern California Gopher
- Washington and Lee University Gopher
- Australian National University Gopher
- Texas Tech Computer Science Gopher

Each page on the internet has an address known as a URL (Universal Resource Locator), which will appear in a form something like: http://www.yahoo.com. When you find a page on the internet that provides information you would like to return to, you can enter a bookmark on your browser. A bookmark is a URL that has been entered into a special location on your browser so that you can find the URL and access its content quickly and easily. Your browser will provide directions for entering bookmarks.

5.3   PHILOSOPHY RESOURCES ON THE INTERNET

The number of philosophy sources on the internet is bewildering. One good place to start looking, as we have mentioned, is the APA home page. In the APA home page you will find the following clickable links, each of which will provide you further information:

- Index of APA resources
- Bibliographies

- Centers
- Content
- Courses
- Departments
- E-texts
- Guides
- Journals
- Libraries
- Online
- Philosophers
- Publishers
- Societies
- Software

By clicking your mouse on these links, you will find many more links to sources of philosophy information. When you enter a search for "philosophy" in the Yahoo search engine, you will be presented with the *Philosophy on the Web* link, which includes information listed in the following categories:

- Directories [of philosophy information]
- Bibliographies
- Departments [of philosophy at major universities]
- E-journals [electronic journals that you can access on-line]
- E-texts [famous philosophy texts, such as Plato's *Republic* that you can access on-line]
- Gophers
- Journals and societies
- Preprints and working papers
- Projects
- Publishers
- Software
- Directories
- Internet Services for Philosophers

You will also discover lists of journals published in printed form. The home pages of these journals will often tell you the contents of articles for recent issues. Examples of journal home pages you will find include:

- *Analysis*
- *Australasian Journal of Philosophy*

- *The British Journal for the Philosophy of Science*
- *Canadian Journal of Philosophy*
- *Environmental Ethics*
- *HOPOS History of the Philosophy of Science*
- *The Journal of Aesthetics and Art Criticism*
- *Journal of Consciousness Studies*
- *Mind*
- *The Monist*
- *Nordic Journal of Philosophical Logic*
- *Philosophia Perennis*
- *Philosophy and Phenomenological Research*
- *Radical Philosophy*
- *Teaching Philosophy*

A recent phenomenon, *electronic journals* are periodicals that are "published" only on the internet. Electronic journals of interest to philosophers include:

- *Bryn Mawr Classical Review*
- *Eidos Journal*
- *Electronic Antiquity: Communicating The Classics*
- *Electronic Journal of Analytic Philosophy*
- *Environmental Ethics Journal*
- *International Society for Environmental Ethics Newsletter*
- *Interscience Review*
- *Logos*
- *Online Journal of Ethics*
- *Qui Parle: An Interdisciplinary Journal*
- *Sorites*
- *The Electronic Journal of Analytic Philosophy*
- *Truth Journal*

Among the links that provide electronic texts is *The Internet Encyclopedia of Philosophy's* Philosophy Text Collection. The collection's editor, James Fieser, has provided copies of famous philosophy texts for you to view and download (for personal educational purposes only, not for publication). These texts include:

- Bentham's *Principles of Morals*
- Berkeley's *Principles of Human Knowledge*
- Berkeley's *Three Dialogues*

- Descartes's *Discourse on the Method*
- Descartes's *Meditations of First Philosophy*
- Epictetus' *Enchiridion*
- Epicurus' *Letter to Menoecius*
- Epicurus' *Principal Doctrines*
- James's *The Will to Believe*
- Lao Tzu's *Tao Te Ching*
- Leibniz's *Monadology*
- Locke's *A Letter Concerning Toleration*
- McCosh's *The Scottish Philosophy*
- Mill's *On Liberty*
- Plato's *Republic*
- Plato's *Crito*
- Presocratic Fragments and Testimonials

Another good source of information is philosophic associations and societies. Some of the groups that have home pages on the web are:

- American Association of Philosophy Teachers
- American Philosophical Association
- American Society for Aesthetics
- Arizona Secular Humanists
- Association for Practical and Professional Ethics
- Association for the Scientific Study of Consciousness
- The Bertrand Russell Society
- British Society for Aesthetics
- British Society for Ethical Theory
- The British Society for the Philosophy of Science
- The Canadian Philosophical Association
- Canadian Society for the History and Philosophy of Mathematics
- Deutsche Zeitschrift für Philosophie
- The Friedrich Nietzsche Society
- History of Science Society
- Hume Society
- International Society for Environmental Ethics
- International Society for the History, Philosophy and Social Studies of Biology
- The Kurt Goedel Society

- Philosophy of Science Association
- Societé Canadienne d'Esthetique
- Society of Christian Philosophers
- Southern Society for Philosophy and Psychology

The purpose of this chapter is to pique your curiosity and help you get started on your exploration of the internet. Once you have begun, you will discover thousands of cites and dozens of types of information that we have not mentioned in this chapter. Some of the things you will find are:

- *Mailing lists.* You can join a mailing list and receive by e-mail or in printed form publications of a wide variety of organizations.
- *Bibliographies.* Numerous extensive bibliographies of philosophic information already appear on the net.
- *Publishers and bookstores.* You will find publishers offering to sell you virtually any title in philosophy, and you will find bookstores that offer not only new books, but old, outdated, and rare editions of many texts.
- *Philosophy projects.* Many philosophy research and discussion projects have home pages on the net, and sometimes you can join in the research and discussions. Of particular interest is the University of Chicago Philosophy Project. Check it out and find out why it is interesting.
- *Philosophy resource guides.* Guides to all these resources and more are on the net, with clickable links that take you directly to the sources they cite.
- *Newsgroups.* Newsgroups are internet pages in which people exchange information on current events.

6

Formats for Philosophy Papers

A mathematician, like a painter or a poet, is a maker of patterns. If his patterns are more permanent than theirs, it is because they are made with ideas.

—Godfrey Harold Hardy (1877–1947)

6.1   GETTING STARTED

Your format makes your paper's first impression. Justly or not, accurately or not, the format of your paper announces your professional competence or lack of competence. A well-executed format implies that your paper is worth reading. More than that, however, a proper format brings information to your readers in a familiar form that has the effect of setting their minds at ease. Your paper's format, therefore, should impress your readers with your academic competence as a philosopher by following accepted professional standards. Like the style and clarity of your writing, your format communicates messages that are often more readily and profoundly received than the content of the document itself.

The format described in this chapter is in conformance with standards generally accepted in the humanities, including instructions for the following elements:

General page format
Title page
Abstract
Table of contents
List of tables and figures

Text

Reference page

Appendix

Except for special instructions from your instructor, follow the directions in this manual exactly.

6.2   GENERAL PAGE FORMAT

Philosophy assignments should be typed or printed on 8½-by-11-inch premium white bond paper, 20 lb. or heavier. Do not use any other color or size except to comply with special instructions from your instructor, and do not use an off-white or a poor-quality (draft) paper. Philosophy that is worthy of your time to write, and worthy of your instructor's time to read, is worthy of good paper. Many of your instructors will have reached the stage in life where they need bifocals. Make their lives a bit more pleasant and improve your chances of getting a good grade by springing for a new ink cartridge or ribbon for your printer or typewriter.

Always submit to your instructor an original typed or computer-printed (preferably laser) manuscript. Do not submit a photocopy! Always print a second copy to keep for your own files in case the original is lost. If you are using a computer, make sure to back up your paper and your research files onto a disk. Beware: Some instructors no longer fall for the excuse that your paper is done but you cannot turn it in until your printer is fixed. They will ask you for the disk or tell you to e-mail it so they can print it themselves. Never fax a paper without prior permission from your instructor. Many fax machines still produce low-quality copies.

Margins, except for theses and dissertations, should be one inch from all sides of the paper. (You will need to consult with the appropriate office at your institution for instructions on theses and dissertations.) Unless otherwise instructed, all paper submissions should be double-spaced in a 12-point word-processing font or typewriter pica type. Typewriter elite type may be used if other fonts or type are not available. Select a font that is plain and easy to read, such as Helvetica, Courier, Garamond, or Times Roman. Do not use script, stylized, or elaborate fonts.

Page numbers should appear in the upper right corner of each page, one inch from the right side and one-half inch from the top of the page. Numbers should begin appearing immediately after the title page. No page number should actually appear on the title page or on the first page of the text, but these pages should still be counted in the numbering. Numbers should proceed consecutively, beginning with the title page (even though the first number is not actually printed on that page). If you choose to use lowercase roman numerals (i, ii, iii, iv, v, vi, vii, viii, ix, x, and so on) for the pages that precede the first page of text (such as the title page, table of contents, and table of figures), these numerals should be centered at the bottom of the page.

Ask your instructor about bindings. In the absence of further directions, *do not bind* your paper or enclose it within a plastic cover sheet. Place one staple in the upper left corner, or use a paper clip at the top of the paper. Note that a paper to be submitted to a journal for publication should not be clipped, stapled, or bound in any form.

Professional philosophy journals do not all require the same preparation style of the manuscripts they publish. The simplest way to determine what a journal requires is to consult an issue. Generally there is an explanation of submission requirements inside the front or back covers. It can become maddening to change styles as you prepare a manuscript for submission to a second or third journal. (Yes, sometimes articles are turned down for publication. It is a good idea to have an alternative journal already in mind when you dispatch your work for consideration the first time.) My experience has been that if you follow a generally accepted style your manuscript will be reviewed and you will only have to reformat it after it has been accepted for publication.

6.3 TITLE PAGE

The following information is centered on the title page:

- Title of paper
- Name of writer
- Course name, section number, and instructor
- College or university
- Date

```
       The Moral Imperative of Vegetarianism
                       by
                  Amber Bovine
          Ethics and Human Happiness
                 Phil 108-03
               Dr. Hayes Fodder
                  Spring 1997
               Harvest College
                March 21, 1997
```

The title should clearly describe the problem addressed in the paper. If the paper discusses the implications of act utilitarianism for animal rights and famine control, for example, the title "Act Utilitarianism, Animal Rights, and Famine Control" is professional, clear, and helpful to the reader. Avoid such titles as "Act Utilitarianism," "Animal Rights," or "Meat and Morals," because they are incomplete or vague.

6.4   ABSTRACT

An abstract is a brief summary of a paper, written to allow potential readers to know the paper's subject matter to see if it contains information of sufficient interest for them to read. People conducting research want specific kinds of information, and they often read dozens of abstracts looking for papers that contain information relevant to their research topic. Abstracts have the designation "Abstract" centered near the top of the page. Next, the title appears, also centered, followed by a paragraph that precisely states the paper's topic, research and analysis methods, and results and conclusions. The abstract itself should be written in one paragraph that does not exceed 250 words. Remember that an abstract is not an introduction but a summary, as demonstrated in the sample below.

Abstract

Bertrand Russell's View of Mysticism

This paper reviews Bertrand Russell's writings on religion, mysticism, and science and defines his perspective on the contribution of mysticism to scientific knowledge. Russell drew a sharp distinction between what he considered to be (1) the essence of religion and (2) dogma or assertions attached to religion by theologians and religious leaders. Although some of his writings, including Why I Am Not a Christian, appear hostile to all aspects of religion, Russell actually asserts that religion, freed from doctrinal encumbrances, not only fulfills certain psychological needs, but evokes many of the most beneficial human impulses. He believes that religious mysticism generates an intellectual disinterestedness that may be useful to science, but that it is not a source of a special type of knowledge beyond investigation by science.

6.5   TABLE OF CONTENTS

A table of contents includes the titles of the major divisions and subdivisions of a paper. Tables of contents are not normally required in papers written as course assignments but may be included. They usually appear, however, in books, theses, and dissertations. The table of contents should consist of the chapter or main section titles, the headings used in the text, with one additional level of titles, along with their page numbers, as the following sample illustrates. (Note that the words "Table of" are not used on the *actual* contents page; they are used only when *referring* to it.)

Contents

6.6   LISTS OF TABLES AND FIGURES

A List of Tables or List of Figures contains the titles of the tables, figures, diagrams, photographs, and pictures included in the paper in the order in which they appear, along with their page numbers. You may list tables, illustrations, and figures together under the title "Figures" (and title them all "Figures" in the text), or, if you have more than a half-page of entries, you may have separate lists for tables, figures, and illustrations (and title them accordingly in the text). The format for all such tables should follow the example below, from a paper entitled "Ethics, Aesthetics, and Immigration."

List of Figures and Illustrations

1. Photograph of the Author 1

2. Drawing of Immanuel Kant 3

3. Painting of a Thing-in-Itself
   by Wilfred Sellars 9

4. Reproduction: John Stewart Curry's "The Migrant
   Workers Camp" 15

5. Venn Diagram of Kant's Categorical
   Imperative 16

6. California Immigration, 1927–1941 23

6.7   TEXT

Ask your instructor for the number of pages required for the paper you are writing. The text should follow the directions explained in Chapters 1 and 2 of this manual and should conform to the format of the page of text printed below.

Sample Page of Text

In the southern waterfront city of Bordeaux, on January 6, 1912, French scholar, sociologist, and lay theologian Jacques Ellul was born. The ensuing years have witnessed production of more than forty books and six hundred articles, earning their author serious critical attention and numerous titles. For most of his career Jacques Ellul was professor of History and Sociology of Institutions on the Faculty of Law and Economic Sciences at the University of Bordeaux.

It would be difficult to overemphasize the influence of his father. Not professionally educated, his father decided that his bright, inquisitive son should enter the practice of law. Ellul had no inclination to legal practice. Respecting his father's wishes, he pushed aside a desire to become a naval officer and went to law school, intent upon teaching Roman law, in which he had some interest. This choice was a gamble. There existed only four or five positions in Roman law in the country, and competition for them was acute. Ellul, however, secured the desired position in his home town of Bordeaux.

His father's character also shaped Ellul's early struggles with money. The elder Ellul's sense of honor kept him from

6.8   CHAPTER HEADINGS

Your papers should include no more than three levels of headings:

1. *Primary,* which should be centered, with each word except articles, prepositions, and conjunctions capitalized:

   `The Development of Social Contract Theory`

2. *Secondary,* which begin at the left margin, also with each word except articles, prepositions, and conjunctions capitalized:

   `Anglo-American Philosophy and the Social Contract`

3. *Tertiary,* which should be written in sentence style (with only the first word and proper nouns capitalized) with a period at the end, underlined:

   `Two contract theorists: Hobbes and Locke.`

6.9   ILLUSTRATIONS AND FIGURES

Illustrations are not normally inserted in the text of a philosophy paper, journal article, or book unless they are necessary to explain the material in the text. Some textbooks and anthologies have begun to include photographs of authors. And certainly pictures are appropriate to aesthetics papers and journals.

Do not paste or tape photocopies of photographs or similar materials to the pages of the text or the appendix. Instead, photocopy each one on a separate sheet of paper and center each photo or illustration, along with its typed title, within the normal margins of the paper. The format of the illustration titles should be the same as the format for tables and figures.

6.10   REFERENCE PAGE

The format for references is discussed in Chapter 7 of this book.

6.11   APPENDICES

Appearing at the back of the paper, after the text, appendices are reference materials that provide information for the convenience of the reader to supplement the important facts contained in the text. Appendices may include maps, charts, tables, and selected documents. They are rarely used in philosophy.

Do not place in your appendix materials that are merely interesting or decorative. Add in an appendix only items that will answer questions raised by the text or are necessary to explain the text. Follow the guidelines for formats for illustrations, tables, and figures when adding material in an appendix. At the top center of the page, label your first appendix "Appendix A," your second appendix "Appendix B," and so on. Do not append an entire government report, journal article, or other publication, but only the portions of such documents that are necessary to support your paper. The source of the information should always be evident on the appended pages.

7

Citing Sources

Man is timid and apologetic; he is no longer upright; he dares not say 'I think,' 'I am,' but quotes some saint or sage. He is ashamed before the blade of grass or the blowing rose. These roses under my window make no reference to former roses or to better ones; they are for what they are; they exist with God today. There is no time to them. There simply is the rose; it is perfect in every moment of its existence.

—Ralph Waldo Emerson

7.1   PRELIMINARY DECISIONS

One of your most important jobs as a research writer is to document your use of source material carefully and clearly. Failure to do so will cause your readers confusion, damage the effectiveness of your paper, and perhaps make you vulnerable to a charge of plagiarism. Proper documentation is more than just good form; it is a powerful indicator of your own commitment to scholarship and the sense of authority that you bring to your writing. Good documentation demonstrates your expertise as a researcher and increases the reader's trust in you and your work; it gives credibility to what you are writing.

Unfortunately, as anybody who has ever written a research paper knows, getting the documentation right can be a frustrating, confusing job, especially for the novice writer. Positioning each element of a single reference citation accurately can require what seems an inordinate amount of time spent thumbing through the style manual. Even before you begin to work on specific citations, there are important questions of style and format to answer.

7.1.1 What to Document

Direct quotes must always be credited, as must certain kinds of paraphrased material. Information that is basic—important dates; facts or opinions universally acknowledged—need not be cited. Information that is not widely known, whether fact or opinion, should receive documentation.

What if you are unsure whether a certain fact is widely known? You are, after all, very probably a newcomer to the field in which you are conducting your research. If in doubt, supply the documentation. It is better to overdocument than to fail to do justice to a source.

7.1.2 Which Citation System to Use

While the question of which documentation style to use may be decided for you in some classes by your instructor, others may allow you a choice. There are several styles available, each designed to meet the needs of writers in particular fields. The documentary note system, in which superscript numbers ([1]) are placed at the end of sentences in the text, is perhaps the one most widely used in the discipline of philosophy, and it is therefore described first, in the next section of this text.

This chapter also includes for your consideration the Student Citation System (SCS), which has been developed for use in all undergraduate college classes, regardless of the discipline. The advantage of the SCS is that it may be used in any college class (English, physics, psychology, philosophy, political science, journalism, economics, and others) in which the instructor permits it. In addition, it is a simple system with few rules. It is easy to type and its punctuation is familiar to students who use the internet. You will find the SCS described below, in section 7.3.

7.1.3 The Importance of Consistency

Whichever style and format you use, the most important rule to remember is, *be consistent.* Sloppy referencing undermines your readers' trust and does a disservice to the writers whose work you are incorporating into your own argument. And from a purely practical standpoint, inconsistent referencing can severely damage your grade.

7.1.4 Using the Style Manual

Read through the following pages before trying to use them to structure your notes. Unpracticed student researchers tend to ignore this section of the style manual until the moment the first note has to be worked out, and then they skim through the examples looking for the one example that perfectly corresponds to the immediate case at hand. But most style manuals do not include every possible documentation model, so the writer must piece together a coherent reference out of elements from several models. Reading through all the models before using them gives you a feel for where to find different aspects of models as well as for how the referencing system works in general.

7.2   DOCUMENTARY-NOTE SYSTEM: NUMBERED REFERENCES

7.2.1   General Format Rules

In the documentary-note system you place a superscript (raised) number after the passage that includes source material. The number refers to a full bibliographical citation given either at the foot of the page (a footnote) or in a list at the end of the paper (an endnote). Information in this section comes from section 15 of the *Chicago Manual of Style* (*CMS*), 14th edition.

7.2.1.1   *Numbering System*

Number the notes consecutively throughout the entire paper, starting with [1]. In other words, do not begin again with [1] at the beginning of each new chapter or section of the paper, as many published works do.

7.2.1.2   *Placement of Superscript Numeral*

Whenever possible, the superscript numeral should go at the end of the sentence:

> Rorty's representation of Sellars as an eliminative materialist is radically mistaken.[1]

If it is necessary to place the reference within a sentence instead of at the end, position the numeral at the end of the pertinent clause.

> In his last editorial Bagley denounces the current city administration[13]—and thousands of others feel the same way.

Notice in the example above that the superscript numeral occurs before the dash. For all other pieces of punctuation—comma, semicolon, period, exclamation mark, question mark—the superscript numeral follows the punctuation.

The numeral also follows the terminal quotation mark of a direct quote:

"This clause," claimed Lindley, "is the most crucial one in the address."[20]

7.2.1.3   *Multiple Notes*

When a passage refers to more than one source, do not place more than one superscript numeral after the passage. Instead, use only one numeral, and combine all the references into a single footnote:

Separate studies by Lovett, Morrison, Collins, and the Anderson Group all corroborate the state's findings.[7]

7.2.2   Models for Documentary Notes and Bibliographical Citations

In each pair of models below, the first model is of a documentary note, and the second is for the corresponding bibliographical entry. A note may appear either as a footnote, placed at the bottom of the page of text on which the reference occurs, or as an endnote, placed in numerical order in a list following the text of the paper. Many word processors are able to change notes from one style to the other.

7.2.2.1   *Differences Between Endnotes and Bibliography*

In the paper's final draft, your endnotes will precede the bibliography, which is usually the final element in the paper. Because its entries are arranged alphabetically, the order of entries in the bibliography will differ from the order of the endnotes, which are arranged according to the appearance of the references within the text. Pay attention to the basic differences between the note format and the bibliography format. Notes are numbered; bibliographical entries are not. The first line of a note is indented; in a bibliography all lines are indented except the first. While the author's name is printed in normal order in a note, the order is reversed in the bibliography to facilitate alphabetizing. There are also variations within the individual references.

If the note refers to a book or an article in its entirety, you need not cite specific page numbers in your references. If, however, you wish to cite material on a specific page or set of pages, give the page numbers in the note.

7.2.2.2   Books

One author

Note

   1. Amanda Collingwood, <u>Metaphysics and the Public</u> (Detroit: Zane Press, 1993), 235-38.

Bibliography

   Collingwood, Amanda. <u>Metaphysics and the Public</u>. Detroit: Zane Press, 1993.

Two authors

Note

   6. Delbert P. Grady and Jane Ryan Torrance, <u>Philosophers and Their Secrets</u>. (New York: Holograph Press, 1989).

Bibliography

   Grady, Delbert P., and Jane Ryan Torrance. <u>Philosophers and Their Secrets</u>. New York: Holograph Press, 1989.

Three authors

Note

   2. Samuel Howard, William J. Abbott, and Jane Hope, <u>Powerbase: How to Increase Your Hold on Your Fellow Philosophy Students</u>. (Los Angeles: Gollum and Smythe, 1986).

Bibliography

   Howard, Samuel, William J. Abbot, and Jane Hope. <u>Powerbase: How to Increase Your Hold on Your Fellow Philosophy Students</u>. Los Angeles: Gollum and Smythe, 1986.

More than three authors

The Latin phrase *et al.,* meaning "and others," appears in roman type after the name of the first author. Note that *al.* (an abbreviation for *alia*) must be followed by a period.

Note

      21. Angela Genessario et al., <u>Religion and the Child</u> (Baltimore: Colgate, 1991), 16-18, 78-82.

Bibliography

    Genessario, Angela, et al. <u>Religion and the Child</u>. Baltimore: Colgate, 1991.

Editor, compiler, or translator as author

Note

      6. Dylan Trakas, comp., <u>Teaching Philosophy</u> (El Paso, TX: Del Norte Press, 1994).

Bibliography

    Trakas, Dylan, comp. <u>Teaching Philosophy</u>. El Paso, TX: Del Norte Press, 1994.

Editor, compiler, or translator with author

Note

      15. Ezra Pound, <u>Literary Essays</u>, ed. T. S. Eliot (New York: New Directions, 1953), 48.

      47. Philippe Aris, <u>Centuries of Childhood: A Social History of Family Life</u>, trans. Robert Baldock (New York: Knopf, 1962).

Bibliography

    Pound, Ezra. <u>Literary Essays</u>. Ed. T. S. Eliot. New York: New Directions, 1953.

    Aris, Philippe. <u>Centuries of Childhood: A Social History of Family Life</u>. Trans. Robert Baldock. New York: Knopf, 1962.

Untranslated book

Note

      8. Henry Cesbron, <u>Histoire critique de l' hystorie</u> (Paris: Asselin et Houzeau, 1909).

Bibliography

    Cesbron, Henry. <u>Histoire critique de l' hystorie</u>. Paris: Asselin et Houzeau, 1909.

Untranslated book with title translated, in parentheses

Note

> 53. Henryk Wereszyncki, <u>Koniec sojuszu trzech cesarzy</u> (The End of the Three Emperors' League) (Warsaw: PWN, 1977).

Bibliography

> Wereszyncki, Henryk. <u>Koniec sojuszu trzech cesarzy</u> (The End of the Three Emperors' League). Warsaw: PWN, 1977.

Two or more works by the same author

In the notes, subsequent works by an author are handled exactly as the first work. In the bibliography, the works are listed alphabetically, with the author's name replaced, in all entries after the first, by a three-em dash (six strokes of the hyphen).

Bibliography

> Russell, Henry. <u>Famous Last Words</u>. New Orleans: Liberty Publications, 1978.
> ———. <u>Famous Philosophical Debates</u>. Denver: Axel & Myers, 1988.

Chapter in a multi-author collection

Note

> 23. Alexa North Gray, "American Philosophers and the Foreign Press," in <u>Current Media Issues</u>, ed. Barbara Bonnard (New York: Boulanger, 1994), 189-231.

Bibliography

> Gray, Alexa North. "American Philosophers and the Foreign Press." In <u>Current Media Issues</u>. Ed. Barbara Bonnard, 189-231. New York: Boulanger, 1994.

You may, if you wish, place the inclusive page numbers in either the note, following the publication information, or in the bibliographical entry, following the name of the editor. If the author of the article is also the editor of the book, you must place her or his name in both locations. If the entire book is written by the same author, do not specify the chapter in the bibliographical reference.

Author of a foreword or introduction

It is not necessary to cite the author of a foreword or introduction in the bibliography unless you have used material from that author's contribution to the volume.

Note

      4. Carla Ferret, foreword to <u>Marital Stress among the Professoriat: A Case Study</u>, by Basil Givan (New York: Bimini, 1997).

Bibliography

      Ferret, Carla. Foreword to <u>Marital Stress among the Professoriat: A Case Study</u>, by Basil Givan. New York: Bimini, 1997.

Subsequent editions

If you are using an edition of a book other than the first, you must cite the number of the edition, or use *Rev. ed.* (for *Revised edition*) if there is no edition number.

Note

      43. Sarah Hales, <u>The Coming Ethics Wars</u>, 2d ed. (Pittsburgh: Blue Skies, 1990).

Bibliography

      Hales, Sarah. <u>The Coming Ethics Wars</u>. 2d ed. Pittsburgh: Blue Skies, 1990.

Multivolume work

Note

      49. Charles Logan August Graybosch, <u>Philosophers Write the Darndest Things</u>, 3 vols. (New York: Starkfield, 1988-89).

Bibliography

      Graybosch, Charles Logan August. <u>Philosophers Write the Darndest Things</u>. 3 vols. New York: Starkfield, 1988-89.

If you are using only one of the volumes in a multivolume work, follow the format below.

Note

>   9. Madeleine Ronsard, Gay Philosophers, vol. 2 of A History of Philosophy, ed. Joseph M. Sayles (Boston: Renfrow, 1992).

Bibliography

>   Ronsard, Madeleine. Gay Philosophers. Vol. 2 of A History of Philosophy. Ed. Joseph M. Sayles. Boston: Renfrow, 1992.

Reprints of older works

Note

>   8. Sterling R. Adams, Debate Strategies (1964; reprint, New York: Starkfield, 1988).

Bibliography

>   Adams, Sterling R. Debate Strategies. 1964. Reprint, New York: Starkfield, 1988.

Modern editions of classics

It is not necessary to give the date of original publication of a classic work.

Note

>   24. Edmond Burke, Reflections on the Revolution in France, ed. J. G. A. Pocock (Indianapolis: Hackett, 1987).

Bibliography

>   Burke, Edmond. Reflections on the Revolution in France. Ed. J. G. A. Pocock. Indianapolis: Hackett, 1987.

7.2.2.3   *Periodicals*

JOURNAL ARTICLES

Journals are periodicals, usually published either monthly or quarterly, that specialize in printing serious scholarly articles in a particular field. One significant distinction between the note format and the bibliographical format for a journal article is that, in the note, you cite only those pages from which you took material from the article, while in the bibliography you report the first and last pages of the article.

Journal with continuous pagination

Most journals are paginated so that each issue of a volume continues the numbering of the previous issue. The reason for such pagination is that most journals are bound in libraries as complete volumes of several issues; continuous pagination makes consulting these large compilations easier.

Note that the name of the journal, which is italicized (or underlined if italics are unavailable), is followed without punctuation by the volume number, which is itself followed by the year, in parentheses, then a colon and the page numbers. Do not use "p." or "pp." to introduce the page numbers.

Note

> 17. Joseph Conlin, "Teaching the Toadies: Cronyism in Academic Philosophy," Reason Today 4 (1987): 253, 260-62.

Bibliography

> Conlin, Joseph. "Teaching the Toadies: Cronyism in Academic Philosophy." Reason Today 4 (1987): 250-262.

Journal in which each issue is paginated separately

Note

> 8. Buck Rogers, "Toward Affirmative Action," Philosophy Revealed 28, no. 3 (1991): 27, 29.

Bibliography

> Rogers, Buck. "Toward Affirmative Action," Philosophy Revealed 28, no. 3 (1991): 27, 29.

The issue number follows the volume number, introduced by "no." It is also permissible to enclose the issue number in parentheses, without the "no.," moving the year to the end of the entry and placing it in a second parentheses: American Philosophy Digest 28 (3): 25-34 (1991).

Whichever format you use, *be consistent.*

MAGAZINE ARTICLES

Magazines, which are usually published weekly, bimonthly, or monthly, appeal to the popular audience and generally have a wider circulation than journals. *Newsweek* and *Scientific American* are magazines. Note that for entries that cite titles beginning with *The,* this word is dropped in the citation, as in *New Yorker* example below.

Monthly magazine

Note

> 10. Bonnie Stapleton, "I Ate Lunch with Socrates," <u>Lifelike Magazine</u>, April 1981, 22-25.

Bibliography

> Stapleton, Bonnie. "I Ate Lunch with Socrates." <u>Lifelike Magazine</u>, April 1981, 22-25.

Weekly or bimonthly magazine

The day of the issue's publication appears before the month. If the article cited begins in the front of the magazine and jumps to the back, then according to *CMS* (15.232) there is no point in recording inclusive page numbers in the bibliographical entry after the year. The specific pages used in your paper, however, must still be cited in the note.

Note

> 37. Connie Bruck, "The World of Philosophy," <u>New Yorker</u>, 18 October 1993, 13.

Bibliography

> Bruck, Connie. "The World of Philosophy." <u>New Yorker</u>, 18 October 1993, 13.

NEWSPAPER ARTICLES

Note that as for magazine titles, *The* is omitted from the newspaper's title, as it is for all English-language newspapers, according to *CMS* (15.242). If the name of the city in which an American newspaper is published does not appear in the paper's title, it should be appended, in italics, as in the second model below. If the city is not well known, the name of the state is added, in italics, in parentheses, as in the second model below.

Notes

> 5. Editorial, <u>New York Times</u>, 10 August 1993.
> 14. Fine, Austin, "Hoag on Trial," <u>Carrollton (Texas) Tribune</u>, 24 November 1992.

Bibliography

CMS (16.117) says that bibliographies usually do not include entries for articles from daily newspapers. If you wish to include such material, however, you may give the name of the paper and the relevant dates in the bibliography:

Carrollton (Texas) Tribune, 22-25 November 1992.

CMS (15.234-42) offers additional suggestions for citations of newspaper material.

7.2.2.4   *Public Documents*

LAWS AND STATUTES

If you wish to make a formal reference for a statute, you must structure the reference according to the place where you found the published law. Initially published separately in pamphlets, as slip laws, statutes are eventually collected and incorporated, first into a set of volumes called *U.S. Statutes at Large*, and later into the *United States Code*, a multivolume set that is revised every six years. You should use the latest publication.

Citing to a slip law

Note

     16. Public Law 678, 103d Cong., 1st sess. (4 December 1993), 16-17.

or

     16. Public Law 678, 103d Cong., 1st sess. (4 December 1993), Library of Congress Book Preservation Act of 1993, 16-17.

or

     16. Library of Congress Book Preservation Act of 1993, Public Law 678, 103d Cong., 1st sess. (4 December 1993), 16-17.

Bibliography

U.S. Public Law 678. 103d Cong., 1st sess., 4 December 1993.

or

U.S. Public Law 678. 103d Cong., 1st sess., 4 December 1993. Library of Congress Book Preservation Act of 1993.

or

Library of Congress Book Preservation Act of 1993. Public Law 678. 103d Cong., 1st sess., 4 December 1993.

Citing to the **Statutes at Large**

Note

> 10. Statutes at Large 82 (1993): 466.

or

> 10. Library of Congress Book Preservation Act of 1993, Statutes at Large 82 (1993): 466.

Bibliography

> Statutes at Large 82 (1993): 466.

or

> Library of Congress Book Preservation Act of 1993. Statutes at Large 82 (1993): 466.

Citing to the **United States Code**

Note

> 42. Library of Congress Book Preservation Act, U.S. Code, vol. 38, sec. 1562 (1993).

Bibliography

> Library of Congress Book Preservation Act. U.S. Code. Vol. 38, sec. 1562 (1993).

UNITED STATES CONSTITUTION

In the documentary-note format, according to *CMS* (15.367), the Constitution is cited by article or amendment, section, and, if relevant, clause. The Constitution is not listed in the bibliography.

Note

> 23. U.S. Constitution, art. 3, sec. 3.

LEGAL REFERENCES

Supreme Court

Note

> 73. State of Nevada v. Goldie Warren. 324 U.S. 123 (1969).

The U.S. in the entry refers to *United States Supreme Court Reports*, which is where decisions of the Supreme Court have been published since 1875. Preceding the "U.S." in the note is the volume number; following is the page number and year, in parentheses. Before 1875, Supreme Court decisions were published under the names of official court reporters. The following reference is to William Cranch, *Reports of Cases Argued and Adjudged in the Supreme Court of the United States,* 1801–1815, 9 vols. (Washington, DC, 1804–1817). The number preceding the clerk's name is the volume number; following the clerk's name is the page number and year, in parentheses:

8. Marbury v. Madison, 1 Cranch 137 (1803).

According to *CMS* (15.369), court decisions are only rarely listed in bibliographies.

Lower courts

Decisions of lower federal courts are published in the *Federal Reporter.* The note should give the volume of the *Federal Reporter* (*F.*), the series, if it is other than the first series (*2d*, in the model below), the page number, and, in parentheses, an abbreviated reference to the specific court (in this case, the Second Circuit Court) and the year.

Note

58. United States v. Sizemore, 183 F. 2d 201 (2d Cir. 1950).

7.2.2.5 *Interviews*

According to *CMS* (15.263), citations to interviews in the documentary-note system should be handled by references within the text. If, however, you wish to include references to interviews, you may use the following formats.

PUBLISHED OR BROADCAST INTERVIEWS

Untitled interview in a book

Note

30. Mary Jorgenson, interview by Alan McAskill, in Hospice Pioneers, ed. Alan McAskill (Richmond: Dynasty Press, 1994), 68.

Bibliography

Jorgenson, Mary. Interview by Alan McAskill. In Hospice Pioneers, ed. Alan McAskill, 62-86. Richmond: Dynasty Press, 1994.

Titled interview in a periodical

Note

> 7. John Simon, "Picking the Patrons Apart: An Interview with John Simon," interview by Selena Fox, <u>Media Week</u>, 14 March 1993, 43-44

Bibliography

> Simon, John. "Picking the Patrons Apart: An Interview with John Simon." By Selena Fox. <u>Media Week</u>, 14 March 1993, 40-54.

Interview broadcast on television

Note

> 4. Clarence Parker, interview by Kent Gordon, <u>Oklahoma Philosophers</u>, WKY Television, 4 June 1994.

Bibliography

> Parker, Clarence. Interview by Kent Gordon. <u>Oklahoma Philosophers</u>. WKY Television, 4 June 1994.

UNPUBLISHED INTERVIEWS

Note

> 17. Melissa Kennedy, interview by author, tape recording, Portland, ME, 23 April 1993.

Bibliography

> Kennedy, Melissa. Interview by author. Tape recording. Portland, ME, 23 April 1993.

7.2.2.6   *Unpublished Sources*

Dissertation

Note

> 16. Richard Rorty, "Sidney Hook's Populism" (Ph.D. diss., University of Virginia, 1980), 88-91.

Bibliography

> Rorty, Richard. "Sidney Hook's Populism." Ph.D. diss., University of Virginia, 1980.

Thesis

Note

> 5. Ellspeth Stanley Sharpe, "Black Women in Philosophy: A Troubled History" (Master's thesis, Oregon State University, 1992), 34, 36, 112-114.

Bibliography

> Sharpe, Ellspeth Stanley. "Black Women in Philosophy: A Troubled History." Master's thesis, Oregon State University, 1992.

Paper presented at a meeting

Note

> 82. Kim Zelazny and Ed Gilmore, "Art for Art's Sake: Funding the NEA in the Twenty-First Century" (presented at the annual Conference of Metropolitan Arts Councils, San Francisco, April 1993), 4-7, 9.

Bibliography

> Zelazny, Kim, and Ed Gilmore. "Art for Art's Sake: Funding the NEA in the Twenty-First Century." Presented at the annual Conference of Metropolitan Arts Councils, San Francisco, April 1993.

Manuscript in the author's possession

The entry should include the institution with which the author is affiliated and a description of the format of the work (typescript, photocopy, or the like).

Note

> 16. Rita V. Borges and Alicia Chamisal, "Mexican-American Border Conflicts, 1915-1970" (University of Texas at El Paso, photocopy), 61-62.

Bibliography

> Borges, Rita V., and Alicia Chamisal. "Mexican-American Border Conflicts, 1915-1970." University of Texas at El Paso. Photocopy.

7.2.2.7 *Subsequent or Shortened References in Notes*

After you have given a complete citation for a source in a note once, it is possible to shorten the reference to that source in later notes. One convenient method of shortening later references to a source, described in *CMS* (15.249), is to give only the last name of the author, followed by a comma and the page number of the reference:

First Reference

  21. Angela Genessario et al., <u>Alimony and the Child: A National Survey</u> (Baltimore: Colgate, 1991), 16-18, 78-82.

Later Reference

  35. Genessario, 46.

If there are citations to more than one work by the same author, you will have to include a shortened form of the title in all later references.

First References

  23. John George, <u>Fringe Groups I Have Known: The Radical Left and Right in American Society</u> (New York: Lear Press, 1995), 45.
  26. John George, "Onward Christian Soldiers: Evangelism on the Plains," <u>Radical Wind Magazine</u>, March 1994, 35,

Later References

  32. George, <u>Fringe Groups</u>, 56.
  48. George, "Christian Soldiers," 34.

Government documents

  Methods for shortening references to government documents vary, depending on the type of source. One rule is to make sure there is sufficient information in the shortened reference to point the reader clearly to the full citation in the bibliography.

Court decisions

First Reference

  58. <u>United States v. Sizemore</u>, 183 F. 2d 201 (2d Cir. 1950).

Later Reference

  67. <u>United States v. Sizemore</u>, 203.

Consult *CMS*, sec. 15, for details on shortening other types of references.

Use of Ibid.

  Ibid., an abbreviation of the Latin term *ibidem*, meaning "in the same place," can be used to shorten a note that refers to the source in the immediately preceding note:

First Reference

> 14. Samuel Howard, William J. Abbott, and Jane Hope, <u>Powerbase: How to Increase Your Hold on Your Fellow Philosophy Students</u> (Los Angeles: Gollum and Smythe, 1986), 35-36.

Following Reference

> 15. Ibid., 38.

7.3   THE STUDENT CITATION SYSTEM (SCS)

As an alternative to the documentary note citation system, you may want to use the Student Citation System (SCS). Be sure to get your instructor's approval before using the SCS system. Why, you may ask, would anyone want another citation system, especially since so many disciplines have their own systems (MLA, APA, and others)? It is precisely because college students are currently required to use several different citation systems that the SCS was created. The SCS is the first system specifically designed for use in all undergraduate college courses. Students who use it will be able to use the same system in their English, psychology, philosophy, math, science, history, political science, and other courses.

How is the SCS different from other citation systems? In addition to the fact that it is designed to be used in courses in all disciplines, the SCS has several other distinctive features:

- The SCS is made for students, not academicians. It is simpler, has fewer rules to learn, and is easier to type than other systems.
- The SCS uses the punctuation and syntax of a new grammar that students are quickly learning around the world: the universal language of the internet. The internet is rapidly becoming the foremost means of a wide range of research and communication activities. SCS symbols are familiar to anyone who has used the internet: / @ + . They allow citations to be constructed with a minimum of space, effort, and confusion.

7.3.1   General Rules and Rules for Notes

Like other citation systems, the SCS requires that each source citation include (1) a note in the text in which the reference to the source cited occurs, and (2) an entry in a reference page. Notes in the text are always placed at the end of the sentence in which the reference is made. Examine the models that accompany the following list of rules for notes.

Rule	Example

1 Notes in the text always contain, in this order:
  1. a forward slash (/)
  2. a source reference numeral (1,2,3, etc.)
  3. a dot (.) that ends the sentence.
	Reagan waved to the convention /1.
	
	(Notice that there is a space before the /, but no spaces between the / and the 1, or between the 1 and the dot.)

2 Direct quotes and references to materials on a specific page both require a page number.	Reagan waved to the convention /1.23. (Note that no spaces occur between the dots and the page number.)
3 You may indicate a range of pages or a page and a range of pages.	Reagan waved to the convention /1.23–25. Reagan waved to the convention /1.19.23–25.
4 Indicate chapters, sections, parts, and volumes in the note with appropriate abbreviations. Note that there is no dot between the abbreviation and the number of the chapter, section, part, or volume.	Reagan waved to the convention /1.c3. Reagan waved to the convention /1.s3. Reagan waved to the convention /1.pt3. Reagan waved to the convention /1.v3.
5 You may cite more than one source in a single note. Separate sources by the / without spaces between any of the characters.	Reagan waved to the convention 1.v3.23/4/13c6. (This note refers to source 1, volume, 3 page 23; source 4; and source 13, chapter 6.)
6 Once used, reference numbers always refer to the same source. They may be used again to refer to a different quote or idea from that same source.	Reagan waved to the convention /1.19. Nancy, who had had a severe headache the evening before, came to join him /5/7. One source reported that they had argued about the color suit he was to wear /1.33. (The second note in this passage refers the reader to two different sources, numbers 5 and 7. The third note is another reference to the first source used in the paper.)
7 Refer to a constitution with article and section number	Bill Clinton fulfilled his obligation to address the state of the nation /18.2.3.
8 Refer to passages in the Bible, the Koran, and other ancient texts that are divided into standard verses with the verse citation in the note.	Jake forgot that "the seventh day shall be your Holy day" /6.Exodus 35.2. (This example refers to the book of Exodus, chapter 35, verse 2. The 6 indicates that this is the sixth source cited in the paper. There is a dot between the source number and the verse citation.)

7.3.2   Rules for Reference Pages

7.3.2.1   General Format Rules

The reference list is usually the final element in the paper. It is entitled "References." Its entries are arranged in the order that citations appear in the paper. The references page has standard page margins (one inch from all sides of the paper). All lines are double spaced. Model references appear at the end of this chapter.

7.3.2.2   Rules of Punctuation and Abbreviation

1. Punctuation imitates the format used on the internet.
2. No spaces occur between entry elements (author, date, and so on) or punctuation marks (/ . + @ ").
3. Dots (.) always follow entry elements with exceptions for punctuation rules 5–6.
4. The number of the source is always followed immediately by a dot.
5. Dots are also used to separate volume and edition numbers in journals.
6. Additional authors are denoted by a plus (+) sign.
7. Subtitles of books and articles are separated from main titles by a colon and a single space: "Crushing Doubt: Pascal's Bleak Epiphany."
8. Book chapters and periodical articles are enclosed in quotation marks (" ").
9. Use the following abbreviations:

c	chapter
comp	compiler
ed	editor
C	College
NY	New York (Use postal abbreviations for all states. Note that NY is unique in that when it is used alone it always means New York City. Cite other New York State locations in this form: "Oswego NY." Cite cities in other states like this: "Chicago IL", "Los Angeles CA", "Boston MA.")
pt	part
s	section
sess	session
tr	translator
v	volume
S	September (Months: Ja F Mr Ap My Je Jl Au S Oc N D)

C   College

I   Institute

U   University

10. Use full names instead of initials of authors whenever they are used in the original source. When listing publishers you may use the commonly used names instead of full titles. For example, use "Yale" for "Yale University Press"; use "Holt" for "Holt, Rinehart and Winston." Use internet abbreviations when known, such as "Prenhall" for "Prentice Hall, Inc." When abbreviating universities in dissertation and thesis citations place no dot between the names of the state or city and the university. For example, use "MaIT" for the Massachusetts Institute of Technology and "UMa" for the University of Massachusetts. Always use the second letter of the state abbreviation, in lower case, to avoid the following type of confusion: "OSU" could be a university in Ohio, Oklahoma, or Oregon.

7.3.2.3   *Rules of Order*

Elements are always entered in the order shown in the following list of examples. Not all elements are available for every citation (authors are sometimes not provided), and the table provides directions for these cases. Further, not all entries are appropriate for every citation. For example, cities of publication are not required for magazines. Carefully examine the order of elements in the examples in the table.

Source	Citation Elements and Examples
Books:	
One author:	3.Edna Applegate.1995.My Life on Earth.4th ed.Howard Press.St. Louis MO.
	Note the order of elements:
	—Reference number of note (1,2,3, etc.), followed by a dot
	—Author's name
	—Year of publication
	—Title of book
	—Number of edition, if other than the first
	—Name of publisher
	—City of publication
	—State of publication (not necessary for New York City)

Two to three authors:	10.William Grimes+Joan Smith+Alice Bailey.1996.Philosophy and Fire.Harvard.Cambridge MA.
More than three authors:	42.Lois Mills+others.1989.Revolution in Thought.Agnew.NY.
Editor, compiler, or translator in place of as author:	1.Michael Schendler ed.1992.Kant's Cosmology.Bloom.NY. (Remember that the citation for New York City does not require a state abbreviation.)
Editor, compiler, or translator with author:	9.Elena White.1997.Nietzsche Was Right.Alexander Nebbs tr.Spartan.Biloxi MS.
No author, editor, compiler, or translator:	5.The Book of Universal Wisdom.1993.4th ed.Northfield Publications, Indianapolis IN. (Reverse the placement of the date and title of the book, beginning the entry with the title.)
Separately authored foreword, afterword, or preface as source:	17.Beulah Garvin.1992.Preface.Down in the Hole by James Myerson.Philosopher's Stone Press.Boston MA.
Separately authored chapter, essay, or poem as source:	5.Jack Wittey.1994."Chickens and People."Animal Rights Anthology.3rd ed.Gene Cayton comp.Palo Duro Press.Canyon TX.73-90.
One volume in a multivolume work:	9.Astrid Schultz+others.1991.The Myth of the West.v3 of The Development of European Thought.8 vols.Muriel Hodgson ed.University of Rutland Press.Rutland ME.

Encyclopedias:

Citation from an encyclopedia that is regularly updated:	24.Ronald Millgate.1985."Mills, John Stuart."Encyclopedia Americana. (The date refers to the edition of the encyclopedia. Cite the name of the article exactly as it appears in the encyclopedia.)
When no name is given for the article's author:	2."Mills, John Stuart."1946.Hargreave's Encyclopedia.
Ancient texts:	24.Holy Bible.New International Version.

Bible, Koran, etc.

(Because the book, chapter, and verse numbers are given in the textual reference, it is not necessary to repeat them here. Remember to cite the traditional divisions of the work instead of the page number and publication information of the specific edition you used.)

Periodicals:

Journal articles:

Article with author or authors named:

30.Ellis Michaels+Andrea Long.1996."How We Know: An Exercise in Cartesian Logic."Philosopher's Stone.12.4.213-227.
(This citation refers to an article published in a journal entitled *Philosopher's Stone,* volume 12, number 4, pages 213-227.)

Article with no author named:

7."Odds and Ends."1995.Philosopher's Stone.12.4.198-199.

Magazine articles:

Article in a weekly or bi-weekly magazine:

11.Lorraine Bond.1994."The Last Epicurean."Mental Health.6Jn.34-41.
(This citation refers to an article published in the June 6, 1994, issue of *Mental Health.*)

Article in a monthly magazine:

3.Allan Hull.1996."My Secret Struggle."Pathology Digest.Mr.17-30.
(The difference between a citation for a monthly magazine and one for a weekly or bi-weekly magazine is that the former does not include a reference to the specific day of publication.)

Newspapers:

Article with named author:

10.Anne Bleaker.1995."Breakthrough in Artificial Intelligence."New York Times.10My.14.
(The word The is omitted from the newpaper's title.)

Article with unnamed author:

22."Peirce Anniversary Celebration Set."1996.Kansas City Times-Democrat.1Ap.14.

When city is not named in newspaper title:

13.Boyd Finnell.1996."Stoic Elected Mayor."(Eugenia TX) Daily Equivocator.30D.1.
(Place the name of the city, and the abbreviation for the state if the city is not well known, in parentheses before the name of the paper.)

**Government
documents:**

Agency publications:

28.U.S. Department of Commerce.1996.Economic
Projections: 1995-2004.GPO.

> (Note that, when no author's name is given, the govern-
> ment department is considered the author. Because the
> Government Printing Office (GPO), the government's pri-
> mary publisher, is located in Washington, D.C., you
> need not list the city of publication.)

Legislative journals:

31.Senate Journal.1993.103Cong.sess1.D10.

> (This citation refers to the record, published in the *Senate
> Journal,* of the first session of the 103rd Congress, held on
> December 10, 1993.)

8.Congressional Record.71 Cong.sess.2.72.8.

> (This citation refers to the account, published in the Con-
> gressional Record, of the second session of the 71st Con-
> gress, volume 72, page 8.)

Bills in Congress:

13.U.S. Senate.1997.Visa Formalization Act of
1997.105Cong.sess1.SR.1437.

> (This citation refers to Senate Resolution 1437, originated
> in the first session of the 105th Congress. Bills originating
> in the House of Representatives are designated by the ab-
> breviation HR.)

Laws:

17.U.S. Public Law 678.1993.Library of Congress Book
Preservation Act of 1993.U.S.Code.38.1562.

> (The law referred to in this citation is recorded in section
> 1562 of volume 38 of the *U.S. Code.*)

Constitutions:

31.U.S.Constitution.
8.MO.Constitution.

> (This citation refers to the Missouri State Constitution.)

Internet documents: 4.Akiko Kasahara and K-lab,Inc.1995.ArtScape of the Far
East: Seminar on the Philosophy of Art.Shinshu.University
Nagano.Japan.@http://Pckiso3.cs.Shinshu-
u.ac.jp/artscape/index.html.Oct27.96.

> (The last item in an Internet citation is always the internet
> address at which the document was found.)

Unpublished materials:

Interview:

12.Lily Frailey.1994.Interview with Clarence Parker.Santa Fe NM.10Ag.

Thesis or Dissertation:

21.Gregory Scott.1973.Mysticism and Politics in the Thought of Bertrand Russell.MA thesis.UVa.

Paper presented at a meeting:

5.Celia Hicks.1995."What Whitehead Would Say."Conference on the Western Imagination.14Ja.Boston MA.

(The citation includes the name of the conference and the date on which the paper was presented, and ends with the city where the conference took place.)

Manuscript housed in a collection:

32.Jose Sanchez.1953?-1982.Journal.Southwest Collection.Arial Library.Chisum Academy.Canyon TX.

(Unpublished manuscripts are sometimes left unnamed and undated by their authors. Use any relevant information supplied by the repository catalogue to complete the citation. When a date is hypothesized, as in the above example, place a question mark after it.)

Manuscript in the author's possession:

14.Jane Fried.1996.Life in California.UTx.Photocopy.

(The citation includes the institution with which the author is affiliated and ends with a description of the format of the work: typescript, photocopy, and so on).

SAMPLE REFERENCE PAGE

REFERENCES

1.Amanda Collingwood.1993.Architecture and Philosophy.Carlington Press.Detroit MI.

2.Tom Barker+Betty Clay, eds.1987.Swamps of Louisiana.Holt.NY.

3.Joan Garth+Allen Sanford.1963."The Hills of Wyoming."Critical Perspectives on Landscape.Prentice Hall.Upper Saddle River NJ.49-75.

4.Hayley Trakas ed.1994.Russell on Space.3rd ed.Harmony Press.El Paso.TX.

5.Philippe Ariès.1962.Centuries of Childhood: A Social History of Family Life in the Northeastern Region of Kentucky.Robert Baldock tr.Knopf.NY.

6.Jesus Gonzolez.1995."The Making of the Federales."Mexican Stories Revisited.Jules Frank ed.Comanche Press.San Antonio TX.54-79.

7.Carla Harris.1994.Foreword.Marital Stress and the Philosophers: A Case Study by Basil Givan.Galapagos.NY.

8.Jasper Craig.1993."The Flight from the Center of the Cities."Time.10S.67-69.

9.Matthew Moen.1996."Evolving Politics of the Christian Right."PS:Political Science and Politics.29.3.461-464.

10.Patrick Swick.1996."Jumping the Gun on the Federal Reserve."New York Times.10My.78.

11.Frances Muggeridge.1993."The Truth is Nowhere."Conundrum Digest.Mr.40-54.

12.Alan McAskill.1994."Interview with Mary Jordan."Hospice Pioneers of New Mexico.Dynasty Press.Enid.OK.62-86.

13.Jane Smith.1997.Interview with Jerry Brown.San Francisco CA.15Oc.

14.Jacob Lynd.1973.Perfidy in Academe: Patterns of Rationalization in College Administrations.Ph.D. diss.UVA.

15.Holy Bible.New King James Version.

16.Paula Thomas.1970-1976.Diary.Museum of the Plains.Fabens TX.

17.U.S. Department of Labor.1931.Urban Growth and Population Projections:1930-1939.GPO.

18.Senate Journal.1993.103Cong.sess1.D10.

19.U.S.Senate.1997.Visa Formalization Act of 1997.105Cong. sess1.SR.1437.

21.Peter Bolen.1995."Creating Designs in Social Systems."The Internet Journal of Sociological Welfare.14.6.http://www.carmelpeak.com.
22.U.S.Public Law 678.1993.Library of Congress Book Preservation Act of 1993.U.S.Code.38.1562.
23.U.S.Constitution.

PART THREE

How to Think and Write Like a Philosopher

8

Principles of Argument

If all mankind minus one were of one opinion, and only one person were of the contrary opinion, mankind would be no more justified in silencing that one person, than he, if he had the power, would be justified in silencing mankind.

—John Stuart Mill

8.1 THE THROWS OF ARGUMENT

Arguments are discussions in which we strive to attain an objective. There are all sorts of objectives: selling our favorite political candidate, gaining a couple of points on an exam, selecting the movie we want to see, returning an item to a department store, or discovering the truth on an important matter. Verbal and nonverbal exchanges of reasons, threats, emotions, or even bricks, in the interest of reaching an objective, are normally called arguments.

The language in which we talk about argument suggests that we conceive argument metaphorically as a war to be won. Words such as "demolished," "overwhelmed," "destroyed," and "thrust," make frequent appearances in our accounts of arguments. And we know that all is fair in love and war. So the very idea that there are rules governing argument may seem questionable from the start, unless the rules are going to show us how to obtain our objectives more effectively.

Let us consider arguments to be verbal wrestling matches. Protagoras (490–421 BCE), a Sophist, boasted that he could make equally strong cases for any side of an argument. Sophists were in great demand in ancient Athens, just as lawyers are in great demand today. People then, like today, needed to know how to argue to defend their lives and property. Sophists knew how to argue well and made a good deal of money by teaching others and by bringing the rich to court. Protagoras wrote a book about argument that he titled *The Throws,* but only the title has survived. The Greek word used in the title was the same term applied to the throws in the sport of wrestling.

Arguments, however, especially legal arguments, are more than mere sport. Unlike the Sophists, who argued for money, the Athenian philosopher Socrates argued for truth. He believed that knowing the truth about matters such as the nature of social justice, piety, the nature of god, and the justification of punishment was essential to living a good and happy life. Socrates was skilled in two strategies essential to good philosophical argument. First, he was adept at keeping the point of an argument from being lost. The Sophists often engaged in long flowery speeches on topics such as the nature of love or justice. Socrates was quick to bring his partners in argument back to the point at issue. This can be a maddening practice for those more interested in style than substance.

Second, during an argument Socrates was skillful at devising examples that undermined definitions offered by his opponents. *Socratic dialectic* is a method of argument in which a definition of an important concept, such as "justice" or "truth," is subjected to a series of questions aimed at testing it. In the Socratic dialogues that Plato wrote, Socrates tests definitions offered by other participants in the discussion. For instance, early in Socrates's dialogue with Euthyphro, Euthyphro defines piety as "that which is pleasing to the gods." Socrates tests this definition by pointing out that the traditional stories of the gods are full of conflicts, which suggests that what pleases one god may well displease another. While one god may be pleased by a person's action, another may be offended by that same action. If this is the case, what happens to Euthyphro's definition of piety? Is it possible for one action to be both pious and impious? Of course not, and so the definition must be given up since it leads to an inconsistency.

Socrates's objective in his dialogues may have been to foster the good life, but despite his public spirit he acquired many enemies in his pursuit of truth. Two respectable Athenian citizens, Anytus and Meletus, charged that Socrates was an atheist who also believed in and taught about gods that were different from those sanctioned by Athens. In his defense, Socrates pointed out that the charge brought against him contained an inconsistency: Reminding his listeners that an atheist is one who believes in no gods, Socrates asked how he could be an atheist and, at the same time, a believer in gods different from those of the state. You can see that Socrates had a good argument for his innocence of the charge on impiety. Anytus and Meletus also charged him, however, with corrupting the youth. The point of our discussion of Socrates is that the goal of philosophical argument is to reach the truth on a particular issue without regard to practical consequences. And it is the goal of truth, or at least justified belief, that leads to the rules of argument expected in good philosophical writing.

Before you can argue effectively, you must know how to identify and analyze arguments presented to you. This requires you first to determine if a series of statements is an argument. If it is an argument, you must then discern if the argument is deductive or nondeductive, valid or invalid, and persuasive or tenuous. In this chapter you will learn:

- The definition of an argument
- The two basic types of argument
- How to evaluate arguments

8.2   THE DEFINITION OF AN ARGUMENT

An *argument* is a series of statements that include at least one premise, a conclusion, and material that links the premise(s) to a conclusion. A *premise* is a statement, offered as evidence for a conclusion, that is assumed or taken for granted. For example, the statements "Cats eat mice" and "Jake is a cat" are premises. Some expressions that indicate premises are: "if," "since," "because," "on the basis of," "on the basis of the following observations," and "the following observation supports my claim." There are also other words that indicate premises.

Philosophers use the expression "connective" to designate the basic linking expressions of logic. The basic connectives are: "it's not the case that," "and," "or," and "if...then." The first connective which is represented by the negation sign does not really connect statements. Instead, it negates a statement or a group of statements connected by the other connectives. "And" joins two or more statements. "Or" also joins two or more statements and is understood in logic in its inclusive sense. A better rendering of this connective would be "at least one." "If...then" does double duty in arguments. It connects two statements. The statement before "then" is the antecedent, the statement after "then" is the consequent. Compound sentences formed by "if...then" are called conditionals. Conditionals often are found as premises in arguments either expressly stated or implied. But "if...then" also functions as the basic connective in any argument connecting the premises to the conclusion. An argument can always be translated into a long conditional sentence in which the premises are the antecedent and the conclusion is the consequent. It is important to know the meanings of antecedent and consequent since they appear in the names of several valid and invalid argument forms.

A *conclusion* is a reasoned judgment resulting from understanding the implications of the premise(s). For example, if we accept the premises that (1) cats eat mice and (2) Jake is a cat, we may reasonably conclude that Jake eats mice. The following are all linking expressions that indicate conclusions: "it follows that," "therefore," "if...then," "hence," "my conclusion is," "consequently," "it is (probably) the case that," and "so."

Here is one of many ways in which we can frame our little discussion about Jake's dining habits in the form of an argument complete with premises, conclusion, and linking material:

Linking expression	Premise	Linking expression	Premise	Linking expression	Conclusion
If	cats eat mice	and	Jake is a cat	then	Jake eats mice.

Here's another phrasing for the argument: "Because cats eat mice and Jake is a cat, it follows that Jake eats mice." How many other ways can you devise for stating the argument, using the connectives given above?

Both premises and conclusions make a claim on us for acceptance. Arguments call for us to take the truth or probable truth of the premises for granted for a moment so that we may determine whether the purported truth of the premises is sufficient to guarantee the truth or probability of the conclusion. In addition to premises and conclusions, arguments may contain extraneous material such as jokes, biographical data, or even personal attacks.

Narratives, which are simply chronological stories of actions or events, are not arguments.

8.3   THE TWO BASIC TYPES OF ARGUMENT

Arguments are either deductive or nondeductive. An argument is *deductive* if it claims that the conclusion must be true if the premises are true. The conclusion is, therefore, guaranteed by the truth of the premises. A deductive argument spends no time, in other words, inquiring into the accuracy of the premises: if they are true, then the conclusion must also be true. The argument given above about Jake the cat is phrased as a deductive argument. The following argument is deductive because its conclusion, given its premises, is presented as being an unarguable matter of fact:

Two million and thirty-seven lottery tickets were sold for Wednesday's drawing. I bought two tickets. So my chance of winning Wednesday is 2 in 2,000,037.

An argument is *nondeductive* (*inductive*) if it claims only a high degree of probability for the conclusion. An inductive argument, then, allows for some doubt of the truth of the conclusion, and it bases its claim of accuracy on the very good chance that its premises are correct. Here is a way to phrase our argument about Jake the cat inductively:

All cats that I have ever seen will eat mice. Jake is a cat. Therefore, Jake will probably eat mice.

Whether we knew it or not at the time, most of us have had the following inductive argument with ourselves:

> Because most commercial aircraft do not crash on routine flights, the flight that I have booked myself on for Christmas break will probably not crash.

It is important to know the difference between deductive and inductive arguments because we must know what an argument demands of us. Does the argument ask us to accept something as true, or only as probably true? The actions we take based upon certainty are different from the actions we take that are based upon mere probability, and we may hold deductive arguments liable for much stronger bases of proof.

8.4   VALIDITY AND SOUNDNESS

8.4.1   Deductive Validity

There are two slightly different definitions of *validity,* which correspond to the two different types of argument, deductive and nondeductive. An argument is *deductively valid* if it is deductive and if the truth of the premises would make it necessary that the conclusion is true also. In other words, an argument is deductively valid if it is deductive and if it cannot be the case that the premises are true and the conclusion is false. The following argument is deductively valid:

PREMISE 1:   If Santa Claus lives at the South Pole, then Tesla invented the light bulb.

PREMISE 2:   Santa Claus lives at the South Pole.

CONCLUSION: Tesla invented the light bulb.

Even though the two premises are false, the argument is still *deductively* valid, that is, the deduction from the assumed true premises is valid. The argument is deductive because it claims certainty for the conclusion, and it is valid because its conclusion would have to be true if the premises were true. When you evaluate an argument for deductive validity, you do not yet check for the truth of the premises. The factual truth of the premises is irrelevant to the validity of an argument. Consequently, a deductively valid argument may have false premises and a true conclusion, or it may have false premises and a false conclusion.

In a deductively valid argument, the relation between premises and conclusions is not a causal relationship. Premises do not cause a conclusion to be true; they merely explain why, if they are true, the conclusion is also true.

8.4.2   Nondeductive Validity

Nondeductive arguments make claims in their conclusions that go beyond the evidence of the premises. If I claim, for example, that "since my chances of winning the lottery are 2 million to 1, then I will probably lose the lottery," then I am making a nondeductive argument because I am claiming only the probability, not the certainty, of my conclusion. An argument is *nondeductively valid* if it is nondeductive and if the truth or high probability of its premises make the conclusion highly probable also. My argument about the probability of my losing the lottery is nondeductively valid because the high odds against winning do indeed produce a high likelihood that I will lose.

Checking for validity is important because it is the first step in examining an argument in order to see if it is worthwhile to check the actual truth of the premises. If an argument is not valid, there is no point in finding out whether or not the premises are true. If an argument is valid, however, the premises become important.

Imagine you are a member of the National Science Foundation and someone presents a grant for funding. The grant's hypothesis is that, since mosquitos carry malaria, then the people of Kentucky are vulnerable to malaria. As you read the grant, you realize that the argument guiding the proposed research is not arranged in a valid way. Not all mosquitoes carry malaria, and the mosquitos that carry malaria have not been found in Kentucky. You would not have to consider funding it, because the project would probably produce invalid information. It needs to be reformulated if it is to be worth funding.

Consider the following deductive arguments. Are they valid?

- If President Clinton did what Paula Jones charged in her deposition that he did, then he is guilty of sexual harassment in the workplace. Paula Jones did indeed speak the truth. Therefore, Clinton is a harasser.
- Republican candidate Bob Dole said he would not raise taxes. But Dole voted many times to raise taxes while he was a senator even while Republicans were in control of the presidency. So Dole was lying.
- When I am in Memphis, I always go to the services at Al Green's church. If I go to Al Green's church, then I will visit Graceland afterward, since it is nearby. So if I go to Memphis, then I will visit Graceland.

If you found yourself asking whether Al Green has a church, how Dole voted, whether Paula Jones spoke the truth, or if Graceland is indeed close to Al Green's church (it is), then you missed the point. *It does not matter to the question of validity whether the statements you questioned are in fact true or false.* It matters only whether, if they and the other premises in their respective arguments were true, the truth of the premise would make it necessary that the conclusion be true also. The anti-Clinton bias of the first argument and the anti-Dole bias of the second argument may irritate you, but these biases have nothing to do with the validity of the arguments. Try to filter your worries about my bias out and attend to the arguments.

Are the following nondeductive arguments nondeductively valid?

- The United States has never elected a third-party candidate as President. So Perot will probably not be elected in 1996.
- When people are transferred to Calvary Hospital they usually die within a week or two. Helene's physician has recommended that she be transferred to Calvary. So the physician has decided she is beyond recovery.

8.4.3   Cogency

To this point, we have discussed three questions that need to be raised when evaluating a passage to test its qualities as an argument:

1. Does it have the components (at least one premise and a conclusion) of an argument?
2. Is the argument deductive (purporting certainty) or nondeductive (purporting probability)?
3. Is the argument valid (the premises lead to the conclusions) or invalid (the premises do not lead to the conclusions)?

A fourth question remains to be asked: Is the argument cogent?

An argument is *cogent* if it is valid and if its premises are true. We may then say that an argument is *deductively cogent* (or sound) if it is deductive, deductively valid, and the premises are in fact true. An argument is *nondeductively cogent* (often called "strong" or "correct") if it is nondeductive, nondeductively valid, and its premises are true or highly probable.

The following argument is deductively cogent:

The electric company charges for electricity. I used electricity from the electric company last month. I will be charged for the use of electricity.

The following argument is nondeductively cogent:

Thousands of tickets are sold for each drawing of the California lottery. I bought one ticket for the next drawing on Wednesday. I will probably lose.

8.5   PATTERNS OF REASONING

Now that we know how to ask four questions that will help us test the quality of an argument, we can add to our argument-testing capabilities by understanding sound and unsound patterns of reasoning. When we discussed validity above, we relied upon simple examples to elicit your agreement on when the premises would guarantee the truth or high probability of a conclusion. Some intuitively appealing forms of argument, however, are invalid. There are mathematically objective ways of demonstrating when an argument form is valid or invalid, but we will not provide mathematical proofs here, for the attempt to do so would take us too far beyond the compass of this book. If you are interested in mathematical proofs, take a course in symbolic logic or look at a good logic textbook.

8.6   VALID FORMS OF ARGUMENT

The practical benefit of learning the valid and invalid argument forms lies in how the forms facilitate argumentative discussion. Once you isolate the author's major thesis and premises for the thesis, you can summarize the argument in argument form. You may discover that the author has structured the argument in a valid form such as modus ponens or a reductio. And so you would not criticize the author's form of argument, but turn immediately to investigate the premises. But if the author has relied upon eliminative induction, then it may be the case that a possibility has been overlooked and a false dilemma presented. Or, if the author relies upon an invalid form such as affirming the consequent, you can identify her error and perhaps find a way to repair the argument. And, of course, if you can cast summaries of your own arguments in valid forms, your writing will be more effective. It is a daunting task to cast most extended arguments in argumentative form, although you might enjoy looking at the attempt to do so found in Spinoza's *Ethics.* It is considerably easier to work with argument summaries. So how do we exhibit the forms of arguments?

In sentential logic ordinary language statements are given letters as their names. Each statement gets only one name, one letter. Take the sentence: "If this is Tuesday, this must be Brussels." This is a compound sentence containing two statements: "This is Tuesday" and "This is Brussels." Some systems of sentential logic use capital letters and begin with the letter A. Others use small letters and begin with p. Whether "This is Tuesday" is named A or p is a convention. The important thing is that in an argument form it keeps the same name and no other statement is given the same name. So "This is Brussels" is going to be B or q, but certainly not A or p. Could we have called it A before we baptized the other statement A? Sure, provided we baptized the other one something else.

When an argument in ordinary language is translated replacing its statements with sentence letters and the connectives with their appropriate symbols then we have exhibited its form. The connectives in sentential logic connect sentences. The connectives are "and," "or," "it is not the case that," and "if...then." They are represented by an upside down v, a right side up v, the ~ or –, and an arrow respectively. Punctuation is also provided with parentheses and brackets.

Two arguments in ordinary language which have the same representation when translated have the same logical or argument form. This is handy because once you know a form is valid and are practiced in recognizing it you can immediately recognize valid arguments about matters you never heard of. Take my argument about Clinton, Paula Jones, and sexual harassment and make it about Rush Limbaugh, Oprah Winfrey, and unfair competition. If one argument is valid the other one is too.

In this section I call your attention to some common valid logical forms.

8.6.1   Tautologies

A *tautology* is a sentence that must be true in all possible worlds. A contradiction is a sentence that must be false in all possible worlds. You can recognize tautologies and contradictions by their forms. "P and not P" is a contradiction. "It is snowing in hell and it is not snowing in hell" is a contradiction. Tautologies are redundant and boring, but they are valid. "P or not P" is a tautology: "It is raining right now in Chico or it is not raining right now in Chico." Notice that a tautology requires no premises. It is true on the basis of form alone. So perhaps tautologies are exceptions to the rules we have looked at governing argument: tautologies are valid argument forms that require no premises. However, philosophers disagree on the question of whether tautologies assert any conclusions at all when sentence names are replaced with ordinary language statements. After all, how much information about the weather is included in the tautology about Chico in this example?

8.6.2   Modus Ponens

A common valid form of argument, *modus ponens* is, as its latin name implies, a "method of putting." A modus ponens argument takes the following symbolic form:

- If p, then q.
- P.
- Therefore q.

A simple example of a modus ponens would be as follows:

- If July 15 is Graybosch's birthday, then he is a Cancer just like O.J. Simpson, Bill Clinton, and Phyllis Diller.
- July 15 is Graybosch's birthday.
- Therefore he is a Cancer just like O.J. and the others.

More complicated modus ponens follow patterns such as the following:

- If p and q and r, then s or t.
- P and q and r.
- Therefore s or t.

8.6.3   Hypothetical Syllogisms

Hypothetical syllogisms are arguments that have the following symbolic form:

- If p, then q.
- If q, then r.
- Therefore if p, then r.

Here is an example of a valid simple hypothetical syllogism:

- If the Yankees win the pennant, then Darryl Strawberry will get a raise.
- If Darryl Strawberry gets a raise, then his ex-wife will take him to court.
- So if the Yankees win the pennant, then Strawberry's ex-wife will take him to court.

Syllogisms come in many forms. One is known as the *disjunctive syllogism,* which has the following symbolic form:

- P or q.
- Not p.
- Therefore q.
  Example: Jill is a lawyer or Jill is a psychologist. Jill is not a lawyer. Therefore Jill is a psychologist.

A knowledge of traditional syllogisms will be helpful to you if you are taking a standardized test for graduate or professional school. Here are several valid syllogisms. Notice that traditional syllogisms are not in sentential form.

- All A's are B's.

- All B's are C's.
- Therefore all A's are C's.

  Example: All talk show hosts are well paid. All well-paid people are happy. Therefore all talk show hosts are happy.

Another valid syllogism follows:

- All A's are B's.
- This is an A.
- This is therefore also a B.

  Example: All Rolling Stones albums have one song on which Keith sings lead. This is a Rolling Stones album. Therefore this album has one song on which Keith sings lead.

Here is a third valid syllogism:

- All A's are B's.
- No B's are C's.
- Therefore no A's are C's.

  Example: All lovers of Champion Jack Dupree are lovers of Jerry Lee Lewis. No lovers of Jerry Lee Lewis are lovers of Johnny Mathis. Therefore no lovers of Champion Jack are lovers of Johnny Mathis.

A fourth valid syllogism is:

- No A's are B's.
- Some C's are A's.
- Therefore some C's are not B's.

  Example: No supporters of President Clinton are Bosnian Serbs. Some Croatians are supporters of Clinton. Therefore some Croatians are not Bosnian Serbs.

Some syllogisms sound valid but are not. What is wrong with the following syllogism?

- God is love.
- Love is blind.
- Ray Charles is blind.
- Ray Charles is God.

8.6.4   Modus Tollens

Modus tollens, latin for "method of removing," is an argument that takes the following symbolic form. Can you see the reason for its name?

- If p, then q.
- Not q.
- Therefore not p.

  Example: If Graybosch finds the Holy Grail, then he will be famous. Graybosch will not be famous. Then Graybosch will not find the Holy Grail.

8.6.5   Dilemmas

A *dilemma* is an argument in which there is a choice between two alternatives, neither of which is particularly desirable. A dilemma takes the following symbolic form:

- P or q.
- If p, then r.
- If q, then s.
- Therefore, r or s.

  Example: Peter either forgot that it was Christmas or did not care enough for his kids to buy them gifts. If Peter forgot it was Christmas, then he needs to see a doctor. If Peter did not care enough for his kids to buy them a gift, then he needs counseling. Therefore, Peter either needs to see a doctor or get counseling.

This is a handy form of argument for use when you know that someone is guilty of one of several offenses but you cannot say which one. You do not have to determine which offense is the real one to convict the person.

8.6.6   Indirect Proof or Reductio ad Absurdum

An indirect proof, also known as *reductio ad absurdum,* or "reduction to the absurd," complies with the following form:

- Suppose: p.
- If p, then q.
- If q, then r.
- Not r.
- Therefore not p.

Example: Suppose Pat Paulsen becomes president. If he becomes president, then he will sell the White House to his cousin Maxine. If he sells the White House to his cousin Maxine, then Maxine will live forever. Maxine will not live forever. Therefore, Pat Paulsen will not become President.

The reductio looks like an extended version of modus tollens. The difference is that the reductio is purposely used to throw doubt on a particular premise. This is a very effective form of argument because it forces an opponent to speak to a matter she might just as soon pass over in silence.

8.6.7   Contradictions

A *contradiction* is a sentence form that must be false no matter what statements are substituted for the statement names. It has the symbolic form "p and not p." For example, the statement "It is raining right now in Chico and it is not raining right now in Chico" is a contradiction. The negation of a contradiction must be true. So if you find a contradiction, you should conclude that its negation is true: "It is not the case that it is raining and not raining in Chico right now." In the charge of atheism against Socrates, outlined above, we would agree with Socrates that it is not the case that he is both an atheist and a believer in gods.

8.6.8   Analogies

In an *analogy* we draw a comparison between the known qualities of a sample population and the partially known qualities of a target population. If, for example, we have several friends who like heavy metal music, alternative rock, mosh pits, and tattoos, and if we make a new friend who likes three of those things, then it would be reasonable to infer by analogy that the new friend will like the fourth thing.

Our analogy works on the basis of similarities. If our friends are similar in three respects, they are probably similar in the fourth. The cogency of this reasoning depends in part on the similar qualities being related to each other. Our first three friends might also like Chopin or falafel, but I would be less inclined to infer that the fourth person shares those likes because an appreciation of falafel does not seem related to an appreciation of mosh pits. Analogies often lead to unsound conclusions because they are not properly grounded.

8.6.9   Induction by Elimination

Induction by elimination is a popular nondeductive form of reasoning in philosophy. It requires three steps. The first is to canvas the alternative perspectives on a question. The second step is to find reasons why all alternatives but one cannot be true. Finally, having eliminated all the unacceptable alternatives, you take step three, which is to accept the remaining alternative as the most probable one. The crucial step in this form of reasoning is the first step. If you have not included all the alternatives, you will commit an informal fallacy called a *false dilemma*. We will talk a little more about false dilemmas in Chapter 9.

8.6.10   Induction by Enumeration

In *induction by enumeration* we infer that a quality probably belongs to a whole population on the basis of a finite number of instances.

Example: Farmer Jones's turkey believes that Farmer Jones will come to feed him every morning on the basis of a finite number of previous feedings.

This is a fairly reliable inference for the turkey; it is correct every morning except the last.

Statistical Induction

A *statistical induction* is similar to induction by enumeration. It involves attributing the statistical frequency of a quality in a sample population to the population as a whole.

Example: Since 75% of the camels we have seen have two humps, we infer that 75% of all camels have two humps.

Both induction by enumeration and statistical induction uncover connections that may be more than coincidences. They may be connections that are based on an underlying causal relationship. Is it a mere coincidence that students begin to fidget in their seats when the end of class approaches? Could it be that the clock makes them fidget?

Higher-level inductions consider a wider variety of objects in their samples than those considered in the inductions, enumerative or statistical, that generate the initial connections that become candidates for causes and effects.

8.6.11   Inference to the Best Explanation

Some philosophers accept *inference to the best explanation* as a valid form of nondeductive inference. Suppose there is a series of events whose occurrence can be most reasonably explained if you posit another event as their cause.

Example: You notice that every time you play cards with me you lose. But when you play cards with other people you do reasonably well. Your losing streak with me might be best explained if you posit that I am a cheat. Perhaps I have marked the cards.

Certainly the explanation will have a stronger initial probability if you have seen me cheat in the past or remember that when we play cards we always use my deck. Your inability to imagine another explanation for your losses does not prove that I am cheating. But it does not follow from the fact that another explanation does not occur to us that the one that does occur is the only possible explanation. An explanation, therefore, is only as good as our knowledge of the conditions and circumstances of the phenomenon that we are trying to explain. Good background knowledge might justify our claim that the explanation that occurs to us is the only possible one, but because our knowledge is so often more limited than we think, we should normally give low probability to conclusions from this form of reasoning.

8.6.12   The Hypothetical-Deductive Method

The *hypothetical-deductive method* is usually attributed to Karl Popper but dates at least from the work of the nineteenth-century American philosopher Chauncey Wright. Popper popularized the method with philosophers of science as his original criterion for differentiating science from nonscience. Popper points out that one can never conclusively verify by empirical means a universal statement, but one can falsify it.

For instance, induction by enumeration cannot establish once and for all that all swans are white. One nonwhite swan can falsify the universal claim about white swans. It may sound odd, but falsifiability is actually more helpful to science than verification via inductions. After all, if you can falsify a claim, then you need not pursue it any longer and can move on to another claim.

Popper urges that scientific investigators select the hypothesis with the lowest initial probability, given our background beliefs, for further investigation. It is the hypothesis that has the highest likelihood to turn out to be wrong when empirically tested. If it survives frequent tests, it is considered corroborated.

Argumentation is the means by which most philosophy gets done. As you read philosophical essays, try to determine which particular modes of argumentation the writers are using. The premises may be more complicated than the ones I have used in my examples above, but the basic forms will be there. Remember, learning the throws of argument now will enhance your ability not only to understand philosophical positions but to find ways to question and, perhaps, improve upon them in your own writing.

9

Avoiding Fallacies

Plato is dear to me, but dearer still is truth.

—Aristotle

9.1 FORMAL FALLACIES

Fallacies are errors in reasoning that lead us to accept conclusions that are not soundly based upon valid premises. Formal fallacies are reasoning errors that occur because the form or structure of an argument is incorrect. There are an infinite number of formal fallacies, yet a few may be identified that are commonly encountered when analyzing arguments. The ability to recognize them may make your job as a critical writer easier.

9.1.1 Denying the Antecedent

Remember the way we formulated arguments in Chapter 8. Consider an argument in this form:

- If p, then q.
- Not p.
- Therefore, not q.

Example: If Graybosch wins the lottery, then he can take a vacation. Graybosch cannot win the lottery. Therefore, Graybosch cannot take a vacation.

It would be a lot easier to take a vacation if I won the lottery, but maybe I will take one anyway. The error in the argument is in assuming that the antecedent (winning the lottery) is necessary to my conclusion (taking a vacation). In actuality, my taking a vacation does not depend upon winning the lottery. Now, it may be true that if I win the lottery, I will take a vacation, but this does not mean the opposite, that if I do not win the lottery, I will not take a vacation. Winning the lottery is one sufficient, but not necessary, condition of taking a vacation.

9.1.2   Affirming the Consequent

Here is another invalid form of reasoning:

- If p, then q.
- Q.
- Therefore, p.

Just because p always leads to q does not mean that q always leads to p. Other sufficient conditions may also result in q. The consequent q is a necessary condition of p in the sense that if p does occur, q must also occur.

9.1.3   The Exclusive Fallacy

This fallacy takes the following form:

- P or q.
- P.
- Therefore, not q.

The fallacy lies in confusing the inclusive and exclusive sense of "or." Example: You are at a party and ask who brought the wine. The host says Fred or Jack brought the wine. If "or" is meant exclusively then once you know that Fred brought wine you could conclude that Jack did not. But if "or" is used inclusively then it means at least Fred and possibly Jack brought wine. Since logic uses the inclusive sense of "ork" you ought not to infer from the fact that Fred brought wine that Jack did not.

Here is an example of the Exclusive Fallacy:

Either Newt Gingrich is guilty of ethics violations or Bill Clinton is guilty of ethics violations.

Newt Gingrich is guilty of ethics violations

Therefore, Bill Clinton is not guilty of ethics violations.

Alas, dear Democrats, the guilt of Newt does not establish Bill's innocence. The inclusive sense of "or" allows both disjuncts to be true. They both could be guilty; both disjuncts could be true.

Of course, we are familiar with detective stories in which each suspect is eliminated until there is only one left who must be guilty. There are eliminative arguments in which the truth or falsity of a disjunct is relevant to the truth or falsity of others. But they must be carefully phrased to show the relevance of the disjuncts to each other. And you will note that the argument example above did not include a premise that said they both could not be guilty. If it did, it would have been a valid argument. But it would also have had a different argument form.

9.2   INFORMAL FALLACIES

Informal fallacies are errors in reasoning based in the content of an argument and not in the argument's form. It is possible to construct arguments with valid forms but still fail to have reasoned properly in one of three general ways. First, the premises of the argument could be false or lack the proper degree of probability. Second, our reasoning could leave out evidence in our possession, or evidence that is not in our possession that we are still responsible for gathering. Ignorance of contrary evidence is not an acceptable excuse. Third, our argument could mistakenly assert that the premises give more support to the conclusion than the truth or probability of the premises would warrant. These three general types of fallacies are found in a number of more specific forms, which we shall now describe.

9.2.1   Susceptibility to Fallacies

Our human desires make us susceptible to fallacies. A common gambling fallacy is to bet on a number that is due because it has not occurred recently. If the dice or the roulette wheel is fair, each outcome has the same probability on each roll or spin regardless of how long it has been since it last occurred. If I throw six snake eyes (two one's) in a row, on the seventh throw it is just as likely that I will throw snake eyes again as it was on the first throw. Snake eyes are not less likely because they have occurred six times in a row, if the dice are fair.

Psychologists have catalogued a number of impediments to reasoning. I am pretty good at math, but I make an increasing number of errors of subtraction in my check book toward the end of the month. Wishful thinking infects my math. Two other interesting impediments to reasoning are our tendencies to have a confirmation bias and to expect one cause for any given event. The confirmation bias allows us to accept horoscopes and psychic hot lines because we remember only the instances when the "predictions" come true and forget the times when they do not. The expectation that every event has just one cause blinds us to other contributing causes and makes us especially prone to give up good causal connections when we run into one exception. For example:

Smoking does not cause cancer because my Dad smoked until he was 97. Perhaps your dad was lucky and had a genetic endowment that helped him resist cancer.

There is also an interesting error made consistently with statistical reasoning that could be called a formal error. Suppose you read of a study that says that 35 percent of people convicted of heroin possession said they had smoked marijuana before becoming involved with heroin. This correlation might lead you to infer that marijuana use causes heroin use; or you might infer that whatever causes marijuana use also causes heroin use. And people commonly make such inferences. The 35% is impressive until you notice that 65% did not say that they smoked marijuana before becoming involved with heroin. When you are presented with a statistical correlation between two factors such as marijuana use and heroin use, you really want to know four correlations before drawing a conclusion about the relevance of one to the other:

What percent of marijuana users also use heroin.

What percent of marijuana users do not use heroin.

What percent of the population use heroin only.

What percent of the population use neither marijuana nor heroin.

But if you studied further, you might find that 50 percent of people convicted of heroin possession are women, 90 percent are coffee drinkers, and 98 percent have at least ten teeth. These figures might lead you to want to test for heroin all the women you can find who drink coffee and have at least ten teeth.

Our human tendency to accept fallacies is, fortunately, counteracted by our ability to identify them. The following list of informal fallacies has been constructed to assist you in identifying fallacies in arguments.

9.2.2   Invalid Appeal to Authority

An *invalid appeal to authority* occurs when we rely on defective expertise. Defective expertise is a source of knowledge that presents itself as authoritative but is not. Michael Jordan is an expert basketball player, but he does not necessarily know the best brand of ice cream. Experts may be subject to bias that can cause them consciously or unconsciously to render unfair judgment. A Toyota salesman will probably not provide an unbiased evaluation of a Nissan. And sometimes the experts disagree, leaving us forced to reason for ourselves. The two founders of the philosophical tradition known as Pragmatism, Charles Peirce and William James, could not agree on a common definition. So Peirce renamed his view Pragmaticism.

The fact that people have positions of authority does not automatically make their beliefs, or our premises, false or unjustified. When the president or the pope speak they do not commit a fallacy of invalid appeal to authority just by saying something. Perhaps their office does not give them expertise in all matters, but each has a sphere of expertise—politics and religion—where it is appropriate to speak and be cited as an authority. And, when they venture into other areas such as the philosophy of love, the arguments they offer ought to be considered. It would be simply unfair to convict them of the fallacy of invalid appeal to authority unless they claim that their position gives them some special expertise. In other words, authorities should have the chance to offer arguments and be given a fair hearing.

9.2.3   Straw Person

A *straw person* is a misrepresentation of the position of an opponent. A straw person is a position or concept that you have formulated because it is more easily attacked than your opponent's real position. The phrase "What so-and-so really means to say" often introduces a straw person argument. Consider this example. "What Pat Robertson really means to say is that if we don't join his church, we will all burn in hell."

9.2.4   Inconsistency

You commit the error of *inconsistency* when you use inconsistent premises to support a conclusion. If you accept as a premise the idea that smoking does not lead to death but admit that diseases caused by smoking lead to death, your two premises conflict. You can also commit this fallacy by being inconsistent in your words and actions. Or you could argue for inconsistent conclusions. Sometimes people change a belief over time without offering an explanation why. And, finally, organizations such as corporations or political parties sometimes take inconsistent positions with different audiences or have spokespersons who take differing stands. You and a friend might take opposing viewpoints on an important issue and send letters to a politician and compare the replies you receive. In many cases, it will look like the politician agrees with both of you.

9.2.5   False Dilemma

A *false dilemma* occurs when all the available alternatives are not considered. Consider this example of a false dilemma often used by parents: "Do you want to go to bed now or after your bath?" Faced with what seem to be only two possible courses of action, the five-year-old child will take the bath and go to bed, without realizing that there may be other, less undesirable alternatives. When she reaches the age of eight or nine, different courses of action, such as continuing to watch television, may occur to her.

In politics, even in the most sophisticated commentaries, false dilemmas appear in questions such as: "Should the United States use military force or economic sanctions against Iraq?"

9.2.6   Complex Question

In this fallacy you ask a question in a way that begs the answer to another, usually negatively perceived, question. The idea is to make your opponents grant a premise that will be useful in constructing an argument against a conclusion they wish to resist. "When are you going to become responsible?" If you answer that question, you admit that you have not been responsible in the past and grant a premise that may then be used against you.

9.2.7   Begging the Question

When you *beg the question*, you argue for a conclusion by assuming at least part of it in your premises. "Why do you doubt that God is good? Does not the Koran say so?" The question assumes that God exists and that the Koran provides an authoritative description of the deity's characteristics.

9.2.8   Suppressed Evidence

Because we cannot spend all our lives in doubt, we must eventually draw conclusions on the basis of the evidence available to us. But whenever we suppress evidence, whether we have it available or not, we engage in fallacious reasoning. It is easier to know when you have suppressed relevant evidence in your possession than it is to know when you have done enough investigation to conclude that there is no conflicting evidence that you have not uncovered. Do you need to have read everything William James ever wrote to know that he believed in free will? Or is reading "The Dilemma of Determinism" enough? The correct answer depends upon your social role and responsibilities, on whether you are a beginning student or an advanced scholar. We often suppress evidence for good motives. When we tell children that bad things will happen to them when they lie, we suppress evidence that not all lies lead to negative consequences.

9.2.9   Lack of Proportion

When we over- or underestimate actions, interests, or outcomes, we are guilty of applying a *lack of proportion* in our arguments. Consider the following exhortation, addressed to a typical teenager: "Go ahead and buy the Smashing Pumpkins concert ticket for $300.00. You only live once!"

9.2.10   Appeal to Unknowable Statistics

It is tempting to insert into our arguments appeals to unknowable statistics. For example: "Let's have one more drink. Nobody has ever died from a six-pack!" Another example: "Battlefield deployment of tactical nuclear weapons has prevented 17 major wars in Europe since 1950."

9.2.11   Ad Hominem

Ad hominem is Latin for "against the person." It is a fallacy that involves attacking people's character, looks, tastes, or some other irrelevant aspect of their lives to avoid dealing with their arguments. Examples: "Clinton's health plan is no good. We know he is a liar." "Dole's tax plan will never work. He's too old."

9.2.12   Guilt by Association

Guilt by association is a form of ad hominen argument in which a person's associates are attacked in attempt to reflect negatively upon that person or her argument. The target person may be beyond reproach but her associates may be easy targets. Vice presidential candidate Richard Nixon used this strategy in his famous 1951 "Checkers" speech to attack Adlai Stevenson, a politician beyond reproach, by associating Stevenson with Harry Truman, who was very controversial. Although Truman had endorsed Stevenson's candidacy for President, Truman and Stevenson were not constant companions. Politicians commonly employ the opposite of this phenomenon, something I call *innocence by association*. When wealthy politicians have themselves photographed with the poor, they take advantage of innocence by association.

9.2.13   Two Wrongs Make a Right

A common fallacy involves defending a wrong action by claiming that someone else has done the same thing or has done something just as bad: "Tommy hit me first!" When we base our argument on the wrong behavior of more than two people, this fallacy is called "common practice": "It's not so bad to cheat on the test; all my friends do it." When a way of doing wrong has become so accepted that it has attained the status of a proverb, it is called "traditional wisdom": "The real speed limit is ten miles per hour above the posted speed limit."

9.2.14   Equivocation

Equivocation is the practice of using different meanings of a term that has more than one meaning to derive a conclusion: "Jesus loved prostitutes, and so do I. That's why I pay them well for their services."

9.2.15   Appeal to Ignorance

We *appeal to ignorance* when we try to get someone to believe that his conclusion is false because he has failed to prove it is true. We may even try to get him to believe that because he has failed to prove his conclusion to be true, then the opposite of his conclusion is true. The failure to prove the existence of extraterrestrial humanoids does not demonstrate that there are none, and the failure to prove that there are no extraterrestrial humanoids does not demonstrate that there are some.

9.2.16   Composition

Composition is a fallacy that occurs when we reason that if the members of a group have a property or characteristic, then the whole group has that characteristic. We might believe, for example, that if all the players on the Oklahoma Sooners football team are individually good players, then the team must be good also. They may not, however, play well together.

9.2.17   Division

Division is the fallacy that occurs when we expect a member of a group to have all the characteristics of a group as a whole: "Native Americans care about the environment." Even if most Native Americans do care about the environment, this does not mean that any individual Native American will.

9.2.18   Hasty Conclusion

When you accept a sweeping conclusion on the basis of a single or small number of incidents, you reach a *hasty conclusion*. For instance, someone may conclude that all New York City taxi drivers are dishonest if she has been overcharged for a ride from the airport to downtown. A hasty conclusion is the result of making a judgment on the basis of too small a sample of experiences. Another example: "From what I've seen, atheists are easier to live with than Christians."

Sometimes hasty conclusions are referred to as small samples. A sample can be too small to reveal a representative trend. You would probably be less likely to accept the conclusion of a survey about pornography and sexual assault if you found out that only twenty-five offenders were surveyed. A sample can also be faulted for being unrepresentative. A survey of New York City cab drivers ought not to be taken as a fair indication of the behaviors of all cab drivers no matter how many cabbies are surveyed.

Humans are inclined to make inductions from single experiences, but rationally we ought not to do so. Calculating a sufficiently large sample size depends on both the size of the population we study and its diversity. I heard a psychologist on the radio this morning say that she had spoken to over fifty women before drawing her conclusion about how best to end a relationship. A sample of fifty is not enough to draw a conclusion about such a large group of persons. Also, people are more complex entities than ping pong balls. One may expect a greater diversity of opinions within the population of women or men, and this should affect sample size. Statisticians would want you to check with at least 1,200 people in a rigorous, scientifically designed study before drawing a conclusion about a country like the United States.

The sample should also be representative of the population. So, if you want to talk about women in general, then you should make sure your sample is not just about a particular ethnic or economic group.

9.2.19   Questionable Cause

The *questionable cause fallacy* is committed when we take an event as the cause of another on the basis of token evidence, such as a correlation that has not been subjected to further investigation. Political candidates are fond of attributing economic improvements to their economic policies. But they rarely consider that there might have been even greater improvements in the economy if their policies had not been followed; that the economy improved despite their policies and not because of them.

9.2.20   Questionable Analogy

A *questionable analogy* is the result of drawing a conclusion on the basis of similarities while ignoring or overlooking relevant differences. For example, electric discharges occur both in a computer that is processing "information" and in the human brain when it is thinking. This might lead us to draw analogies between what goes on in the brain and the computer as support for the conclusion that computers and humans both process information in the same sense. But there are many dissimilarities between human brains and computers; in fact, there may be too many relevant dissimilarities to compare "artificial intelligence" to human intelligence.

9.2.21   Appeal to Pity

Sometimes we are tempted to accept a conclusion or a premise because we have sympathetic feelings either for the person who advances it or for the person's current situation. Perhaps we may accept a job applicant's argument that he deserves a teaching position because, if he does not receive it, he and his family will suffer.

9.2.22   Appeal to the Stick

Appeals to the stick are actions that mistake threats for arguments. When we appeal to the stick we urge someone to accept a conclusion or else suffer stated or implied negative consequences. "Why should I attend class?" asks the student. "Because if you do not, I will lower your grade one level for each absence in excess of two," replies the authoritarian philosophy instructor. The instructor has not persuaded the student of the reasonableness of attending class but instead has tried to supply a motivation.

9.2.23   Appeal to Loyalty

Sometimes we accept a conclusion because it comes from a revered public figure, or it is crucial to our national interest, or its contradiction reflects unfavorably on our nation or another cherished institution such as a church, school, or family. Some Americans have refused, for example, to believe that our armed forces have committed atrocities.

9.2.24   Provincialism

Like the appeal to loyalty, *provincialism* blinds us to the value of beliefs and practices of other cultures. We are provincial when we reject the ideas of others not for verified reasons but simply because we are familiar with our own practices but not theirs. We may attend a Christian communion service without questioning its value but reject a harvest dance as having no religious value.

9.2.25   Popularity

We rely upon *popularity* or appeal to the crowd (argument ad baculum) when we argue for a conclusion on the grounds of its widespread acceptance or acceptance by an important group that is not composed of appropriate experts. If we go to church because all our neighbors do, we are basing our actions upon popularity.

9.2.26   Double Standard

A *double standard* occurs when we treat similar cases in a dissimilar manner. If we expect men but not women to experience premarital sex, we subscribe to a double standard.

9.2.27   Invincible Ignorance

Some people actually take pride in refusing to listen to argument. This severe form of evading the issue is usually fed by faith, frustration, and self-righteousness. Extremists on both sides of the abortion issue, for example, sometimes exhibit invincible ignorance by demonstrating pride in not listening to arguments of the other side.

9.3   EXERCISES IN IDENTIFYING FALLACIES

Here are some exercises to sharpen your argument skills. Although the examples presented here may not at first appear to be arguments, if you examine them closely you will find an argument within each one, and all of them contain fallacies. Your task, to identify the fallacies, will be easier if you approach each example by taking the following steps, in this order:

1. Identify the conclusion that you are being asked to accept.
2. Identify the reasons (premises) that are offered for accepting the conclusion.
3. Determine the appropriateness of the premises, that is, the extent to which the premises lead to the conclusion.
4. Determine adequacy of the premises, that is, the extent to which the premises provide sufficient reason to accept the conclusion.
5. If the premises are inappropriate or inadequate, select the fallacy from the list above that most adequately explains the error in the argument.

1. Gas Company Commercial: "Heat pumps [which run on electricity] will not last as long as gas furnaces. Just look at the warranty. Electricity is fine for air conditioning, but in our state most people prefer to heat with gas."

2. From "Pretty Boy Floyd," a song by Woody Guthrie:

It was in Oklahoma City, it was on a Christmas Day/A whole carload of groceries with a letter that did say:/"You say that I'm an outlaw. You say that I'm a thief./Well, here's a Christmas dinner for the families on relief."/As through this life you travel, you'll meet some funny men./Some rob you with a six gun, some with a fountain pen./As through this land you ramble, as through this lot you roam,/You'll never see an outlaw take a family from their home.

3. Letter to the editor of a newspaper addressing reparations to Japanese Americans interned in camps in California during World War II:

There is no question that these people of Japanese ancestry were wronged, and for this I am truly sorry. But the idea that this specific historical act should be selected for me to help pay for, when I had absolutely nothing to do with it nor even know of anyone who did is outrageous. . . . As for American historical wrongs that should be righted, coming from ancestors of the old cotton South, I personally would rather give the money to American blacks. . . . But finally, I don't believe that the sins of the father should be exacted from his children. One man's sin is another man's virtue.

4. Excerpt from a newsletter touting investment in government bonds:

We know that the federal government will always pay the interest on Treasury Bills and will always redeem them at full value at maturity for two reasons. One, the whole edifice of the U.S. Government financial system is built on the foundation of the Treasury Bill. If the U.S. Government should default on the U.S. Treasury Bill, the entire financial system of the United States and in fact of much of the world would collapse. The second reason: it is inflationary but all the government has to do is print some more money or sell some more Treasury Bills to pay for the old ones.

5. A university announced the conversion of an unrestricted but metered parking area containing thirteen spaces to a nonmetered student parking area. The Director of Auxiliary Enterprises announced, "We are trying to provide more parking for students."

6. *Tulsa World* AP Wire Story from South Africa, 8/27/88:

When his company's trucks kept being stolen, Norman Asch called the doctor—the witch doctor. "He poured some liquids into various parts of the vehicles and marked the underside of some parts," Asch said. "He left a small, plastic doll hanging from each rear-view mirror." Asch said none of the company's vehicles has been stolen since.

7. Pope John Paul II, Apostolic Letter on the Role of Women, 10/01/88.

In the name of liberation from male domination, women must not appropriate to themselves male characteristics contrary to their own feminine originality. If they take this path, women will not reach fulfillment, but instead will deform and lose what constitutes their essential richness.

8. Television commentator on the defeat of conservative Judge Bork's nomination to the United States Supreme Court after a lengthy, and at times highly personal, debate: "Bork lived and died by the bash. He bashed gays, civil rights, and women. And when he was nominated they bashed him back. What else should he have expected?"

9. Newspaper story about punishment and rehabilitation:

[A] former college president, having served 7 months of a 10-year sentence for embezzling funds from the college, was let out of prison to attend the season opening football game. The Corrections Department spokesperson said, "You can't just lock them up in prison forever and throw away the key. We've got to prepare them to function in society when they're released."

10. Wire story: "Racism was on the increase in the United States in 1988. There were 258 incidents of racial discrimination as opposed to 169 the previous year."

9.4   CALCULATING PROBABILITIES

Now that we understand how valid arguments are formed and how to identify fallacies, we may consider how to calculate the probability that certain types of arguments (those whose elements are quantifiable) may be valid. We stated in the previous chapter that a nondeductive argument is one that claims that a conclusion follows from the premises with a high probability of truth. But how high must the probability of truth be in order for us to believe that a conclusion is sufficiently probable? The answer is not clear.

We may begin, however, with the proposition that the probability's sufficiency depends upon the context. In other words, the strength of the proof that we demand will depend upon the importance of what the conclusion demands of us, and the costs to us of ignoring the conclusion. For instance, if I owned a truck whose manufacturer sent a recall notice because one in ten thousand have exploding ashtrays, I would take the truck in for service. Taking the truck in for service is a relatively minor inconvenience compared to the potential damage of an explosion, even if the chance of an explosion is remote.

There are some rules you can use in determining probabilities. If you want to know the probability of winning a lottery, you should find out how many tickets are sold. Your probability of being a winner when the ticket is just pulled out of a drum is equal to the number of tickets you bought divided by the number sold. But lotteries are designed for suspense. They are meant to be presented as television drama. You have seen on television the little Ping-Pong balls floating around until they are sucked into a tube and displayed at the bottom of the television screen. This means of selection allows there to be lotteries with no winner in a given drawing, since no one may have picked the right combination. There can also be several winners, since more than one person may pick the right set of numbers.

The odds of winning in such a lottery depend upon the number of possible values and the number of values you have to pick. Perhaps your state lottery asks you to pick seven numbers from a field of fifty. No lotteries I know of allow a number to repeat. A winning ball is not thrown back in before the next is picked. So in a lottery with seven values picked from a field of fifty, the odds of any one ticket being the winner would be one in 50 times one in 49 times one in 48 times one in 47 times one in 46 times one in 45 times one in 44. This is because there are fifty candidates for the first pick and one less candidate on each subsequent draw when the selected ball is not replaced. Likewise, the probability of getting heads on two successive tosses of a fair coin is calculated by multiplying the probability of each separate occurrence. One-half times one-half equals one-fourth, a one-in-four chance.

If you wanted to know the probability of a disjunction (a particular number on either of two dice)—let's say the chance of getting a six or a three on a single throw of a single die—you would add the individual probabilities. One-sixth plus one-sixth gives us two-sixths or one-third, which is one chance in three. So the probability of getting a three or a six on a throw of a die is three to one.

But when events are not independent, we must include the effect of one outcome on the other in the calculation of probabilities. In our fifty-number lottery, each numbered ball has a one-in-fifty chance of being selected on the first draw. After the first draw, the numbers not selected have a one-in-forty-nine chance of being selected on draw two. The joint probability of the selection of any two particular numbers is one in fifty times one in forty-nine, because on the second draw there are only forty-nine candidates left: $1/50 \times 1/49 = 1/2,450$. This means you have a one-in-2,450 chance to draw, say, a five and a twenty-six.

The task of calculating probabilities is complex and requires more than one textbook to explain, but we have presented here a sample of the types of considerations that are used in calculation.

9.5   EMOTIVE LANGUAGE

Words are used to do many more things than just describe a factual occurrence or convey our thoughts. When someone says "I promise" she may not be describing what is going on in her head. Perhaps she has no intention at all of doing what she promised. But she promises anyway by saying, "I promise." We also use words to convey feelings of surprise, approval, or disgust. Sometimes we select and use words in ways that allow us to increase our chances of persuading others to accept a conclusion without doing the hard and honest work required by rational argumentation. Perhaps you noticed how I just used the word "honest" to nudge you in the direction of accepting my view that such forms of non-argumentative persuasion are not only nonrational but immoral? You will be a better critic if you are able to notice these forms of manipulation and a better philosophical writer if you do not use them yourself.

Certain words have positive overtones for the majority of people. It always helps your case if you are an advocate of freedom and self-determination. The positive or negative overtones attached to other words vary with the audience. Certainly you will be more inclined to grant the presumption of legitimacy to the political actions of a foreign government official if he or she is a premier and not a dictator. A colleague in Israel once remarked that he knew Nicolae Ceausescu, the head of Romania, was doomed the day the Israeli radio began to refer to him as a dictator after calling him premier for years.

A careful choice of words can allow you the opportunity to significantly manipulate others. One common form of manipulation we are all familiar with is doublespeak. Often doublespeak, using positive or neutral expressions to hide an unpleasantness or a barbarity, actually appears to be a kindness. Corporations "re-engineer" or "downsize," instead of firing or laying off workers.

Academics and other professionals often resort to difficult language to convey what could be conveyed in much more straightforward ways. Sometimes it is because we are expected to write in an unintelligible manner; sometimes we are trying to demonstrate that we are highly educated and deserve respect. Some writers seem to get a thrill out of making others feel stupid, and some professions actually create employment opportunities by writing in a special jargon. You need a lawyer to interpret the legalese that some other lawyer used to draw up your lease. The first lawyer creates an employment opportunity for the second.

Language can be used to separate you from your money. Disclaimers on contracts are good examples. The most common application seems to be the small print flashed briefly on television screens during automobile leasing commercials. Sure, you can drive a Mustang for $299 a month—if you have $2000 down, drive only 12,000 miles a year, and do not mind owning nothing when the three year lease is up.

Legalese is popular with landlords, bureaucrats, and health maintenance organizations. It is a way of depriving clients of just treatment and washing your hands of guilt at the same time. Opponents at a community debate are silenced by procedures that allow only for two-minute statements. Security deposits disappear to cover cleaning expenses. And HMOs seem to enjoy postponing approval of treatment long enough to tell you that, since it is more than sixty days since an injury occurred, you are no longer eligible for the treatment you requested.

Besides these manipulative moves that are connected to the choice of particular expressions, there are other ways of non-argumentative persuasion. One way to discount the legitimate arguments of others and strengthen your own position is to be in a position to interpret their remarks in a way that slants them in your favor. As I am writing this chapter on July 18, 1996, the story of TWA flight 800 is still unfolding on television. Yesterday the media began speculating that the incident was a result of terrorism. At the afternoon press conference I just watched, the chief FBI officer on the scene referred to the possibility that terrorists were involved and said that if they were involved, they were cowards. In the question and answer session afterwards the press used his hypothetical reference as "evidence" that the terrorism hypothesis was not just speculation. The FBI investigator responded to this move by emphasizing that he was speaking hypothetically. Yet the network reporter who provided the follow-up summary when we went back to the studio again used the remark as evidence that the terrorism was not just media speculation. Even if it turns out that terrorism was involved, the media slanted the remark to support their case.

Sometimes slanting is accomplished just on the basis of social position. Administrators make it clear that opposition to a redeployment of resources will be regarded as a lack of loyalty. It is also fairly easy to convey that a view should not be taken seriously through the tone of presentation. There are modes of expression, material that can be juxtaposed, or even rhetorical questions or pictures in the text to suggest that while a reporter is doing her duty in presenting a view it ought not to be taken seriously.

Another way in which we can make a weak case seem stronger is to claim only a weak degree of justification for a conclusion. "Terrorists may be involved." If we are right we look good. If we are wrong we still look good because we only said it was a possibility. Writers making a case also hope that the weak claim they substantiate will be taken as the stronger one they cannot support and pass unchallenged.

How you handle objections and questions is also important to how strong a case appears to others. If you can wander away from an issue to one you feel more comfortable with, many people will wander with you. You can also dismiss a question with the attitude that it is inappropriate, immoral, insulting, or farfetched.

Finally, I have a word to offer about humor. Ridicule of an opponent is an ad hominem attack. It is fallacious. It is also very effective in slanting an argument. If you become the target of humor you might try to portray your opponent as superficial for using humor in connection with a serious issue. Humor is, however, a very useful way of presenting an objection to those who have more power than you do. It allows you to be heard and provides the other person with the opportunity to retrench while saving face. When emotive and persuasive uses of language are substituted for argument, then they are fallacious. You may fool most of the people most of the time with such strategies, but you will not fool your philosophy instructor.

10

An Introduction to Ethics

Two things fill the mind with ever new and increasing admiration and awe . . . the starry heavens above and the moral law within.

—Immanuel Kant

10.1 WHAT IS ETHICS?

This chapter provides an introduction to the basic concepts of philosophical ethics. To start, consider the following story by William Gass:

Imagine I approach a stranger on the street and say to him, "If you please, sir, I desire to perform an experiment with your aid." The stranger is obliging, and I lead him away. In a dark place conveniently by, I strike his head with the broad of an ax and cart him home. I place him, buttered and trussed, in an ample electric oven. The thermostat reads 450 degrees. Thereupon I go off to play poker with friends and forget all about the obliging stranger in the stove. When I return, I realize I have overbaked my specimen, and the experiment, alas, is ruined. Something has been done wrong. Or something wrong has been done. (William H. Gass. *Fiction and the Figures of Life.* New York: Alfred A. Knopf, 1970. 225.)

Gass's story illustrates different concepts of wrong and right. A person (we will call him a sadist) first kills and then overbakes a stranger. To kill may be called wrong, and to overbake may be called wrong, but we seem to sense that if both actions are wrong, they are not in the same category of "wrong."

Such distinctions form the subject matter of ethics. As ethicists, we are not satisfied if the sadist only perceives the wrong involved in having overbaked the stranger. We want the sadist to perceive the killing as wrong, too. We agree further that the actions described in the example are matters of morality. But from this point forward, we may agree on little else. You, for instance, might believe that killing is sometimes justified, whereas I might believe that killing is always wrong. And this is just the beginning of the argument. You might suggest that ethics is always interpersonal. I might believe that we also have ethical duties to ourselves, the environment, and animals.

At this point we seem to be happy to agree to disagree. Simple. Morality is our sense of right and wrong. Ethics is nothing but different opinions about moral issues. We shall study no further. But, aha! The matter is not so easily settled. Consider that ethical theories almost universally condemn the baking of an obliging stranger. It would seem, therefore, that there is some common ground among ethical theories, and so, as ethicists, we explore the limits and extent of this common ground. *Philosophical ethics, therefore, is the development of ethical principles by reflection upon human interactions.* When we define our ethical theories, we build a firm foundation for our morality.

Whence comes morality? Most of us acquire our morals from our families, religion, friends, television, and schools. We acquire them in a more or less haphazard manner. We have morals. We make moral judgments. But we do not notice inconsistencies between the principles at the bottom of our various moral judgments unless our beliefs are challenged.

Notice that we have to go to such an extreme case as the one posited by William Gass to come up with examples of a morally transparent situation: one in which almost everyone agrees that an act is immoral. There are persons who see nothing morally wrong with the action described by Gass. Sometimes you read about them in the morning's paper. But we quickly redescribe them as moral monsters, not really persons at all, and preserve the morally transparent.

All of the ethical theories you will run across in philosophy would condemn the baking of the obliging stranger. And so, while clear cases like that of the obliging stranger may lead us to generate ethical principles which we synthesize into a theoretical stand toward right and wrong, they do not serve to sort one theory from the others. Clear cases generate no conflicts of judgment about the cases. I might believe that the correct theory is some form of utilitarianism that maximizes the happiness of all people affected by an action. You might be an advocate of the golden rule. We would both still condemn the action. The case does not offer an opportunity to discuss why your theory is right and mine inferior.

It does seem that anyone who needed a reason for condemning this action would be morally blind. Talking to such a person about ethics would be like talking to the colorblind about red and yellow. And, of course, if you accept the view that there are morally transparent cases that are the logical or causal foundations of our ethical theories, you will be less inclined to see the theories as needing explanation.

So clear cases serve to introduce us to situations which have an ethical dimension, and they also provide illustrations of ethical theories. Despite the oddness of asking for reasons why the action was wrong, it can be enlightening to hear how a utilitarian and a social contract theorist would explain the wrongness differently.

Where ethical reasoning can bring theories into conflict is over hard cases. The challenges to our current theoretical stance can be created by new technologies which unsettle our previously consistent ethics. Perhaps you are opposed to abortion on the grounds that it disrespects human life. What position shall you adopt on in vitro fertilization, which allows people to have children but also leads to the disposal of extra embryos?

Another source of hard cases is the conflict of loyalties caused by a complex society in which we have a variety of duties. When I was doing research on Ralph Waldo Emerson at the Houghton Library I used to stay with my friend Ed in Brookline. I would take public transportation to the library, and I always passed an abortion clinic. During business hours there was a police officer stationed outside. The officer's job was to uphold the law and in this case that meant separating the pickets from those seeking services. I remember wondering what the officer's personal view of abortion was and if it reconciled with his current job. Could we, even in that city so close to the homes of Emerson and Thoreau, tolerate police who objected to a particular assignment on the grounds of conscience?

By starting with a case, even an imaginary one, I illustrated the bottom up approach to ethics. Some theorists work from the top down. They believe they can offer non-empirical justifications of ethical principles. Kant is an example of such a philosopher, and we will discuss his view below.

Most commonly, challenges to our beliefs occur when we are called upon to act on them. Consider an example. I do not believe I should buy bootlegged tapes of rock concerts. However, when I got the chance to buy a copy of the Rolling Stones' 1978 concert in Memphis (when they sang "Hound Dog"), I bought it. (This is just an example. I would never do such a thing.) Now I really do not believe in buying bootleg tapes. I was simply (and hypothetically!) too weak to live up to my convictions.

10.2   THE DISTINCTION BETWEEN FACT AND VALUE

If you take an ethical theory course you will be exposed to a problem that has troubled philosophers since it was formulated by David Hume in the eighteenth century. Hume pointed out that ethicists tend to move tacitly from statements of fact to statements of value without justifying the transitions. Examples of statements of fact are "God exists," "Pain is to be avoided," "Pleasure is regarded as a good," and "Business depends upon the keeping of contracts." Value statements, according to Hume, look quite a bit like statements of fact, except they include the term "ought" or a synonym. Examples are "You ought to obey God's commandments," "You ought to choose actions that maximize pleasure and minimize pain," and "You ought to keep your contracts." Hume doubted that we could derive "ought" statements, also called normative statements, from statements of fact. In other words, even if we accept the statement "speed kills" as a statement of fact, we cannot automatically assume that speed is wrong. In order to come to the conclusion that speed is wrong, we must be able to show that killing is wrong. The problem is that the statement "killing is wrong" is a moral judgment, not a statement of fact. For Hume, moral statements cannot be based upon facts, only upon our emotive reactions to the effects of facts.

You should be sensitive to the distinction of fact and value when you are arguing for a position in an applied or professional ethics class. People disagree about the facts of the cases discussed and about what the important values are. If you find yourself realizing that a disagreement is based upon what happened in a case or the statistics about a social practice, then your disagreement is one of fact. Disagreements of fact are more easily settled because, for one thing, they do not have to be settled. You can treat your disagreement as two different hypothetical cases and discuss each in turn. This way your discussion focuses on the ethical issues. But when you write a paper or an exam, make sure you give a descriptive exposition of your understanding of a case or social practice before launching an evaluative discussion. This will prevent misunderstanding of your position by the instructor when there may not be the opportunity to clear it up at a later time.

10.3   TWO BASIC APPROACHES TO ETHICS: CONSEQUENTIALISM AND DEONTOLOGY

Consequental theories propose that actions are right or wrong depending upon their outcome. For a consequentialist, action is good if we reasonably expect it to have good results. Deontological theories hold that the rightness or wrongness of an action depends upon the intent of the actor, and the word *deontologist* comes from the Greek word meaning "having to do with assuming responsibility." For a deontologist an action is good if my intentions when I commit the act are good.

Suppose that I promise to have dinner with you on Saturday night. But then I am offered a chance to go to the opera with my new friend Keith. I decide to tell you that I had already been asked to the opera by Keith and simply forgot. You and I will have dinner Sunday night. Is it good to lie and break my promise? The consequentialist says yes; the deontologist says no.

10.3.1   Consequentialism

Among the important varieties of consequentialists are hedonists, eudaimonists, and egoists.

- *Hedonists* believe the only intrinsic good is pleasure, and by pleasure they mean the pleasant feelings associated with our senses.
- *Eudaimonists* (a phrase derived from the Greek word for "living well") believe that pleasure is part of happiness but insist that the intrinsic good is more complicated than just pleasure. For instance, they might include intellectual happiness and the companionship of friends as important elements in achieving a good life.
- *Psychological egoists* believe that humans always choose what appears to be the greatest good for themselves. In other words, they believe that humans act only in their own interests. Psychological egoists deny that humans can act from altruistic motives, but they do not deny that they can commit altruistic actions.

Depending upon their definition of what constitutes the greatest good, psychological egoists may also be acting as either hedonists or eudaimonists. (This does not mean that hedonists and eudaimonists must be psychological egoists. They could also be altruists.) The psychological egoist sees our motivational structure as the result of a combination of genetic and social conditioning. Thus, since people do not choose their parents, society, sexual orientation, ethnicity, religion, or nationality, it is difficult, in the view of the psychological egoist, to hold people responsible for their actions. What makes psychological egoism so difficult to refute is that any human action can be redescribed to make an altruistic action look like it was done for selfish, and not altruistic, motives.

Ethical egoism maintains that we *ought* to act only in our own interests, and that we have a responsibility to maximize our own concept of what is good. There are at least three types of ethical egoism: personal, individual, and universal. All three types believe that people have the right to decide what is right for themselves. In regard to the acts of others, however, they differ.

- A *personal egoist* makes no claim and has no opinion about what someone else should do.
- An *individual egoist* assumes that it is your responsibility to maximize his expected good.
- A *universal egoist* declares that your responsibility is to maximize your own happiness.

Just imagine that these persons were on your basketball team. Whenever any one of them got the ball, he would shoot it. But the expectations each of them has of your behavior when you get the ball are very different. The first player does not care what you do. The second wants you to pass it to him so he can shoot. And the third envisions a basketball game in which everyone has a ball and everyone shoots.

Utilitarianism

Another school of consequentialist philosophical ethics, *utilitarianism* is based on the principle of utility, or usefulness. Utilitarianism tells me that my moral duty is to select from the available alternatives that action which would lead to the greatest amount of happiness for the greatest number of all those with an interest in the matter. The two major historical figures in the development of utilitarianism were nineteenth-century British philosophers Jeremy Bentham and John Stuart Mill.

The first insight of utilitarianism is that pleasure is intrinsically valuable. Both Bentham and Mill were hedonists, in that they believed the pleasure of any one person is worth as much or as little as anyone else's pleasure. Bentham proposed that most of us had developed rules by which we could readily decide between pleasures. Further, if an action is going to affect only ourselves, according to Bentham we need not be concerned with the attitudes of others towards our action. But if my action affects several others as well as myself, I must prefer the interests of others to my own, unless the costs or benefits of my actions to others are far less than the consequences of my actions to myself. John Stuart Mill argued that there are qualitative differences in pleasures. Mill would maximize the pleasure of the greatest number of those with a stake in the matter, but when there are conflicts between pleasures of qualitatively different orders he urges us to choose the qualitatively better.

If you believe, for example, that classical music is superior to country music, Mill would probably agree with you. How do we know what pleasures are qualitatively superior? Is it not the case that bowling is as good as philosophy; that Johnny Paycheck is as good as Mozart? Mill says no. When we want to know the nature of something we should ask the experts, and experts are people with experience. I should not ask someone who has not experienced the pleasures of Mozart whether I should buy Mozart's *Eine Kleine Nachtmusik* or Dolly Parton's "Joline." I should ask someone who has experienced and appreciated both. So according to Mill, not everyone has an equal voice in determining which pleasures should be maximized. Perhaps this explains why you are taking a general education course in philosophy.

It is not especially important to utilitarians whom the others affected by your actions are. They could be strangers, illegal aliens, a fetus, an animal. In order to have moral standing, you need only be an organism susceptible to feeling pain and pleasure. You might guess that utilitarians often turn out to be vegetarians. The pleasure of eating chicken nuggets is not great enough to justify the pain to chickens raised under the conditions prevalent on factory farms. But you might not anticipate that they would consider hunting for food morally superior to buying meat at the supermarket. The animal that is killed in the wild at least had a natural life and an opportunity for pleasure, while those raised on factory farms that end up in the meat case had a miserable existence.

We have noted how Mill and Bentham disagree over the question of whether there are qualitative differences in pleasures. But both agree that in most cases we will readily follow utilitarian rules and that, when the interests of others are affected, we should count their interests as equal to ours. Of course, Mill would add the proviso that they too are interested in the higher order pleasure. Bentham actually provided a calculus for our use in estimating pleasures when we are uncertain which to prefer.

Bentham's calculus urges us to give a quantitative value to six features of pleasures: intensity, duration, certainty, propinquity, fecundity, and purity. There is the additional seventh condition that when others will be affected by our actions we consider the extent of pleasure to them also as equals. The first three measures of pleasure are straightforward enough. We should prefer pleasures that are more intensely pleasurable, longer lasting, and more certain to be attained.

Propinquity commits us to choosing, other factors being equal, the nearest of competing pleasures: the "sooner" pleasure. This would leave the time of the more distant pleasures available for filling with another pleasure later. Fecundity refers to the ability of a pleasure to lead to pleasures of a similar kind. If I could learn to take pleasure in Green Day, then I might also get other pleasures from many alternative rock bands. And finally, purity refers to the relative amount of pain the pleasure in question is going to cause me.

It might be said that there is no generally accepted way to measure the value of the aspects of pleasures Bentham refers us to. But this objection misunderstands Bentham. Each person is in the best position, according to Bentham but not Mill, to estimate the value of a pleasure to himself of herself. The simplest way I know to measure the aspects of pleasures is to ask how much I would be willing to pay for a pleasure of this intensity or that duration. By placing dollar amounts on the elements of the calculus, each person gives a public measure to private, subjective preferences.

There are two kinds of utilitarianism. *Act utilitarians* calculate benefits for each specific situation. *Rule utilitarians* attempt to define general policies that if consistently followed would lead to the greatest good for the greatest number, and they follow that policy in each situation.

Act Utilitarians are guided by rules of thumb or the calculus as needed in each situation. Rule Utilitarians, again relying on rules of thumb or the calculus, select the general policy that if consistently followed would lead to the greatest good for the greatest number. And they follow that policy in each situation.

Why would they not make an exception to a rule when a situation calls for it? Rule Utilitarians point out that each of us is especially prone to make errors of judgment about when an exception is called for in our own cases. And they are quick to add that even if you are a person who is not prone to such errors your action in making an exception to a rule will give a bad example to those who are.

When they discuss rule utilitarianism, my students tend to fall into two confusions. One comment I get is that rule utilitarians believe in following the law. In most cases they do, but if there were a rule that would lead to more happiness than a law, they would be obligated to work for its acceptance. And in some cases they might even have an obligation to follow that rule instead of the law.

Another misunderstanding of rule utilitarianism is to think that it commits itself to coming up with perfect rules. It does not. It is committed to the rules that would lead to the greatest good for the greatest number, and those rules may not be perfect. Rule utilitarians may accept the necessity of enduring some pain, and even what nonutilitarians would call injustice, as the price of greater happiness.

10.3.2   Deontology: Kant

Perhaps the most famous deontologist is Immanuel Kant, who believed that we can derive correct ethical theory from reason alone. In Kant's view the only unconditional and hence intrinsic good is the good intention. Pleasure or happiness is not intrinsically good. Kant understands "good intention" to mean something like respect for duty and law. Yet the law in question is not the law of the state, but moral law. Moral actions are those done with the good intention, with respect for duty and love of the moral law.

Imagine, for example, that you inherit a large sum of money. Kant would commend you if you decide to donate some of it to your college (and maybe some of it to the Philosophy Department). But Kant would not be sure that your action fits within the moral dimension. It may be the case that you made the donation for the purpose of maximizing your own happiness. Maybe you need the tax deduction. A moral action, for Kant, is one you are *obligated to do regardless of the consequences.* Now, if the good will is one that acts regardless of consequences, it is not going to be governed by our personal inclinations. Where, then, will the content of our moral duty come from? Kant's position is that morality is based in what he calls the categorical imperative. The categorical imperative is an absolute command, not dependent upon one's inclinations or personal desires or goals; it is the product of reason alone and is capable of being formulated in three ways:

1. Act so that the maxim of your action could be a universal law.
2. Treat all humans as ends in themselves and never as merely means.
3. All humans are universal law givers.

According to the categorical imperative, when I consider an action I should not calculate its consequences to myself or society. Rather I should submit the action in question to the universalization test: I should ask myself if the maxim (the rule) on the basis of which I am acting could be followed by all rational creatures.

So, if I think of breaking a promise, I should ask myself if I could logically imagine a world in which all people broke promises when it suited them.

Perhaps you are the type of person who does not make promises and does not expect others to keep theirs. You might be tempted to accept a world in which people break promises. Kant is asking us if there could be a world in which there were promises and people routinely broke them. He is not asking if the real world is like that or if the real world could be like that. Kant wants you to answer that there could be no world with promising in it in which all people routinely broke promises. And since there can be no world in which people all get to act as you would on the basis of your maxim, you ought not to act that way either in this world. After all, you are not special.

Kant believed that the universalization test could be used to show that various actions were always wrong. These included murder, suicide, lying, stealing, and breaking promises. What he seems to have had in mind is that there is a purely logical inconsistency in advocating ethical principles or maxims which parallel those found in statements. If I tell you that it is raining in Chico this morning and you want to check the truth of my statement, you have to look or call the national weather service. If I tell you that it is raining and it is not raining in Chico this morning then you do not have to gather any empirical evidence. You know my statement is false because it is a contradiction. You also know that its negation, "It is not the case that it is raining and it is not raining," must be true.

The inconsistency Kant finds in ethical maxims is that if I advocate the maxim of lying when it suits me I advocate a world in which there is lying and there is not lying. Since I am advocating such a world, I ought also to advocate not only my lying but the lying of all my equals. But paradoxically, this involves advocating a world in which there can be no lying since in this sort of world trust has been destroyed. Therefore, since I cannot advocate a world in which there is and is not lying, such a world is morally unjustified. I ought to advocate its opposite: a world with no lying. And, of course, the way to do what I can to advocate such a world is to tell the truth regardless of consequences.

This way of understanding the universalization test works best with Kant's views on lying and breaking promises. When he discusses suicide and murder the meaning of the universalization test seems to change to a consideration of whether there would be moral value in a universe in which humanity had been eliminated via everyone murdering others or taking their own lives. And just exactly what Kant meant to be the universalization test still occupies scholars. But we can at least agree here that Kant meant to emphasize the equality of human beings, their intrinsic worth, and their special ability to be moral beings.

The second formulation of the categorical imperative is commonly referred to as the respect for persons principle. Kant calls attention to the special worth of human beings as possessors of the good will. Since humans are the source of moral goodness, they should never be treated as merely a means to an end. This does not mean that when you are about to leave Safeway with your groceries you have to obtain consent from the checker to pay for your goods. While it is wrong to treat people as merely means, Kant tells us that you can treat them as means to an extent. But if the checkers were slaves, or were perhaps paid substandard wages, then Kant would urge you to take your business elsewhere.

So respect for persons will make us opponents of slavery and prostitution perhaps. But more importantly, the respect for persons principle tells us to respect the human ability to direct one's own life. And if I respect persons, I respect their autonomy and creativity. If I am a doctor I will try to provide opportunities for patients to make informed health care choices. I will do my best to provide others with as much personal autonomy as I can.

The third formulation of the catogorical imperative is the one that is most often misunderstood. It does not say that every human creates his or her own ethics; it does not say that each human legislates an ethics he or she wishes to be binding on all others like the individual ethical egoist. It says that each human has reason and that on the basis of reason alone a person can discover the categorical imperative. The categorical imperative gives people access to the objective moral law which applies to every rational creature. There is one morality that can be discovered by every rational creature.

It probably has not escaped your notice that Kant's morality is similar to the principle of habitual morality called the golden rule. There are two ways of stating the golden rule: positive and negative. Some people say, "Do unto others as you would want them to do unto you." Others advise us, "Don't do unto others what you would not want them to do to you." The first formulation, the positive one, is very difficult to satisfy without becoming a saint. Imagine what your life would be like if you took it to be your duty to always treat people exactly the way you would like them to treat you. You would be so busy doing things for others you would have no time even to think about your own life.

The positive golden rule seems to have been advocated by Christ. Bertrand Russell once shocked quite a few people in his essay "Why I Am Not a Christian" by using it to explain why there are so few real Christians. The negative formulation is probably what most people feel is binding. But notice that a hermit could satisfy this version of the golden rule. All it enjoins you to do is leave other people alone. Or, as Pascal pointed out, there would be no trouble in the world if everybody stayed in his or her own room.

Kant was aware of these two ways of looking at the golden rule. And he spoke about acts of justice and beneficence. We are required to do justice to others by never lying or breaking promises. These duties and others are fixed by the categorical imperative. And performing them makes us only a basically good person. If you like, think of someone who follows the specific dictates of the categorical imperative as a C person.

Kant was aware that we could not follow the positive golden rule all the time, but he did feel that we should sometimes aid others. After all, if we are committed to the special value of humans and respect for persons, then we should act in a way that enhances their autonomy and creativity at least on occasion. So Kant does not argue that I have a duty to engage in specific beneficent acts so many times a week or give ten per cent of my income to charity. Rather, his position is that I should act in a beneficiary manner in proportion to my talents and resources. So although I have no specific duties to benefit others, to give money or time to the AIDS Walk or the United Fund, if I do not give something to some people or charity sometimes then I am at best a C person. To earn moral praise I must do more than what is enjoined by the categorical imperative in line with my abilities and means.

I hope that this material on Kantianism and Utilitarianism has been helpful to you. Most of you will find these views phrased in terms of principles in your applied and professional ethics courses. Your instructors will refer to the principles of autonomy, respect for persons, and utility. I would just like to add that utilitarians regard Kant as a rule utilitarian. The question they would put to him is why we should be moral. And the answer they expect is that being moral leads to the greatest good for the greatest number. In other words, Kantianism is justified on the grounds of the principle of utility. But Kant cannot accept that view and keep the moral maxims he bases on the categorical imperative.

There are other ethical theories which compete with utilitarianism and deontology. Naturalism, advocated by Aristotelians and Thomists, is the view that organisms fall into categories based upon distinguishing constitutional elements. The moral life is one that leads to the proper use of the essential characteristics. Aristotle saw humans as rational animals and the good life as one in which the satisfaction of the rational nature was given priority over physical pleasures. The good person had both intellectual and moral virtues which enabled the intellectual and physical parts of the self to flourish. A good deal of luck and a well run state were necessary to the good life. Aristotle's views had a great deal of influence on the Christian advocates of natural law theories.

Another alternative is an ethics based on empathy or care. David Hume thought morality was based in empathic feelings for others. Hume has received a good deal of attention recently from feminists who see parallels with their emphasis on care as the basics of ethics.

And there is also currently a resurgence of interest in virtue ethics. Philosophers involved in courses in professional ethics naturally find themselves asking questions about the character that facilitates being a good police officer, business person, or medical professional. And so their interest has turned to understanding the role of virtues in the particular professions. Here I can only make you aware of these alternatives and urge you to consult a philosophical dictionary, an introductory textbook, *The Encyclopedia of Ethics*, a web page devoted to ethics, or the writings of the philosophers mentioned for further clarification.

10.4 PERENNIAL ISSUES FOR POLITICAL ETHICS: JUSTICE AND RIGHTS

The study of ethics includes many divisions that are taught not only by philosophy departments but by other disciplines as well. Ethics courses are taught by professors of economics, business, law, medicine, science, sociology, and many other fields. Political science departments offer courses in political philosophy that normally spend considerable time discussing ethical issues. Justice and rights are two concepts that are found at the heart of political philosophy, for they help to define structures of government, the extent of our freedoms, and the patterns of our lives in society. Because they are so important to our daily lives, we shall take a moment to discuss justice and rights.

Many discussions of justice in political philosophy classes begin with Socrates's definition of justice as recorded in Plato's *Republic*. Socrates begins by refuting the definitions of justice most common in Athens in the fifth century BCE. Cephalus, a politically prominent Athenian, has declared that justice is honesty and repaying debt. Socrates, finding this definition inadequate, replies:

> But take this matter of doing right: can we say that it really consists in nothing more nor less than telling the truth and paying back anything we may have received? Are not these actions sometimes right and sometimes wrong? Suppose, for example, a friend who had lent us a weapon were to go mad and then ask for it back, surely anyone would say we ought not to return it. It would not be "right" to do so; nor yet to tell the truth without reserve to a madman. (*Republic* I: 331)

Socrates then tackles another definition of justice, this one posed by Cephalus's friend Polemarchus. Polemarchus maintains, "That it is just to render every man his due," which Polemarchus believes means essentially helping friends and harming enemies. Socrates insists, however, that it can never be just to harm someone, because injury diminishes people's lives and abilities, leaving them less just. It cannot be just to make someone less just.

Thrasymachus, a compatriot of Cephalus who dislikes Socrates, then asserts that justice is the will of the stronger. This is the famous "might makes right" argument. Justice, according to this argument, is neither more nor less than the will of the powerful. For Thrasymachus, philosophers can talk all day about different concepts of justice, but their discussions affect nothing in the real world. People in power decide who gets what, who lives and who dies, who is free and who is in slavery. But Socrates is undaunted. Through skillful questioning—that is, through use of the Socratic method—Socrates compels Thrasymachus to admit that the strong are not perfect and that they sometimes harm themselves by not clearly thinking through the consequences of their actions. If justice is always that which is in the interest of the stronger, and if the strong sometimes do that which is not in their own interests, then it is not always just to obey the commands of the strongest. Might does not necessarily make right.

Having destroyed the most common conceptions of justice of his time, Socrates proposes a new definition. Each human being, he asserts, is composed of three aspects, body (physical appetites), spirit (courage), and mind (intelligence, or rationality). Justice occurs within individuals when the mind, which is rational, rules over both the impulse to courage (the spirited nature) and the physical appetites. When the spirited nature rules the mind, the result is excessive courage, which leads to unnecessary conflict. When physical appetites rule over the mind, excessive indulgence in physical pleasure is the result. But when the mind rules, reason can direct courage and appetite to appropriate expression, and justice is achieved.

The same principles that govern individuals govern society. When people who have superior minds govern those who are brave or who have common abilities, then society achieves justice. Socrates says that the logical conclusion of this reasoning is that a philosopher king, the person in any society who has the greatest reasoning abilities, is best qualified to rule society in the interests of all. Justice results when philosophers rule.

Since the time of Socrates many other definitions of justice have been proposed, and so have many categories for different types of justice. *Retributive justice,* for example, involves situations in which harm has been done. One set of categories within the concept of retributive justice is a distinction between substantive justice and procedural justice. Suppose that an assassin murders a United States Senator on the floor of the Senate in full view of Senators, television cameras, and the nation. There is no doubt that the assassin is guilty. When the police arrest her, however, they do not advise her of her rights. When her case comes to trial, she is set free because her constitutional rights were violated. Has justice been done? Those who answer yes advocate *procedural justice,* which asserts that justice is achieved whenever the rules of law, such as constitutional rights, have been followed. Those who answer no support *substantive justice,* which declares that justice is done only when the guilty are punished and the innocent absolved, regardless of the rules of law. Procedural justice focuses upon the means by which cases are decided, whereas substantive justice focuses upon the ends achieved by criminal proceedings.

Students of retributive justice are also interested in justifying punishment. Rehabilitation, deterrence, and retribution are three common justifications for punishing those guilty of committing a harmful act. Advocates of *rehabilitation* believe that the primary purpose of punishment is to return the guilty to full membership in society. Some rehabilitationists see criminals as diseased and punishment as a cure. Others see the criminal as someone who freely does evil, but they regard the infliction of punishment as justified only if it benefits the criminal or at least does no further harm. Since the purpose of punishment is to cure the criminal, rehabilitationists support indeterminate sentences and alternative forms of punishment like community service.

Advocates of *deterrence* are convinced that prisons cannot rehabilitate criminals and that the only thing that forestalls further crime is incarceration. In this view, the purposes of prison are: (1) to remove criminals from society for a period of time so that the opportunity to commit another crime is not available, and (2) to demonstrate to potential criminals that the penalty for crime is sure and severe. *Retributionists,* on the other hand, see themselves as respecting the humanity of the criminal by holding the criminal responsible for his or her actions. Criminals are not diseased individuals or even examples to be used to instruct others, but free individuals who intentionally act immorally and illegally. They should be punished according to the damage they have done.

If retributive justice concerns punishment for harmful acts, then *distributive justice* concerns how to fairly apportion either the resources of society or the access to those resources. Harvard professor John Rawls' book *A Theory of Justice* (1971) is a leading recent work on distributive justice. Rawls defines justice as fairness, which is, essentially, political and social equality. Rawls proposes, "Each person possesses an inviolability founded on justice that even the welfare of society as a whole cannot override. For this reason justice denies that the loss of freedom for some is made right by a greater good shared by others" (John Rawls. *A Theory of Justice.* Cambridge, MA: Belknap Press of Harvard University. 1971. 3–4).

If any group of people should come together today to set up the rules for a new society, all of them would naturally strive to protect their own interests. In the struggle to preserve privileges or advantages that already exist, valid principles of fairness would be lost. Rawls proposes, therefore, that to ensure justice for all, the contracting parties make an "original agreement" based upon the principle that "free and rational persons concerned to further their own interests would accept an initial position of equality as defining the fundamental terms of the association" (11). To write this agreement, the people will need to come together under an assumed "veil of ignorance," in which they do not know in advance the attributes they will have in the society that they construct. In a way, they are to write a plan for society as if they have not yet been born. Since they would not know in advance whether they personally will be rich or poor, mentally impaired or highly intelligent, attractive or unattractive, healthy or physically impaired, they will design principles that will be fair to anyone under any of these circumstances. As Rawls explains, the veil of ignorance is not an actual historical condition. If people write the rules for society under this veil of ignorance, Rawls believes, reason will lead them to adopt, as a minimum, the following two principles:

1. Each person is to have an equal right to the most extensive basic liberty compatible with similar liberty for others.
2. Social and economic inequalities are to be arranged so that they are both (a) reasonably expected to be to everyone's advantage, and (b) attached to positions and offices open to all. (60)

Robert Nozick, another Harvard philosopher, disagrees fundamentally with Rawls on the nature of justice. Whereas Rawls is concerned with fairness and equality, Nozick is concerned with the role of the state. Nozick contends that justice maintains maximum freedom for individuals, and that an active state constricts freedom. Only a minimal state, therefore, assures justice. Nozick calls his version of justice the "entitlement view." For Nozick, then, individuals are entitled to freedom from government interference, whereas for Rawls, individuals are entitled to an equal opportunity to share the benefits of society.

For both Nozick and Rawls, however, justice is secured by defining, establishing, and respecting rights. Think of rights as valid claims. These valid claims can be based on the kind of entity you are, or a natural characteristic you have, or your membership in a social group; we will call these claims, respectively, human, natural, and social rights. If you believe that all humans have a right not to be slaves, you might base this claim on either their membership in the human species or their possession of the ability to reason. The first approach says that freedom is a human right, the second that it is a natural right. Notice that if you become convinced that animals or computers can reason, then if you advocate natural rights you should extend freedom to animals and computers. (Of course, the human rights advocate is not immediately committed to enfranchising thinking animals or computers.) Both natural and human rights are commonly regarded as politically valid, which is why President Jimmy Carter felt justified, both during his presidency and afterward, in talking about violations of rights performed within other nations.

Sometimes people assert unalienable rights, as Thomas Jefferson did in the Declaration of Independence. *Unalienable rights* are intrinsic. Not only may they not be taken from you, but you may not give them up even if you want to do so. Jefferson said: "We hold these Truths to be self-evident, that all Men are created equal, that they are endowed by their Creator with certain unalienable Rights." Jefferson wrote this, and yet he held slaves. Were Jefferson's actions consistent with his words? What if he believed that unalienable rights are natural rights, and that slaves lack the ability to reason? Some of Jefferson's statements seem to lead to this conclusion. If it is true that Jefferson did indeed believe slaves lacked the ability to reason, he was following a misguided but popular ancient tradition whose proponents included Aristotle.

Another way of looking at rights is to contrast positive and negative rights. *Positive rights* assume the obligation of others to perform a service for you. For example, you have a positive right to a social security check when the government has a corresponding duty to provide it to you. *Negative rights* assume a lack of interference by others. You have a negative right to freedom of speech when the government or other people are constrained from interfering with your opportunity to speak. As we can see from our discussion above, John Rawls's concern for social equality led him to advocate a positive concept of justice (freedom to enjoy a share of society's benefits), whereas Robert Nozick's interest in individual freedom led him to propose a negative concept of justice (freedom from state control).

Most rights, however, are neither purely positive nor purely negative. They may be compared to coins, which have two sides. Two individuals, for example, are asked if they have a right to travel. One replies, "Yes, I have a right to travel; there are no barriers on the road, and the police do not care where I go." Another replies, "No, you may claim that I have a right to travel, but you mock me. It costs money to travel, and I have no money. I am old and cannot walk beyond a short distance. If I really had a right to travel, the government would be obligated to buy me an airline ticket." The right to travel is therefore positive for some and negative for others, depending upon which side of the coin they are looking at. To consider one further example, it is easy to see that voting is both a positive and a negative right. You exercise the right to vote when the government provides you a ballot (a positive right) and when the Ku Klux Klan is constrained, by the voting Rights Acts of 1957 and 1965, from interfering with your visit to the polls (a negative right).

Considerations of justice and rights such as the ones discussed above are merely the tip of the political ethics iceberg. In your philosophy classes you will have the opportunity to participate in discussions of medical, legal, environmental, and social ethics, and there are more categories of ethics besides these. The chapters that follow contain directions for writing assignments that are designed to help you understand your own ethical standards and develop your awareness of many different ethical issues.

PART FOUR

Specific Philosophy Writing Assignments

11

Writing Sound Arguments:
Position Papers

I wish to propose for the reader's favourable consideration a doctrine which may, I fear, appear wildly paradoxical and subversive. The doctrine in question is this: that it is undesirable to believe a proposition when there is no ground whatever for supposing it true.

—Bertrand Russell

11.1 WHAT IS A POSITION PAPER?

A philosophical position paper is a written argument. It is an attempt to convince someone to accept a conclusion. It contains:

- A conclusion, stated in the beginning of the paper
- Premises that lead to the conclusion
- Information that supports the premises

You may not be aware that you encounter position papers every day. They come in many forms. You see them in television commercials. You hear politicians giving campaign speeches. You listen to sermons in church. All of these events are written arguments: they are forms of position papers. The ability to write an effective argument is an essential skill in many professions, including, but not limited to:

- Politics
- Law

- Ministry
- Advertising
- Sales
- Teaching
- Business management

A position paper is a basic written argument that may be used for many different purposes and occupations. The directions in this chapter provide help in writing position papers with a method that is applicable to a wide range of topics.

11.2   THE STEPS TO WRITING A POSITION PAPER

There are nine basic steps to writing a position paper:

1. Select a topic.
2. Conduct research.
3. Select a position (a point you wish to make, your conclusion).
4. Define one or more premises that lead to the conclusion.
5. Construct an outline of the argument you plan to make.
6. Check the outline for fallacies.
7. Write the argument.
8. Test your argument.
9. Revise your argument.

As you write, remember that the writing process is *recursive*. This means that the steps outlined above, although taken basically in the order in which they are given, may be repeated during the writing process. For example, once you have constructed some premises, you may decide to change your conclusion. Or, when you have tested your argument, you may feel a need to go back and redefine your premises.

11.2.1   Selecting a Topic

Several considerations govern the selection of topics for position papers for courses in philosophy. First, the topic should be a matter of personal concern to you. It should interest you, and, even better, be important to you. Topics related to your religious faith, your career choice or major, or your political views are likely to hold your interest, but remember: a position paper assignment is not written merely to confirm your own prejudices. It provides an opportunity for you to consider new information and perhaps even change your opinion, or at least make it a better-informed one.

A second parameter for selecting position paper topics is that papers should address current problems and issues, not historical ones. When you write a paper on an issue that is yet to be resolved, you are participating in the relevant discussions of your own times. A current issue is more likely to be of interest than one that has already been decided. There is even a possibility that the paper, properly submitted to a newspaper or magazine editor, may influence the opinions of others.

This is not to say that all questions about issues from the past have been resolved. People still argue about the various possible causes of World War I and the reasons behind Harry S Truman's upset victory over Thomas E. Dewey in the 1948 presidential election. And such arguments can yield useful insights for today's world. But right now, we are focusing on issues and events that are accessible to all members of society—and all the members of your philosophy class—in ways that historical topics, which require specialized reading and research, are not. Chapter 14, which focuses on historical philosophy, offers help for papers dealing with historical concerns. So, of course, do classes offered in the history department of your school.

A third requirement is that philosophy position paper topics should have an appropriate scope. A common mistake of students is to choose topics that are too complex or that require special technical knowledge or skills beyond those normally available. A good general rule for your position paper is to confine the topic to a matter that you can address without special expertise and with only a moderate amount of research. (Again, this is one reason why we are avoiding historical issues in this chapter.) The availability of relevant data is very important to your choice of topic. Here are some examples of topics. Which of them are obviously sufficiently narrow to be suitable for position papers in philosophy courses? Which are obviously too vague or complex? Which might be appropriate if sufficient data are available?

1. "Deterrence Does Not Justify Capital Punishment"
2. "Humans: Innately Good or Evil?"
3. "The Concept of Freedom in Western Thought"
4. "All Parents Should be Licensed by the State"
5. "The World Views of Plato and Aristotle"
6. "The Morality of In Vitro Fertilization: A Consequentialist Perspective"
7. "Police Use of Deadly Force Against Fleeing Felons Deters Crime"

Topics 1 and 4 are very likely to be suitable; topics 2, 3, and 5 are either too vague or too complex, and topics 6 and 7 are possibly suitable if sufficient data are available.

If you have difficulty in thinking up a topic, your local newspaper will help you. It features articles about dozens of possible topics every day. Scan through the paper until you find an article that interests you. Then ask yourself, "What is it about the article that interests me?" Perhaps something about the article makes you angry, or happy, or sad. Remember what you have learned from Chapters 8 and 9 about invalid argument patterns. Is there a position taken on the paper's editorial page that does not hold up to rigorous scrutiny? When you find an article that makes you think, "Something has to be done about this!" then you are on the right track.

11.2.2   Conducting Research

No matter how basic your topic is, you will no doubt have to do at least some research on it. Part Two of this manual explains how to conduct research for topics in philosophy. Many arguments are strengthened by the use of factual data and statistics, so, in addition to the books and articles that you will find in your college library and the materials you will find on the internet, be sure to ask the librarian about the statistical data available in government documents and reports from research institutes.

Also, be aware that it is highly unlikely that you are the first person who has ever investigated the topic you have chosen, whatever it may be. Periodicals will contain arguments that have already been written on your topic. This does *not* mean that your job has been done for you. It does mean that you can select the best elements of other writers' arguments, restate and reorganize them in your own words, add new thoughts that they have overlooked, and produce an argument of your own.

11.2.3   Selecting a Position

Once you have collected some relevant information, you need to identify a conclusion, which is sometimes called a thesis or a position. A position is a declarative statement that sums up the argument you are making. Often the position gives you the title of your paper, as you can see from the list of positions in the exercise given above. Consider your first attempt to formulate a position to be a hypothesis, a temporary conclusion that allows you to identify premises to support it. As you conduct further research you may well change your position to reflect the implications of your premises.

11.2.4   Defining Premises

Let's suppose the conclusion you wish to argue is "Premarital sex is immoral." In order to define the premises for your argument, you need to state why premarital sex is immoral. A good way to begin is to try to define the predicate of your sentence. What is morality? When is something either moral or immoral? Suppose you decide that something is immoral when it results in harm. If this is the case, then you need to demonstrate that premarital sex causes harm. If you can establish that premarital sex has harmful consequences, such as unwanted pregnancy, sexually transmitted diseases, infant mortality, and abortions, then you may construct a list of premises leading to a conclusion. The result may look something like the following:

Main Argument

PREMISE 1: Activities that cause harm are immoral.

PREMISE 2: Premarital sex results in unwanted pregnancies.

PREMISE 3: Premarital sex results in sexually transmitted diseases.

PREMISE 4: Premarital sex results in infant mortality.

PREMISE 5: Premarital sex results in abortions.

PREMISE 6: Unwanted pregnancies, sexually transmitted diseases, infant mortality and abortions are harmful to the people who experience them.

PREMISE 7: Premarital sex is a harmful activity.

CONCLUSION: Premarital sex is immoral.

Notice that most if not all the premises you list will require supporting evidence. For example, your premise "premarital sex results in unwanted pregnancies" will be strengthened if you provide *supporting details* like the following ones:

- Thirty-four percent of pregnancies of unmarried people are terminated in abortions.
- Thirty-one percent of pregnancies of unmarried people result in adoptions.

Notice further that some of the premises you list may also require arguments to sustain them. For example, Premise 1, which claims that harmful activities are immoral, may not be automatically accepted by your reader and may require a *subordinate argument* (one that is not the main argument of the paper but which supports a single premise within the main argument) such as the following:

Subordinate Argument

PREMISE 1: Morality is the knowledge of the difference between right and wrong.

PREMISE 2: The knowledge of the difference between right and wrong allows us to make choices between moral and immoral actions.

PREMISE 3: Moral actions are actions taken as a result of choices to decrease or eliminate direct or indirect harm to other living beings.

PREMISE 4: Immoral actions are actions taken as a result of choices to create or increase direct or indirect harm to other living beings.

CONCLUSION: Activities that cause harm are immoral.

Notice that the conclusion of the subordinate argument directly above becomes a premise (Premise 1) for the major argument.

11.2.5   Constructing an Outline

Your list of premises is the first step in outlining your argument. As the passage on outlining in Chapter 1 makes clear, an outline is an essential step in the process of building your argument because it allows you to see the strengths and weaknesses of the logical structure of your argument.

Construct an outline using the heading format described in Chapter 1. For your convenience, the pattern of a generic paper outline is repeated here:

I. First main idea
   A. First subordinate idea
      1. Reason, example, or illustration
      2.   Reason, example, or illustration
         a. Detail supporting reason 2
         b. Detail supporting reason 2
         c. Detail supporting reason 2
   B. Second subordinate idea
II. Second main idea

The outline for your position paper will follow the principles embodied in the generic outline above. Notice that premises may be supported by any combination of arguments, subpremises, and supporting details. Examine the sample format below:

I. Premise 1
   A. Argument 1 for Premise 1
      1. Subpremise 1
         a. Detail supporting Subpremise 1
         b. Detail supporting Subpremise 1
         c. Detail supporting Subpremise 1
      2. Subpremise 2
         a. Detail supporting Subpremise 1
         b. Detail supporting Subpremise 1

       B. Argument 2 for Premise 1
          1. Subpremise 1
             a. Detail supporting Subpremise 1
             b. Detail supporting Subpremise 1
             c. Detail supporting Subpremise 1
          2. Subpremise 2
             a. Detail supporting Subpremise 1
             b. Detail supporting Subpremise 1
  II. Premise 2
     A. Detail supporting Premise 2
     B. Detail supporting Premise 2
 III. Premise 3
 IV. Conclusion

If we apply the outline format to our partially developed argument about premarital sex, we have the following partially developed outline:

    I. Activities that cause harm are immoral. [Premise 1]
       A. Morality is the knowledge of the difference between right and wrong.
       B. The knowledge of the difference between right and wrong allows us to make choices between moral and immoral actions.
       C. Moral actions are actions taken as a result of choices to decrease or eliminate, directly or indirectly, harm to other living beings.
       D. Immoral actions are actions taken as a result of choices to create or increase, directly or indirectly, harm to other living beings.
   II. Premarital sex results in unwanted pregnancies. [Premise 2]
       A. Thirty-four percent of pregnancies of unmarried people are terminated in abortions.
       B. Thirty-one percent of pregnancies of unmarried people result in adoptions.
  III. Premarital sex results in sexually transmitted diseases. [Premise 3]
  IV. Premarital sex results in infant mortality. [Premise 4]
   V. Premarital sex results in abortions. [Premise 5]
  VI. Unwanted pregnancies, sexually transmitted diseases, infant mortality and abortions are harmful to the people who experience them. [Premise 6]
 VII. Premarital sex is a harmful activity. [Premise 7]
VIII. Premarital sex is immoral. [Conclusion]

Construct an outline as soon as you can in the writing process. You may change it several times, but each time you do, you will have a clearer picture of the argument you are forming.

11.2.6   Checking for Fallacies

Chapter 9 of this book provides a description of common fallacies. The following checklist is taken from that chapter. Use it as a checklist to make sure that your argument is not a victim of any one of them.

Checklist of Fallacies

- ☐ Denying the Antecedent
- ☐ Affirming the Consequent
- ☐ The Exclusive Fallacy
- ☐ Invalid Appeal to Authority
- ☐ Straw Person
- ☐ Inconsistency
- ☐ False Dilemma
- ☐ Complex Question
- ☐ Begging the Question
- ☐ Suppressed Evidence
- ☐ Lack of Proportion
- ☐ Appeal to Unknowable Statistics
- ☐ Ad Hominen
- ☐ Guilt by Association
- ☐ Two Wrongs Make a Right
- ☐ Equivocation
- ☐ Appeal to Ignorance
- ☐ Composition
- ☐ Division
- ☐ Hasty Conclusion
- ☐ Questionable Cause
- ☐ Questionable Analogy
- ☐ Appeal to Pity
- ☐ Appeal to the Stick
- ☐ Appeal to Loyalty
- ☐ Provincialism
- ☐ Popularity
- ☐ Double Standard
- ☐ Invincible Ignorance

11.2.7   Writing the Argument

While it is vital to plan adequately, it is also vital that you not plan your paper to death. Once you have what seems to be a viable outline, it is time to begin writing your first draft. The outline, especially in the early stage of your writing, can provide you with the topics—and even the topic sentences—of your paper's individual paragraphs. But writing the first draft also tests your outline, showing you places where the outline holds and places where it may need to be changed. Don't be afraid to depart from the outline if your growing concept of the paper requires you to do so. If such changes do occur, it might be a good idea to pause occasionally in your writing of the first draft to rework the outline, integrating your new insights into it to see where they will finally lead you.

Remember that one of the great benefits of adequate planning is that the confidence it gives you in your material and its organization can transmit itself to your writing. This confidence can help you to write a narrative with a crisp, clear style that allows the reader to understand exactly what you are saying. At the end of this chapter a sample position paper is provided.

11.2.8   Testing the Argument

Test your argument by having someone read your draft and then discuss it with you. Ask the person to state the argument you have made in his own words. This allows you to determine if you have been understood correctly. Ask your reader if your argument is convincing. Ask him to point out both the strengths and weaknesses of your argument, as you see them. Testing the argument is a good exercise to conduct in class. Remember, though, that the classmate who is helping you is very probably not experienced at critiquing a colleague's paper and may feel a bit awkward at trying to help you improve your draft. If time allows, it would be a good idea to let your reader take the draft home and read it more than once in a quiet setting before talking with you about it.

11.2.9   Revising the Argument

After you have tested your argument, revise it. You may have picked up a few points since the time you wrote your draft that are worth including in your paper.

11.3   THE FORMAT OF A POSITION PAPER

Position papers contain five basic elements:

1. Title page
2. Outline page, which summarizes the paper

3. Text, or body of the paper
4. Bibliography (references to sources of information)
5. Appendices

The format of each of these elements should follow the directions provided in Chapter 6 of this manual. The outline listed as item number 2 above should be the final outline that you write, when your paper is completed. It should resemble the sample outline provided in this chapter and should not exceed two pages in length. Do not exceed three levels of headings in the outline you submit with your position paper, even though you may have had several more levels in the outline you used to write the paper.

Two general rules govern the amount of information presented in the body of the paper. First, content must be *adequate for the reader to draw a reasonable conclusion*. All the facts necessary to accepting the conclusion must be present. The second guideline for determining the length of a position paper is to *omit extraneous material*. Include only the information that is relevant to the conclusion at hand.

All sources of information in a position paper must be properly cited. Follow the directions for reference formats given in Chapter 7.

Appendices can be helpful to the reader of position papers by providing information that supplements the important facts contained in the text. You should attach the appendices to the end of the paper, after the bibliography. You should not append entire government reports, journal articles, or other publications, but selected charts, graphs, or other pages may be appended. The source of the information should always be evident on the appended pages.

11.4   AN EXERCISE: *UNITED STATES v. VIRGINIA*

11.4.1   Directions

As we noted at the beginning of this chapter, position papers are written in many forms for many purposes. Opinions of the United States Supreme Court are position papers that affect our lives directly in many ways. Before proceeding to write your own position paper, you will find it well worth your time to read and outline Justice Ruth Bader Ginsburg's opinion in the case of *United States v. Virginia.*

To outline the opinion, read the text carefully. As you read, make a list on a sheet of paper or on your computer of the following:

- All statements that you believe are premises of the argument
- All statements that you believe are supporting details of the premises
- The conclusion of the argument

Once you have made your list, number the entries according to the outline format provided in this chapter. Your main task is to distinguish the main points from the subpoints that support them. As you assign and reassign the statements in your list to different levels in your outline, the structure of Justice Ginsburg's argument will appear.

The following text is an exact copy of a Supreme Court case and therefore adheres to the Court's formal rules. Single-numeral references to incidental documents have been eliminated.

11.4.2   *United States v. Virginia*

The decision in the case of *United States v. Virginia* was announced in the United States Supreme Court on June 26, 1996. The Court decided, voting seven to one (Justice Thomas did not take part in the case), that the Virginia Military Institute's policy barring women from admission was unconstitutional because it denied women the equal protection of the laws that is guaranteed to them under the fourteenth amendment to the Constitution. Justice Ruth Bader Ginsburg delivered the opinion for the Court. Excerpts of her opinion follow.

SUPREME COURT OF THE UNITED STATES
Nos. 94-1941 AND 94-2107
UNITED STATES, PETITIONER 94-1941v.
VIRGINIA ET AL.

Virginia's public institutions of higher learning include an incomparable military college, Virginia Military Institute (VMI). The United States maintains that the Constitution's equal protection guarantee precludes Virginia from reserving exclusively to men the unique educational opportunities VMI affords. We agree.

Founded in 1839, VMI is today the sole single-sex school among Virginia's 15 public institutions of higher learning. VMI's distinctive mission is to produce "citizen-soldiers," men prepared for leadership in civilian life and in military service. VMI pursues this mission through pervasive training of a kind not available anywhere else in Virginia. Assigning prime place to character development, VMI uses an "adversative method" modeled on English public schools and once characteristic of military instruction. VMI constantly endeavors to instill physical and mental discipline in its cadets and impart to them a strong moral code. The school's graduates leave VMI with heightened comprehension of their capacity to deal with duress and stress, and a large sense of accomplishment for completing the hazardous course.

VMI has notably succeeded in its mission to produce leaders; among its alumni are military generals, Members of Congress, and business executives. The school's alumni overwhelmingly perceive that their VMI training helped them to realize their personal goals. VMI's endowment reflects the loyalty of its graduates; VMI has the largest per-student endowment of all undergraduate institutions in the Nation.

Neither the goal of producing citizen-soldiers nor VMI's implementing methodology is inherently unsuitable to women. And the school's impressive record in producing leaders has made admission desirable to some women. Nevertheless, Virginia has elected to preserve exclusively for men the advantages and opportunities a VMI education affords.

From its establishment in 1839 as one of the Nation's first state military colleges, see 1839 Va. Acts, ch. 20, VMI has remained financially supported by Virginia and "subject to the control of the [Virginia] General Assembly," . . . VMI today enrolls about 1,300 men as cadets. Its academic offerings in the liberal arts, sciences, and engineering are also available at other public colleges and universities in Virginia. But VMI's mission is special. It is the mission of the school "'to produce educated and honorable men, prepared for the varied work of civil life, imbued with love of learning, confident in the functions and attitudes of leadership, possessing a high sense of public service, advocates of the American democracy and free enterprise system, and ready as citizen-soldiers to defend their country in time of national peril.'" 766 F. Supp. 1407, 1425 (WD Va. 1991) (quoting Mission Study Committee of the VMI Board of Visitors, Report, May 16, 1986).

In contrast to the federal service academies, institutions maintained "to prepare cadets for career service in the armed forces," VMI's program "is directed at preparation for both military and civilian life"; "[o]nly about 15% of VMI cadets enter career military service." 766 F. Supp., at 1432.

VMI produces its "citizen-soldiers" through "an adversative, or doubting, model of education" which features "[p]hysical rigor, mental stress, absolute equality of treatment, absence of privacy, minute regulation of behavior, and indoctrination in desirable values." Id., at 1421. As one Commandant of Cadets described it, the adversative method "dissects the young student," and makes him aware of his "limits and capabilities," so that he knows "how far he can go with his anger, . . . how much he can take under stress, . . . exactly what he can do when he is physically exhausted." Id., at 1421–1422 (quoting Col. N. Bissell).

VMI cadets live in spartan barracks where surveillance is constant and privacy nonexistent; they wear uniforms, eat together in the mess hall, and regularly participate in drills. Id., at 1424, 1432. Entering students are incessantly exposed to the rat line, "an extreme form of the adversative model," comparable in intensity to Marine Corps boot camp. Id., at 1422. Tormenting and punishing, the rat line bonds new cadets to their fellow sufferers and, when they have completed the 7-month experience, to their former tormentors. Ibid.

VMI's "adversative model" is further characterized by a hierarchical "class system" of privileges and responsibilities, a "dyke system" for assigning a senior class mentor to each entering class "rat," and a stringently enforced "honor code," which prescribes that a cadet "'does not lie, cheat, steal nor tolerate those who do.'" Id., at 1422–1423.

VMI attracts some applicants because of its reputation as an extraordinarily challenging military school, and "because its alumni are exceptionally close to the school." Id., at 1421. "[W]omen have no opportunity anywhere to gain the benefits of [the system of education at VMI]." Ibid.

In 1990, prompted by a complaint filed with the Attorney General by a female high-school student seeking admission to VMI, the United States sued the Commonwealth of Virginia and VMI, alleging that VMI's exclusively male admission policy violated the Equal Protection Clause of the Fourteenth Amendment. Id., at 1408.3 Trial of the action consumed six days and involved an array of expert witnesses on each side. Ibid.

In the two years preceding the lawsuit, the District Court noted, VMI had received inquiries from 347 women, but had responded to none of them. Id., at 1436. "[S]ome women, at least," the court said, "would want to attend the school if they had the opportunity." Id., at 1414. The court further recognized that, with recruitment, VMI could "achieve at least 10% female enrollment"—"a sufficient 'critical mass' to provide the female cadets with a positive educational experience." Id., at 1437–1438. And it was also established that "some women are capable of all of the individual activities required of VMI cadets." Id., at 1412. In addition, experts agreed that if VMI admitted women, "the VMI ROTC experience would become a better training program from the perspective of the armed forces, because it would provide training in dealing with a mixed-gender army." Id., at 1441.

The District Court ruled in favor of VMI, however, and rejected the equal protection challenge pressed by the United States. That court correctly recognized that *Mississippi Univ. for Women v. Hogan*, 458 U.S. 718 (1982), was the closest guide. 766 F. Supp., at 1410. There, this Court underscored that a party seeking to uphold government action based on sex must establish an "exceedingly persuasive justification" for the classification. *Mississippi Univ. for Women*, 458 U.S., at 724 (internal quotation marks omitted). To succeed, the defender of the challenged action must show "at least that the classification serves important governmental objectives and that the discriminatory means employed are substantially related to the achievement of those objectives." Ibid. (internal quotation marks omitted).

The District Court reasoned that education in "a single-gender environment, be it male or female," yields substantial benefits. 766 F. Supp., at 1415. VMI's school for men brought diversity to an otherwise coeducational Virginia system, and that diversity was "enhanced by VMI's unique method of instruction." Ibid. If single-gender education for males ranks as an important governmental objective, it becomes obvious, the District Court concluded, that the only means of achieving the objective "is to exclude women from the all-male institution—VMI." Ibid.

"Women are [indeed] denied a unique educational opportunity that is available only at VMI," the District Court acknowledged. Id., at 1432. But "[VMI's] single-sex status would be lost, and some aspects of the [school's] distinctive method would be altered" if women were admitted, id., at 1413: "Allowance for personal privacy would have to be made," id., at 1412; "[p]hysical education requirements would have to be altered, at least for the women," id., at 1413; the adversative environment could not survive unmodified, id., at 1412–1413. Thus, "sufficient constitutional justification" had been shown, the District Court held, "for continuing [VMI's] single-sex policy." Id., at 1413.

The Court of Appeals for the Fourth Circuit disagreed and vacated the District Court's judgment. The appellate court held: "The Commonwealth of Virginia has not . . . advanced any state policy by which it can justify its determination, under an announced policy of diversity, to afford VMI's unique type of program to men and not to women." 976 F. 2d 890, 892 (1992).

The appeals court greeted with skepticism Virginia's assertion that it offers single-sex education at VMI as a facet of the State's overarching and undisputed policy to advance "autonomy and diversity." The court underscored Virginia's nondiscrimination commitment: "'[I]t is extremely important that [colleges and universities] deal with faculty, staff, and students without regard to sex, race, or ethnic origin.'" Id., at 899 (quoting 1990 Report of the Virginia Commission on the University of the 21st Century). "That statement," the Court of Appeals said, "is the only explicit one that we have found in the record in which the Commonwealth has expressed itself with respect to gender distinctions." Ibid. Furthermore, the appeals court observed, in urging "diversity" to justify an all-male VMI, the State had supplied "no explanation for the movement away from [single-sex education] in Virginia by public colleges and universities." Ibid. In short, the court concluded, "[a] policy of diversity which aims to provide an array of educational opportunities, including single-gender institutions, must do more than favor one gender." Ibid.

The parties agreed that "some women can meet the physical standards now imposed on men," id., at 896, and the court was satisfied that "neither the goal of producing citizen soldiers nor VMI's implementing methodology is inherently unsuitable to women," id., at 899. The Court of Appeals, however, accepted the District Court's finding that "at least these three aspects of VMI's program—physical training, the absence of privacy, and the adversative approach—would be materially affected by coeducation." Id., at 896–897. Remanding the case, the appeals court assigned to Virginia, in the first instance, responsibility for selecting a remedial course. The court suggested these options for the State: Admit women to VMI; establish parallel institutions or programs; or abandon state support, leaving VMI free to pursue its policies as a private institution. Id., at 900. In May 1993, this Court denied certiorari. See 508 U.S. 946; see also ibid. (opinion of SCALIA, J., noting the interlocutory posture of the litigation).

In response to the Fourth Circuit's ruling, Virginia proposed a parallel program for women: Virginia Women's Institute for Leadership (VWIL). The 4-year, state-sponsored undergraduate program would be located at Mary Baldwin College, a private liberal arts school for women, and would be open, initially, to about 25 to 30 students. Although VWIL would share VMI's mission—to produce "citizen-soldiers"—the VWIL program would differ, as does Mary Baldwin College, from VMI in academic offerings, methods of education, and financial resources. See 852 F. Supp. 471, 476–477 (WD Va. 1994).

The average combined SAT score of entrants at Mary Baldwin is about 100 points lower than the score for VMI freshmen. See id., at 501. Mary Baldwin's faculty holds "significantly fewer Ph.D.'s than the faculty at VMI," id., at 502, and receives significantly lower salaries, see Tr. 158 (testimony of James Lott, Dean of Mary Baldwin College), reprinted in 2 App. in Nos. 94-1667 and 94-1717 (CA4) (hereinafter Tr.). While VMI offers degrees in liberal arts, the sciences, and engineering, Mary Baldwin, at the time of trial, offered only bachelor of arts degrees. See 852 F. Supp., at 503. A VWIL student seeking to earn an engineering degree could gain one, without public support, by attending Washington University in St. Louis, Missouri, for two years, paying the required private tuition. See ibid.

Experts in educating women at the college level composed the Task Force charged with designing the VWIL program; Task Force members were drawn from Mary Baldwin's own faculty and staff. Id., at 476. Training its attention on methods of instruction appropriate for "most women," the Task Force determined that a military model would be "wholly inappropriate" for VWIL. Ibid.; see 44 F. 3d 1229, 1233 (CA4 1995).

VWIL students would participate in ROTC programs and a newly established, "largely ceremonial" Virginia Corps of Cadets, id., at 1234, but the VWIL House would not have a military format, 852 F. Supp., at 477, and VWIL would not require its students to eat meals together or to wear uniforms during the school day, id., at 495. In lieu of VMI's adversative method, the VWIL Task Force favored "a cooperative method which reinforces self-esteem." Id., at 476. In addition to the standard bachelor of arts program offered at Mary Baldwin, VWIL students would take courses in leadership, complete an off-campus leadership externship, participate in community service projects, and assist in arranging a speaker series. See 44 F. 3d, at 1234.

Virginia represented that it will provide equal financial support for in-state VWIL students and VMI cadets, 852 F. Supp., at 483, and the VMI Foundation agreed to supply a $5.4625 million endowment for the VWIL program, id., at 499. Mary Baldwin's own endowment is about $19 million; VMI's is $131 million. Id., at 503. Mary Baldwin will add $35 million to its endowment based on future commitments; VMI will add $220 million. Ibid. The VMI Alumni Association has developed a network of employers interested in hiring VMI graduates. The Association has agreed to open its network to VWIL graduates, id., at 499, but those graduates will not have the advantage afforded by a VMI degree.

Virginia returned to the District Court seeking approval of its proposed remedial plan, and the court decided the plan met the requirements of the Equal Protection Clause. Id., at 473. The District Court again acknowledged evidentiary support for these determinations: "[T]he VMI methodology could be used to educate women and, in fact, some women . . . may prefer the VMI methodology to the VWIL methodology." Id., at 481. But the "controlling legal principles," the District Court decided, "do not require the Commonwealth to provide a mirror image VMI for women." Ibid. The court anticipated that the two schools would "achieve substantially similar outcomes." Ibid. It concluded: "If VMI marches to the beat of a drum, then Mary Baldwin marches to the melody of a fife and when the march is over, both will have arrived at the same destination." Id., at 484.

A divided Court of Appeals affirmed the District Court's judgment. 44 F. 3d 1229 (CA4 1995). This time, the appellate court determined to give "greater scrutiny to the selection of means than to the [State's] proffered objective." Id., at 1236. The official objective or purpose, the court said, should be reviewed deferentially. Ibid. Respect for the "legislative will," the court reasoned, meant that the judiciary should take a "cautious approach," inquiring into the "legitima[cy]" of the governmental objective and refusing approval for any purpose revealed to be "pernicious." Ibid.

"[P]roviding the option of a single-gender college education may be considered a legitimate and important aspect of a public system of higher education," the appeals court observed, id., at 1238; that objective, the court added, is "not pernicious," id., at 1239. Moreover, the court continued, the adversative method vital to a VMI education "has never been tolerated in a sexually heterogeneous environment." Ibid. The method itself "was not designed to exclude women," the court noted, but women could not be accommodated in the VMI program, the court believed, for female participation in VMI's adversative training "would destroy . . . any sense of decency that still permeates the relationship between the sexes." Ibid.

Having determined, deferentially, the legitimacy of Virginia's purpose, the court considered the question of means. Exclusion of "men at Mary Baldwin College and women at VMI," the court said, was essential to Virginia's purpose, for without such exclusion, the State could not "accomplish [its] objective of providing single-gender education." Ibid.

The court recognized that, as it analyzed the case, means merged into end, and the merger risked "bypass[ing] any equal protection scrutiny." Id., at 1237. The court therefore added another inquiry, a decisive test it called "substantive comparability." Ibid. The key question, the court said, was whether men at VMI and women at VWIL would obtain "substantively comparable benefits at their institution or through other means offered by the [S]tate." Ibid. Although the appeals court recognized that the VWIL degree "lacks the historical benefit and prestige" of a VMI degree, it nevertheless found the educational opportunities at the two schools "sufficiently comparable." Id., at 1241.

Senior Circuit Judge Phillips dissented. The court, in his judgment, had not held Virginia to the burden of showing an "'exceedingly persuasive [justification]'" for the State's action. Id., at 1247 (quoting *Mississippi Univ. for Women*, 458 U.S., at 724). In Judge Phillips' view, the court had accepted "rationalizations compelled by the exigencies of this litigation," and had not confronted the State's "actual overriding purpose." Ibid. That purpose, Judge Phillips said, was clear from the historical record; it was "not to create a new type of educational opportunity for women, . . . nor to further diversify the Commonwealth's higher education system[,] . . . but [was] simply . . . to allow VMI to continue to exclude women in order to preserve its historic character and mission." Ibid.

Judge Phillips suggested that the State would satisfy the Constitution's equal protection requirement if it "simultaneously opened single-gender undergraduate institutions having substantially comparable curricular and extracurricular programs, funding, physical plant, administration and support services, and faculty and library resources." Id., at 1250. But he thought it evident that the proposed VWIL program, in comparison to VMI, fell "far short . . . from providing substantially equal tangible and intangible educational benefits to men and women." Ibid.

The Fourth Circuit denied rehearing en banc. 52 F. 3d 90 (1995). Circuit Judge Motz, joined by Circuit Judges Hall, Murnaghan, and Michael, filed a dissenting opinion. Judge Motz agreed with Judge Phillips that Virginia had not shown an "'exceedingly persuasive justification'" for the disparate opportunities the State supported. Id., at 92 (quoting *Mississippi Univ. for Women*, 458 U.S., at 724). She asked: "[H]ow can a degree from a yet to be implemented supplemental program at Mary Baldwin be held 'substantively comparable' to a degree from a venerable Virginia military institution that was established more than 150 years ago?" Id., at 93. "Women need not be guaranteed equal 'results,'"

Judge Motz said, "but the Equal Protection Clause does require equal opportunity . . . [and] that opportunity is being denied here." Ibid.

The cross-petitions in this case present two ultimate issues. First, does Virginia's exclusion of women from the educational opportunities provided by VMI—extraordinary opportunities for military training and civilian leadership development—deny to women "capable of all of the individual activities required of VMI cadets," 766 F. Supp., at 1412, the equal protection of the laws guaranteed by the Fourteenth Amendment? Second, if VMI's "unique" situation, id., at 1413—as Virginia's sole single-sex public institution of higher education—offends the Constitution's equal protection principle, what is the remedial requirement?

We note, once again, the core instruction of this Court's pathmarking decisions in *J. E. B. v. Alabama* ex rel. T. B., 511 U.S. 127, 136–137, and n. 6 (1994), and *Mississippi Univ. for Women*, 458 U.S., at 724 (internal quotation marks omitted): Parties who seek to defend gender-based government action must demonstrate an "exceedingly persuasive justification" for that action.

Today's skeptical scrutiny of official action denying rights or opportunities based on sex responds to volumes of history. As a plurality of this Court acknowledged a generation ago, "our Nation has had a long and unfortunate history of sex discrimination.". . .

Without equating gender classifications, for all purposes, to classifications based on race or national origin, the Court, in post-Reed decisions, has carefully inspected official action that closes a door or denies opportunity to women (or to men). See J. E. B., 511 U.S., at 152 (KENNEDY, J., concurring in judgment) (case law evolving since 1971 "reveal[s] a strong presumption that gender classifications are invalid"). To summarize the Court's current directions for cases of official classification based on gender: Focusing on the differential treatment or denial of opportunity for which relief is sought, the reviewing court must determine whether the proffered justification is "exceedingly persuasive." The burden of justification is demanding and it rests entirely on the State. See *Mississippi Univ. for Women*, 458 U.S., at 724. The State must show "at least that the [challenged] classification serves 'important governmental objectives and that the discriminatory means employed' are 'substantially related to the achievement of those objectives.'" Ibid. (quoting *Wengler v. Druggists Mutual Ins. Co.*, 446 U.S. 142, 150 (1980)). The justification must be genuine, not hypothesized or invented post hoc in response to litigation. And it must not rely on overbroad generalizations about the different talents, capacities, or preferences of males and females. See *Weinberger v. Wiesenfeld*, 420 U.S. 636, 643, 648 (1975); *Califano v. Goldfarb*, 430 U.S. 199, 223–224 (1977) (STEVENS, J., concurring in judgment).

The heightened review standard our precedent establishes does not make sex a proscribed classification. Supposed "inherent differences" are no longer accepted as a ground for race or national origin classifications. See *Loving v. Virginia*, 388 U.S. 1 (1967). Physical differences between men and women, however, are enduring: "[T]he two sexes are not fungible; a community made up exclusively of one [sex] is different from a community composed of both." *Ballard v. United States*, 329 U.S. 187, 193 (1946).

"Inherent differences" between men and women, we have come to appreciate, remain cause for celebration, but not for denigration of the members of either sex or for artificial constraints on an individual's opportunity. Sex classifications may be used to compensate women "for particular economic disabilities [they have] suffered," *Califano v. Webster*, 430 U.S. 313, 320 (1977) (per curiam), to "promot[e] equal employment opportunity," see *California Federal Sav. & Loan Assn. v. Guerra*, 479 U.S. 272, 289 (1987), to advance full development of the talent and capacities of our Nation's people. But such classifications may not be used, as they once were, see *Goesaert*, 335 U.S., at 467, to create or perpetuate the legal, social, and economic inferiority of women.

Measuring the record in this case against the review standard just described, we conclude that Virginia has shown no "exceedingly persuasive justification" for excluding all women from the citizen- soldier training afforded by VMI. We therefore affirm the Fourth Circuit's initial judgment, which held that Virginia had violated the Fourteenth Amendment's Equal Protection Clause. Because the remedy proffered by Virginia—the Mary Baldwin VWIL program— does not cure the constitutional violation, i.e., it does not provide equal opportunity, we reverse the Fourth Circuit's final judgment in this case.

The Fourth Circuit initially held that Virginia had advanced no state policy by which it could justify, under equal protection principles, its determination "to afford VMI's unique type of program to men and not to women." 976 F. 2d, at 892. Virginia challenges that "liability" ruling and asserts two justifications in defense of VMI's exclusion of women. First, the Commonwealth contends, "single-sex education provides important educational benefits," Brief for Cross-Petitioners 20, and the option of single-sex education contributes to "diversity in educational approaches," id., at 25. Second, the Commonwealth argues, "the unique VMI method of character development and leadership training," the school's adversative approach, would have to be modified were VMI to admit women. Id., at 33–36. We consider these two justifications in turn.

Single-sex education affords pedagogical benefits to at least some students, Virginia emphasizes, and that reality is uncontested in this litigation. Similarly, it is not disputed that diversity among public educational institutions can serve the public good. But Virginia has not shown that VMI was established, or has been maintained, with a view to diversifying, by its categorical exclusion of women, educational opportunities within the State. In cases of this genre, our precedent instructs that "benign" justifications proffered in defense of categorical exclusions will not be accepted automatically; a tenable justification must describe actual state purposes, not rationalizations for actions in fact differently grounded. See *Wiesenfeld*, 420 U.S., at 648, and n. 16 ("mere recitation of a benign [or] compensatory purpose" does not block "inquiry into the actual purposes" of government-maintained gender-based classifications); *Goldfarb*, 430 U.S., at 212–213 (rejecting government-proffered purposes after "inquiry into the actual purposes") (internal quotation marks omitted).

Mississippi Univ. for Women is immediately in point. There the State asserted, in justification of its exclusion of men from a nursing school, that it was engaging in "educational affirmative action" by "compensat[ing] for discrimination against women." 458 U.S., at 727. Undertaking a "searching analysis," id., at 728, the Court found no close resemblance between "the alleged objective" and "the actual purpose underlying the discriminatory classification," id., at 730. Pursuing a similar inquiry here, we reach the same conclusion.

Neither recent nor distant history bears out Virginia's alleged pursuit of diversity through single-sex educational options. In 1839, when the State established VMI, a range of educational opportunities for men and women was scarcely contemplated. Higher education at the time was considered dangerous for women; reflecting widely held views about women's proper place, the Nation's first universities and colleges—for example, Harvard in Massachusetts, William and Mary in Virginia—admitted only men. See E. Farello, *A History of the Education of Women in the United States* 163 (1970). VMI was not at all novel in this respect: In admitting no women, VMI followed the lead of the State's flagship school, the University of Virginia, founded in 1819.

"[N]o struggle for the admission of women to a state university," a historian has recounted, "was longer drawn out, or developed more bitterness, than that at the University of Virginia." 2 T. Woody, *A History of Women's Education in the United States* 254 (1929) (History of Women's Education). In 1879, the State Senate resolved to look into the possibility of higher education for women, recognizing that Virginia "'has never, at any period of her history,'" provided for the higher education of her daughters, though she "'has liberally provided for the higher education of her sons.'" Ibid. (quoting 10 *Educ. J. Va.* 212 (1879)). Despite this recognition, no new opportunities were instantly open to women.

Virginia eventually provided for several women's seminaries and colleges. Farmville Female Seminary became a public institution in 1884. See supra, at 3, n. 2. Two women's schools, Mary Washington College and James Madison University, were founded in 1908; another, Radford University, was founded in 1910. 766 F. Supp., at 1418–1419. By the mid-1970's, all four schools had become coeducational. Ibid.

Debate concerning women's admission as undergraduates at the main university continued well past the century's midpoint. Familiar arguments were rehearsed. If women were admitted, it was feared, they "would encroach on the rights of men; there would be new problems of government, perhaps scandals; the old honor system would have to be changed; standards would be lowered to those of other coeducational schools; and the glorious reputation of the university, as a school for men, would be trailed in the dust." 2 *History of Women's Education* 255.

Ultimately, in 1970, "the most prestigious institution of higher education in Virginia," the University of Virginia, introduced coeducation and, in 1972, began to admit women on an equal basis with men. See *Kirstein v. Rector* and *Visitors of Univ. of Virginia,* 309 F. Supp. 184, 186 (ED Va. 1970). A three-judge Federal District Court confirmed: "Virginia may not now deny to women, on the basis of sex, educational opportunities at the Charlottesville campus that are not afforded in other institutions operated by the [S]tate." Id., at 187.

Virginia describes the current absence of public single-sex higher education for women as "an historical anomaly." Brief for Cross-Petitioners 30. But the historical record indicates action more deliberate than anomalous: First, protection of women against higher education; next, schools for women far from equal in resources and stature to schools for men; finally, conversion of the separate schools to coeducation. The state legislature, prior to the advent of this controversy, had repealed "[a]ll Virginia statutes requiring individual institutions to admit only men or women." 766 F. Supp., at 1419. And in 1990, an official commission, "legislatively established to chart the future goals of higher education in Virginia," reaffirmed the policy "of affording broad access" while maintaining "autonomy and diversity." 976 F. 2d, at 898–899 (quoting *Report of the Virginia Commission on the University of the 21st Century*). Significantly, the Commission reported:

"'Because colleges and universities provide opportunities for students to develop values and learn from role models, it is extremely important that they deal with faculty, staff, and students without regard to sex, race, or ethnic origin.'" Id., at 899 (emphasis supplied by Court of Appeals deleted).

This statement, the Court of Appeals observed, "is the only explicit one that we have found in the record in which the Commonwealth has expressed itself with respect to gender distinctions." Ibid. . . .

In sum, we find no persuasive evidence in this record that VMI's male-only admission policy "is in furtherance of a state policy of 'diversity.'" See 976 F. 2d, at 899. No such policy, the Fourth Circuit observed, can be discerned from the movement of all other public colleges and universities in Virginia away from single-sex education. See ibid. That court also questioned "how one institution with autonomy, but with no authority over any other state institution, can give effect to a state policy of diversity among institutions." Ibid. A purpose genuinely to advance an array of educational options, as the Court of Appeals recognized, is not served by VMI's historic and constant plan—a plan to "affor[d] a unique educational benefit only to males." Ibid. However "liberally" this plan serves the State's sons, it makes no provision whatever for her daughters. That is not equal protection.

Virginia next argues that VMI's adversative method of training provides educational benefits that cannot be made available, unmodified, to women. Alterations to accommodate women would necessarily be "radical," so "drastic," Virginia asserts, as to transform, indeed "destroy," VMI's program. See Brief for Cross-Petitioners 34–36. Neither sex would be favored by the transformation, Virginia maintains: Men would be deprived of the unique opportunity currently available to them; women would not gain that opportunity because their participation would "eliminat[e] the very aspects of [the] program that distinguish [VMI] from . . . other institutions of higher education in Virginia." Id., at 34 (internal quotation marks omitted). . . .

The United States does not challenge any expert witness estimation on average capacities or preferences of men and women. Instead, the United States emphasizes that time and again since this Court's turning point decision in *Reed v. Reed*, 404 U.S. 71 (1971), we have cautioned reviewing courts to take a "hard look" at generalizations or "tendencies" of the kind pressed by Virginia, and relied upon by the District Court. See O'Connor, *Portia's Progress*, 66 N.Y.U.L. Rev. 1546, 1551 (1991). State actors controlling gates to opportunity, we have instructed, may not exclude qualified individuals based on "fixed notions concerning the roles and abilities of males and females." *Mississippi Univ. for Women*, 458 U.S., at 725; see J. E. B., 511 U.S., at 139, n. 11 (equal protection principles, as applied to gender classifications, mean state actors may not rely on "overbroad" generalizations to make "judgments about people that are likely to . . . perpetuate historical patterns of discrimination").

It may be assumed, for purposes of this decision, that most women would not choose VMI's adversative method. As Fourth Circuit Judge Motz observed, however, in her dissent from the Court of Appeals' denial of rehearing en banc, it is also probable that "many men would not want to be educated in such an environment." 52 F. 3d, at 93. (On that point, even our dissenting colleague might agree.) Education, to be sure, is not a "one size fits all" business. The issue, however, is not whether "women—or men—should be forced to attend VMI"; rather, the question is whether the State can constitutionally deny to women who have the will and capacity, the training and attendant opportunities that VMI uniquely affords. Ibid.

The notion that admission of women would downgrade VMI's stature, destroy the adversative system and, with it, even the school, is a judgment hardly proved, a prediction hardly different from other "self-fulfilling prophec[ies]," see *Mississippi Univ. for Women,* 458 U.S., at 730, once routinely used to deny rights or opportunities. When women first sought admission to the bar and access to legal education, concerns of the same order were expressed. . . . Field studies did not confirm these fears. See *Women in Control?* supra, at 92–93; P. Bloch & D. Anderson, Policewomen on Patrol: Final Report (1974).

Women's successful entry into the federal military academies, and their participation in the Nation's military forces, indicate that Virginia's fears for the future of VMI may not be solidly grounded. The State's justification for excluding all women from "citizen-soldier" training for which some are qualified, in any event, cannot rank as "exceedingly persuasive," as we have explained and applied that standard.

Virginia and VMI trained their argument on "means" rather than "end," and thus misperceived our precedent. Single-sex education at VMI serves an "important governmental objective," they maintained, and exclusion of women is not only "substantially related," it is essential to that objective. By this notably circular argument, the "straightforward" test *Mississippi Univ. for Women* described, see 458 U.S., at 724–725, was bent and bowed.

The State's misunderstanding and, in turn, the District Court's, is apparent from VMI's mission: to produce "citizen-soldiers," individuals "'imbued with love of learning, confident in the functions and attitudes of leadership, possessing a high sense of public service, advocates of the American democracy and free enterprise system, and ready . . . to defend their country in time of national peril.'" 766 F. Supp., at 1425 (quoting Mission Study Committee of the VMI Board of Visitors, Report, May 16, 1986).

Surely that goal is great enough to accommodate women, who today count as citizens in our American democracy equal in stature to men. Just as surely, the State's great goal is not substantially advanced by women's categorical exclusion, in total disregard of their individual merit, from the State's premier "citizen-soldier" corps. Virginia, in sum, "has fallen far short of establishing the 'exceedingly persuasive justification,'" *Mississippi Univ. for Women,* 458 U.S., at 731, that must be the solid base for any gender-defined classification. . . .

As earlier stated, see supra, at 24, generalizations about "the way women are," estimates of what is appropriate for most women, no longer justify denying opportunity to women whose talent and capacity place them outside the average description. Notably, Virginia never asserted that VMI's method of education suits most men. It is also revealing that Virginia accounted for its failure to make the VWIL experience "the entirely militaristic experience of VMI" on the ground that VWIL "is planned for women who do not necessarily expect to pursue military careers." 852 F. Supp., at 478. By that reasoning, VMI's "entirely militaristic" program would be inappropriate for men in general or as a group, for "[o]nly about 15% of VMI cadets enter career military service." See 766 F. Supp., at 1432.

In contrast to the generalizations about women on which Virginia rests, we note again these dispositive realities: VMI's "implementing methodology" is not "inherently unsuitable to women," 976 F. 2d, at 899; "some women . . . do well under [the] adversary model," 766 F. Supp., at 1434 (internal quotation marks omitted); "some women, at least, would want to attend [VMI] if they had the opportunity," id., at 1414; "some women are capable of all of the individual activities required of VMI cadets," id., at 1412, and "can meet the physical standards [VMI] now impose[s] on men," 976 F. 2d, at 896. It is on behalf of these women that the United States has instituted this suit, and it is for them that a remedy must be crafted, a remedy that will end their exclusion from a state-supplied educational opportunity for which they are fit, a decree that will "bar like discrimination in the future." Louisiana, 380 U.S., at 154. . . .

Virginia, in sum, while maintaining VMI for men only, has failed to provide any "comparable single-gender women's institution." Id., at 1241. Instead, the Commonwealth has created a VWIL program fairly appraised as a "pale shadow" of VMI in terms of the range of curricular choices and faculty stature, funding, prestige, alumni support and influence. See id., at 1250 (Phillips, J., dissenting).

Virginia's VWIL solution is reminiscent of the remedy Texas proposed 50 years ago, in response to a state trial court's 1946 ruling that, given the equal protection guarantee, African Americans could not be denied a legal education at a state facility. See *Sweatt v. Painter,* 339 U.S. 629 (1950). Reluctant to admit African Americans to its flagship University of Texas Law School, the State set up a separate school for Herman Sweatt and other black law students. Id., at 632. As originally opened, the new school had no independent faculty or library, and it lacked accreditation. Id., at 633. Nevertheless, the state trial and appellate courts were satisfied that the new school offered Sweatt opportunities for the study of law "substantially equivalent to those offered by the State to white students at the University of Texas." Id., at 632 (internal quotation marks omitted).

Before this Court considered the case, the new school had gained "a faculty of five full-time professors; a student body of 23; a library of some 16,500 volumes serviced by a full-time staff; a practice court and legal aid association; and one alumnus who ha[d] become a member of the Texas Bar." Id., at 633. This Court contrasted resources at the new school with those at the school from which Sweatt had been excluded. The University of Texas Law School had a full-time faculty of 16, a student body of 850, a library containing over 65,000 volumes, scholarship funds, a law review, and moot court facilities. Id., at 632–633.

More important than the tangible features, the Court emphasized, are "those qualities which are incapable of objective measurement but which make for greatness" in a school, including "reputation of the faculty, experience of the administration, position and influence of the alumni, standing in the community, traditions and prestige." Id., at 634. Facing the marked differences reported in the Sweatt opinion, the Court unanimously ruled that Texas had not shown "substantial equality in the [separate] educational opportunities" the State offered. Id., at 633. Accordingly, the Court held, the Equal Protection Clause required Texas to admit African Americans to the University of Texas Law School. Id., at 636. In line with Sweatt, we rule here that Virginia has not shown substantial equality in the separate educational opportunities the State supports at VWIL and VMI.

When Virginia tendered its VWIL plan, the Fourth Circuit did not inquire whether the proposed remedy, approved by the District Court, placed women denied the VMI advantage in "the position they would have occupied in the absence of [discrimination]." *Milliken,* 433 U.S., at 280 (internal quotation marks omitted). Instead, the Court of Appeals considered whether the State could provide, with fidelity to the equal protection principle, separate and unequal educational programs for men and women.

The Fourth Circuit acknowledged that "the VWIL degree from Mary Baldwin College lacks the historical benefit and prestige of a degree from VMI." 44 F. 3d, at 1241. The Court of Appeals further observed that VMI is "an ongoing and successful institution with a long history," and there remains no "comparable single-gender women's institution." Ibid. Nevertheless, the appeals court declared the substantially different and significantly unequal VWIL program satisfactory. The court reached that result by revising the applicable standard of review. The Fourth Circuit displaced the standard developed in our precedent, see supra, at 13–16, and substituted a standard of its own invention.

We have earlier described the deferential review in which the Court of Appeals engaged, see supra, at 10–11, a brand of review inconsistent with the more exacting standard our precedent requires, see supra, at 13–16. Quoting in part from *Mississippi Univ. for Women,* the Court of Appeals candidly described its own analysis as one capable of checking a legislative purpose ranked as "pernicious," but generally according "deference to [the] legislative will." 44 F. 3d, at 1235, 1236. Recognizing that it had extracted from our decisions a test yielding "little or no scrutiny of the effect of a classification directed at [single-gender education]," the Court of Appeals devised another test, a "substantive comparability" inquiry, id., at 1237, and proceeded to find that new test satisfied, id., at 1241.

The Fourth Circuit plainly erred in exposing Virginia's VWIL plan to a deferential analysis, for "all gender-based classifications today" warrant "heightened scrutiny." See J. E. B., 511 U.S., at 136. Valuable as VWIL may prove for students who seek the program offered, Virginia's remedy affords no cure at all for the opportunities and advantages withheld from women who want a VMI education and can make the grade. See supra, at 31–36.20 In sum, Virginia's remedy does not match the constitutional violation; the State has shown no "exceedingly persuasive justification" for withholding from women qualified for the experience premier training of the kind VMI affords. . . .

A prime part of the history of our Constitution, historian Richard Morris recounted, is the story of the extension of constitutional rights and protections to people once ignored or excluded. VMI's story continued as our comprehension of "We the People" expanded. See supra, at 29, n. 16. There is no reason to believe that the admission of women capable of all the activities required of VMI cadets would destroy the Institute rather than enhance its capacity to serve the "more perfect Union."

For the reasons stated, the initial judgment of the Court of Appeals, 976 F. 2d 890 (CA4 1992), is affirmed, the final judgment of the Court of Appeals, 44 F. 3d 1229 (CA4 1995), is reversed, and the case is remanded for further proceedings consistent with this opinion.

It is so ordered.

12

Introductory Ethics Assignment: A Personal Ethics Statement

The heart has reasons of which reason knows nothing.

—Blaise Pascal

A fool must now and then be right, by chance.

—William Cowper

This chapter provides some materials that will help you write your own personal code of ethics. You may have given it little thought, but you have one. Each day you make many decisions relating to what to do and what not to do. You may lend your friend money for lunch. You may drive through an automated toll booth without paying the fare. You may volunteer at a hospital or steal to support a drug habit. Whatever you do, you probably justify it to yourself in one way or another. The justifications that you use for your actions all add up to a code of ethics.

When you write your code of ethics you have an opportunity to understand more clearly the ethical principles by which you live. You have a chance to examine them, review them, and perhaps even revise them.

Before you begin to write your own ethics statement, read some that other people have written. A few examples are provided, but your library contains hundreds of them, which can be found under many headings, including philosophy, religion, theology, and politics. The following examples are not comprehensive, systematic statements of ethics. Instead, they are excerpts from longer statements that address a wide variety of ethical considerations. As you read, write down notes about things you agree with, things you disagree with, and other thoughts that occur to you. You will find these notes very helpful when you begin to write your own paper.

12.1 EXAMPLES OF FAMOUS STATEMENTS OF ETHICS

12.1.1 Kindergarten Wisdom

ALL I REALLY NEED TO KNOW about how to live and what to do and how to be I learned in kindergarten. Wisdom was not at the top of the graduate-school mountain, but there in the sand pile at Sunday School. These are things I learned:

Share everything.

Play fair.

Don't hit people.

Put things back where you found them.

Clean up your own mess.

Don't take things that aren't yours.

Say you're sorry when you hurt somebody.

Wash your hands before you eat.

Flush.

Warm cookies and cold milk are good for you.

Live a balanced life—learn some and think some and draw and paint and sing and dance and play and work every day some.

Take a nap every afternoon.

When you go out into the world, watch out for traffic, hold hands, and stick together.

Be aware of wonder. Remember the little seed in the Styrofoam cup: the roots go down and the plant goes up and nobody really knows how or why, but we are all like that.

Goldfish and hamsters and white mice and even the little seed in the Styrofoam cup—they all die. So do we.

And then remember the Dick-and-Jane books and the first word you learned—the biggest word of all—LOOK. (Robert Fulghum. *All I Really Need to Know I Learned in Kindergarten.* New York: Ivy Books, 1988. 4–6.)

12.1.2   Ten Commandments

And God spoke all these words:

I am the Lord your God, who brought you out of Egypt, out of the land of slavery.

You shall have no other gods before me.

You shall not make for yourself an idol in the form of anything in heaven above or on the earth beneath or in the waters below. You shall not bow down to them or worship them; for I, the Lord your God, am a jealous God, punishing the children for the sin of the fathers to the third and fourth generation of those who hate me, but showing love to a thousand generations of those who love me and keep my commandments.

You shall not misuse the name of the Lord your God, for the Lord will not hold anyone guiltless who misuses His name.

Remember the Sabbath day by keeping it holy. Six days you shall labor and do all your work, but the seventh day is a Sabbath to the Lord your God. On it you shall not do any work, neither you, nor your son or daughter, nor your manservant or maidservant, nor your animals, nor the alien within your gates. For in six days the Lord made the heavens and the earth, the sea, and all that is in them, but He rested on the seventh day. Therefore the Lord blessed the Sabbath day and made it holy.

Honor your father and your mother, so that you may live long in the land the Lord your God is giving you.

You shall not murder.

You shall not commit adultery.

You shall not steal.

You shall not give false testimony against your neighbor.

You shall not covet your neighbor's house. You shall not covet your neighbor's wife, or his manservant or maidservant, his ox or donkey, or anything that belongs to your neighbor.

12.1.3   Tao

Horses

When a nation follows the Way,
Horses bear manure through its fields;
When a nation ignores the Way,
Horses bear soldiers through its streets.

There is no greater mistake than following desire;
There is no greater disaster than forgetting contentment;
There is no greater sickness than seeking attainment;
But one who is content to satisfy his needs
Finds that contentment endures.

12.1.4   Declaration of Independence

We hold these truths to be self-evident, that all men are created equal,
that they are endowed by their Creator with certain unalienable rights, that
among these are life, liberty and the pursuit of happiness. That to secure these
rights, governments are instituted among men, deriving their just powers from
the consent of the governed. That whenever any form of government becomes
destructive to these ends, it is the right of the people to alter or to abolish it,
and to institute new government, laying its foundation on such principles and
organizing its powers in such form, as to them shall seem most likely to effect
their safety and happiness. (Preamble to the Declaration of Independence.)

12.1.5   Humanist Manifesto II

In the best sense, religion may inspire dedication to the highest ethical
ideals. The cultivation of moral devotion and creative imagination is an expression of genuine "spiritual" experience and aspiration. . . .

We believe, however, that traditional dogmatic or authoritarian religions
that place revelation, God, ritual, or creed above human needs and experience
do a disservice to the human species. Any account of nature should pass the
tests of scientific evidence; in our judgment, the dogmas and myths of traditional religions do not do so. Even at this late date in human history, certain elementary facts based upon the critical use of scientific reason have to be restated.
We find insufficient evidence for belief in the existence of a supernatural; it is
either meaningless or irrelevant to the question of survival and fulfillment of
the human race. As nontheists, we begin with humans not God, nature not
deity. Nature may indeed be broader and deeper than we now know; any new
discoveries, however, will but enlarge our knowledge of the natural. . . .

We affirm that moral values derive their source from human experience.
Ethics is autonomous and situational needing no theological or ideological

sanction. Ethics stems from human need and interest. To deny this distorts the whole basis of life. Human life has meaning because we create and develop our futures. Happiness and the creative realization of human needs and desires, individually and in shared enjoyment, are continuous themes of humanism. We strive for the good life, here and now. The goal is to pursue life's enrichment despite debasing forces of vulgarization, commercialization, and dehumanization. (American Humanist Association. Humanist Manifesto II).

12.1.6   Thus Spake Zarathustra

I teach you the Superman. Man is something that is to be surpassed. What have ye done to surpass man?

All beings hitherto have created something beyond themselves: and ye want to be the ebb of that great tide, and would rather go back to the beast than surpass man?

What is the ape to man? A laughing-stock, a thing of shame. And just the same shall man be to the Superman: a laughing-stock, a thing of shame. . . . Lo, I teach you the Superman!

The Superman is the meaning of the earth. Let your will say: The Superman shall be the meaning of the earth! . . . Once blasphemy against God was the greatest blasphemy; but God died, and therewith also those blasphemers. To blaspheme the earth is now the dreadfulest sin, and to rate the heart of the unknowable higher than the meaning of the earth! . . .

Verily, a polluted stream is man. One must be a sea, to receive a polluted stream without becoming impure.

Lo, I teach you the Superman: he is that sea; in him can your great contempt be submerged. (Friedrich Nietzsche. 1891. *Thus Spake Zarathustra*. Trans. Thomas Common. http://www.republic.k12.mo.us/highschool/sstudies/block/eur/nietzsche/zara.txt.)

12.2   WRITING YOUR OWN PERSONAL CODE OF ETHICS

How do you write a code of ethics? There is no one set way, but this chapter has some suggestions. First, construct a list of questions pertaining to right and wrong, or the basis on which you might determine right or wrong. Your list may have many entries but should include at least the following questions:

- Is there an objective basis for ethics? In other words, is there a set of universal moral principles available for everyone to find?
- If there is an objective basis for ethics, what is that basis? Is it revelation, the nature of humanity, our moral feelings, reason alone?

- If there is no objective basis for ethics, is there a reasonable subjective basis for ethics? In other words, can I make up my own ethical system?
- What are my most important ethical values?
- What do my ethical values have to say about the value of human life?
- What do my ethical values have to say about the value of nonhuman life?
- What do my ethical values have to say about my obligations to others?
- What do my ethical values have to say about my obligations to myself?
- What do my ethical values have to say about what I am free to do?
- What do my ethical values have to say about what I am not free to do?

After you have written your list of questions, take some time to answer each one. This whole exercise can be much more fun if you do it with others, who may have ideas very different from your own. Invite your philosophically minded friends, the ones you are always arguing with, for some Pepsi and pizza. Remember not to copy their ideas as you develop your own.

After you have answered your list of questions, explore the implications of your answers by applying them to concrete situations. You may begin with the following hypothetical situations, but do not feel confined to them. Read each of the following situations and explain on paper what you would do in each situation and the ethical basis or reasons for your actions.

When you finish, reread with CARE in mind. CARE is an acronym for Consequences, Autonomy, Rights, and Equality. It sums up the considerations which most people think have relevance to ethical decisions. Have you considered all four major factors in developing your personal code?

12.2.1 Situation 1

You are driving Route 66 in your 1962 Corvette. It's a beautiful day. The speed limit is 55, but, hey, everyone drives 65 on this road, and it sure would be nice to go over 55. What will you do?

12.2.2 Situation 2

Your cousin Alfred is a computer whiz. You are virtually helpless when it comes to things that run with electricity. Alfred notices that on your new PC you are running Windows 3.1, and he just happens to have a CD-ROM that carries Windows95. He offers to install it on your computer for free, even though doing so is a violation of copyright law. Of course, Microsoft will never know that you are using their product without paying them for it. Will you accept the software?

12.2.3   Situation 3

Late at night you hear an intruder breaking into your home. You grab your grandfather's shotgun, hastily load it, and wait as the intruder breaks down the door. You shout a warning but the intruder surges toward you with a knife. Do you fire the gun?

12.3   THE CONTENTS OF A PERSONAL ETHICS STATEMENT

Your personal ethics statement may be very different from those of your class-mates, for your concerns will in many ways be different from theirs. Your paper, however, should conform to the format described in Chapter 6 of this manual and should include a title page and the text of the paper. References to sources are necessary if you quote from or derive ideas from authors to whom credit is due. Your paper should be in essay form, and should address at least the following three issues:

- From what or whom do you derive the basis of your ethical principles?
- What are your most important ethical principles?
- How do your ethical principles apply to situations you have encountered or may encounter in life (provide some examples)?

You will find printed below two sample student essays. Notice that they each approach ethical problems differently, but that both students begin the attempt to define their own ethical systems.

12.4   TWO SAMPLE STUDENT ETHICS STATEMENTS

12.4.1   Jeremy Scott's Essay

The following essay was written by Jeremy Scott, who, at the time he wrote it in the fall of 1996 had not yet had a course in the history of philosophy but used this assignment as an opportunity to sort out his own values. He achieved the ob-jective of the assignment because, rather than attempting to copy someone's philosophy, he explored his own beliefs and experiences and arrived at some new insights about them.

A Statement of Personal Ethics

Jeremy Scott

University of Kansas

October 1996

I have a problem when it comes to ethics. My actions do not always line up with my beliefs. My beliefs come from many places, most notably my experiences in life and people I have known. The most simple daily decisions I make, such as deciding what I will eat, seem to influence my beliefs. I find that I can examine each of the questions asked in the directions to this writing assignment and arrive at a conclusion that seems to be rational and ethical. However, when I find myself in situations that call for an ethical decision, I do not always do what my personal ethics seem to demand. I would, for example, break the speed limit because I always do. Since I am a student with a limited budget, and Bill Gates is so rich, I would be tempted to install Windows95 on my computer illegally and not feel like I am a terrible person. The more I think about doing this, however, the more uncomfortable I feel. I need a reason to pay for the software. Why shouldn't I take the Windows95 when it is offered to me: because it is illegal, or because I would be stealing?

Since I need some way to answer these questions, I will try to get to the bottom of my ideology, my ethical system. I guess it all begins with happiness. Sorting through my values has led me to a relatively simple conclusion. Happiness is the foundation of my ideology, which is my personal set of ethical values. Without happiness life is not life at all, but is merely existence controlled by emotions and the decisions of other people. First, I must decide what happiness is and then I must determine what ethical decisions I should make to promote happiness.

The times I am happiest are when I am relatively independent, making my own decisions for myself. When I find myself feeling like I have to make most of my decisions in an effort to make someone else happy, that is when I am the least happy. It's not that I don't want to do things to make other people happy. Ironically, I also find happiness when I do something for someone spontaneously, completely of my own free will, like when I help someone pick something up that she just dropped. I feel good about myself because I have helped someone. Maybe I helped brighten someone's day. I feel this way because if I drop something and someone picks it up for me, then I feel a certain amount of gratitude towards that person. I therefore experience happiness when someone appreciates what I have done. The times when I am most unhappy are the times when I experience guilt and grief. What I am saying is that I am not happy when I find myself constantly worried about someone else, like my girlfriend. When I start thinking about her needs all the time, I start to get resentful. Happiness is having the choice to do something for someone when I want to, not because I feel I have to.

If happiness is the basic principle of my ideology, and if happiness is freedom to do things for myself and others when I want to, what then can I say about ethical problems such as exceeding the speed limit or stealing software? Should I abide by the law because a group of individuals decided that it was best for me not to drive more than 65 miles per hour? No, I am too independent for that. Following other people's wishes is what makes me unhappy. Would I be happier going 120 miles per hour and spending the night in jail, or abiding by the rules and going 65 miles per hour? Since I don't have the money to pay the fine, or would have to borrow it, I will not drive 120 miles per hour. Maybe 80. And should I "borrow" Windows95 from my friend? I don't know what the penalty is for copyright infringement. I know I can't afford it.

Getting caught speeding or stealing does not make me happy, or increase my freedom to do what I want; it brings me grief and makes me do what other people want. I do not necessarily agree with all the laws that I live by, but until I can change them, I will abide by most of them, because the less grief I experience, the happier I am.

Another problem I have not resolved is this: does my happiness come first when it is in conflict with someone else's happiness? Certainly I would be happy if you sold me your father's brand new Porsche for five dollars. Would your father be happy? Do I care? Since my happiness is the most important thing in my life, I do care because I care about other people. Therefore, my own happiness cannot be the single most important value in my life. I realize that I have no set formulas for how to treat others in various situations. My obligations to other people are therefore hazy at best. But part of my happiness is affected by whether my loved ones are happy. I know from experience that a few kind words or actions from a loved one, friend, or stranger, can completely change the way I visualize life. This does not mean I feel obligated to make other people, friends or strangers, happy. I realize their happiness is out of my control.

Furthermore, simple ethical dilemmas like speeding and stealing cannot be compared to decisions that other people have confronted. For example, the decision to drop an atom bomb that would kill thousands of people is certainly not one that anyone should be able to make. How can I choose the happiness of one group of people over the happiness of another group? I do not know. It has taken me a while to figure out what makes me happy, and I certainly cannot assume that I know what makes other people happy.

I understand that I have a lot more thinking to do about my personal ethics. I have come, however, to one preliminary conclusion: ethics needs to begin with allowing people the freedom to find their own happiness as much as possible. Maybe the more I am allowed to find out what truly makes me happy, the more able I will be to solve the problem with which I started this essay: I will be better able to have my actions agree with my personal ethical standards.

12.4.2   Chris Allen's Essay

The second essay was written by Chris Allen, who, at the time she wrote it in the fall of 1996, was studying sociology and ethics. Chris used this assignment as an opportunity to clarify her ethical values. She also achieved the objective of the assignment because she defined in clear and simple terms her current understanding of the origin and implications of her personal ethical system.

A Statement of Personal Ethics

Chris Allen

Mount Holyoke College

October 1996

Ethics creates the fabric of who we are as human beings, affecting every decision that we make and every objective we pursue. We need a personal code of ethics the most when the need for it is least apparent; it is the most difficult yet important aspect of life to develop. It forms who we are as individuals and as members of society. If we fail to define our personal ethical code we will live by expediency, justifying our actions with pretexts rather than principle. For this assignment I tried at first to outline my code of ethics by setting up a list of rules to live by, but I found rules are a poor substitute for ethical character. Ethics are broader and deeper than rules, and yet I must find some guiding principles, so this is what I came up with:

> Treat others as you would want to be treated.
>
> Be sincere to everyone, including yourself.
>
> Use sound judgment.
>
> Listen objectively before you pass judgment.

These are the values that express, most accurately, how I try to live my life. It is important to value others' lives in the same way that you expect your life to be valued. If you live in a manner that expresses kindness towards others, in most cases you will be treated kindly. Kindness makes you responsible for following laws and abiding by regulations because your conscience tells you it's right, not because you are afraid of being caught. My ethics have not come from a single experience in life or from something that people have told me. They were formed from a number of experiences, from reading the simple teachings of the Bible to walking in the woods, where I learned not to touch the wild flowers so that others could appreciate them as I had. Everyone learns these ethical ideas, but they are important in shaping how I respond to the world. The most important ethical principle is treating other people as I would want to be treated. I cannot clarify this principle by saying "do not kill" or "it is always wrong to steal" because situations will inevitably arise in which I would have to break my code. If someone breaks into my home and threatens my life, I might have to make the decision to protect myself, but the intruder also made an ethical decision by threatening me. If I threatened someone else's life, I would expect her to protect herself. It is important to remain sincere and objective when making ethical decisions. As long as I am protecting myself because I know it's right and not to get revenge, then I will know that I have not broken my code.

Protecting my life may be difficult in practice, but it does not pose a challenging ethical problem, for violence clearly violates a basic principle: treat others as you would be treated. Ironically, the more subtle the situation, the greater the ethical complexity. When considering if I would exceed the speed limit on the open highway, for example, I face an ethical dilemma greater than the one posed by self-defense.

What are the forces that prevent me from speeding? Are they bigger than the forces that are encouraging me to speed? A criminal with a gun presents a problem that seems ethically clear cut. Driving on the highway presents a more difficult issue because I am not affecting anyone by speeding, and following the rules, therefore, seems less important. The effects of speeding would be detrimental, however, if a small child ran out in the road in front of my car. The possibility of a child entering my path seems to present an extreme scenario, because is does not happen very often, but the thought of a child being killed because of my recklessness forces me to realize that speeding is wrong. It is true that driving five miles an hour over the speed limit would probably not affect my reaction time, but going thirty miles an hour over the speed limit certainly would.

Other ethical issues are even less clear because they arise from actions for which there are no real ramifications. In these cases it seems that the only motivating force is honor. Illegal use of software is an example. If I copy Windows95 onto my computer, and have not paid for the software license, I will not be physically hurting anyone or putting anyone in danger. I will most likely avoid getting caught and even if I am caught the punishment will probably not be severe. But does this justify theft? In this subtle ethical situation I cannot escape my nagging conscience. While most people would probably copy the software, and feel little remorse for it, I don't think any one of them would say that what they did was right.

Problems like stealing software confront us every day. Our ethical code, therefore, is something that arises in some manner in virtually every situation we face, whether we recognize it or not. We cannot escape ethics, for we must consider and take into account the ramifications and implications of every action we take. We neglect ethics at our peril, and when we seem to need a code of ethics the least is when we need it most.

13

Ethics Assignments for Intermediate and Advanced Students

Though sages may pour out their wisdom's treasure, There is no sterner moralist than pleasure.

—Lord Byron

An Englishman thinks he is moral when he is only uncomfortable.

—George Bernard Shaw

Grub first, then ethics.

—Bertholt Brecht

13.1 ASSIGNMENT FOR INTERMEDIATE STUDENTS: AN APPLIED ETHICS PAPER

13.1.1 Introduction: The Unabomber as Ethicist

John Hauser had been accepted into NASA's astronaut training program. An Air Force pilot and student at the University of California at Berkeley, Hauser was working on a research project on May 15, 1985, when he opened a box that exploded, obliterating the fingers of his right hand, and ending his long-cherished dream of a career exploring the last frontier. He was, however, fortunate to be alive, for he was one of twenty-two victims of the Unabomber who had been injured and yet survived. Hugh Scrutton, who had owned a computer store; Thomas Mosser, who was in advertising; and Gilbert Murray, an executive in the lumbering

245

business, all died when the Unabomber's packages exploded in their hands. It took the efforts of dozens of federal agents to catch Theodore Kaszynski, in his primitive cabin in Montana in 1996, but before he was apprehended, he was able to get major newspapers to publish his letters and what is now known as his "manifesto," a statement entitled "Industrial Society and its Future."

The manifesto is a statement of social and political ethics. It is a commentary on what is right and wrong in the world, and what should and should not be done about social problems. It provides you, as student of ethics, with an opportunity to define more clearly your own social and political ethics by writing an applied ethics paper which critiques the manifesto. Kaszynski's manifesto also provides an opportunity for you to address other considerations, such as the circumstances under which it was written and its author. Is the document merely a pretext for murder?

The Unabomber manifesto is, of course, by no means the only ethical statement that you can critique. In this chapter we shall first explain how to write an applied ethics paper and then present the manifesto and several other ethics declarations as examples of statements that you can critique. You may also select another statement from a newspaper editorial, a magazine article, a book of philosophy, or another source. It is always a good idea to ask your instructor if your selection is appropriate for the assignment.

13.1.2   Writing a Critique of a Brief Ethics Statement

An applied ethics paper is a writing exercise in which you analyze and evaluate someone's ethical statement by applying to it the principles of your own ethical system or another system that you have selected. This process occurs in seven steps:

1. Target statement selection
2. Target statement analysis
3. System definition
4. Criteria definition
5. Verity identification
6. Error identification
7. Conclusion

13.1.2.1   Target Statement Selection

The first step in the process of writing an applied ethics paper is to select a statement (we shall call this the "target statement") to be analyzed and evaluated. The Unabomber manifesto is a potential target statement, but be sure to ask your instructor if it is acceptable or if you should select another statement. Please be aware that the authors of this text do not in any way endorse the ideas contained in the manifesto. It is selected only because it provides an opportunity to discover fallacies and to generate interesting class discussions. Any essay, proclamation, or editorial that contains significant ethical content may be an appropriate target statement for an ethical analysis paper. The more substantial the statement, the more opportunities it affords for analysis. If you select a major work of philosophy as your target statement, however, be prepared to write a very substantial paper. Ask your instructor about the appropriate scope for a paper assignment in your class, but a good general rule is to select one that does not exceed the length of a normal journal article (20 to 30 pages).

You should select a paper that addresses a topic that personally interests you. Excerpts from several statements are included at the end of this chapter. You may select one of them, or simply read them to get an idea of the types of ethics statements that are appropriate subjects for your critique.

13.1.2.2   *Target Statement Analysis*

Analyze the target statement by precisely describing what it says and explaining its major implications. The best way to begin this analysis is to outline the target statement. Chapters 1 and 11 give directions by which you can construct a useful outline, meaning one that identifies the target statement's premises, the data supporting its premises, and its conclusion. Once you have completed your outline it is time to begin writing a first draft. Your primary job is to describe the major elements of the target statement in such a manner that your readers understand clearly what the target statement proposes.

13.1.2.3   *System Definition*

Your next job is to describe the ethical system (we shall call this "the system") that you will use to evaluate the target statement. This section need not be more than two or three pages in length, but it should contain a series of statements which summarize the philosophy which you will use as a guide in judging the target statement. If you consider yourself to be a utilitarian (or a stoic, or a Platonist), then briefly describe your fundamental ethical beliefs. If you wish you may adopt, for the purposes of this paper, a set of beliefs you do not actually hold, so that when you apply them to the target statement you will gain a better understanding of the belief system you have adopted. Examining the target statement from the point of view of an ultra-right-wing conservative, for example, may give you insights not only into the nature of the target statement but also into the nature of political conservatism.

13.1.2.4   *Criteria Definition*

Once you have described the belief system within which you will operate for the purposes of this assignment, you must deduce from your ethical system a list of specific criteria to use to evaluate the target statement. Make your criteria as specific as possible. Suppose, for instance, that you are a police officer. Your statement of criteria might look like this: I believe that a good code of ethics will:

- Keep the peace and enforce the laws of society
- Allow me to exhibit loyalty to my fellow officers
- Allow me to not engage in or support actions that violate my religious convictions and protect the innocent and facilitate the punishment of the guilty

The above criteria may at first appear specific but are, in fact, so general that they leave excessive room for interpretation. The following criteria are more specific:

- Keep the peace through the minimal use of force as a last resort
- Enforce the laws of society in the interests of peace and justice and not embrace full enforcement as an end in itself
- Exhibit appropriate loyalty to fellow officers in their proper enforcement of the law
- Refuse to engage in actions that violate my most cherished religious beliefs such as the right of children to a safe home environment

Notice that as you make your position more specific, you provided opportunities for dialogue with people who do not share your acculturation processes. The process of making your system more specific provides bridges to other systems.

13.1.2.5   *Verity Identification*

By completing the tasks above you will have chosen a target statement and established criteria by which to judge it. The next challenge is a two-step process through which you will apply your criteria to the target statement. First, identify the elements of the target statement that are "correct," that is, those elements that meet the qualifications established by your criteria, and then explain why they are correct. Second, proceed to error identification.

13.1.2.6   *Error Identification*

Identify the elements of the target statement that are "incorrect," that is, those that conflict with or fail to conform to your evaluation criteria, and explain why they are incorrect. These two steps, verity identification and error identification, will be the longest sections of your paper.

It is important to understand that by "correct" and "incorrect" we are not suggesting that elements of the target statement are "right" or "wrong" in some absolute sense, only that they correspond or fail to correspond with elements of the ethical system by which we are judging them.

13.1.2.7   Conclusion

Finally, write a general summary evaluation of the target statement, based upon the insights you have gained in the steps above. Tell your reader the specific strengths and weaknesses of the target statement and then make some general evaluatory comments.

13.1.3   Contents of an Applied Ethics Paper

An applied ethics paper will include the following elements:

- Title page
- Text or body of the paper, including the elements listed above (target statement selection, target statement analysis, and so on)
- Reference page
- Appendices

For all of the elements above, follow basic format directions presented in Chapter 6 of this manual. It is not necessary to cite references to the target statement that you have selected. If you select as a target statement something other than the samples provided in this chapter, however, attach a copy of the target statement to your paper as an appendix. (If the target statement is a published pamphlet or a book, you may attach a note to your instructor requesting that it be returned to you). If you adopt a published statement (such as the "Humanist Manifesto," Aristotle's Nichomachean Ethics, or the Koran) as your own ethical system for the purposes of this paper, cite references to the system either by page or by chapter and verse numbers. You will also need source citations for ideas or quotations taken from other published sources. Chapter 7 gives models of reference formats you can use.

13.1.4   Excerpts from Selected Statments of Ethics

13.1.4.1   The Unabomber Manifesto

1. The Industrial Revolution and its consequences have been a disaster for the human race. They have greatly increased the life-expectancy of those of us who live in "advanced" countries, but they have destabilized society, have

made life unfulfilling, have subjected human beings to indignities, have led to widespread psychological suffering (in the Third World to physical suffering as well) and have inflicted severe damage on the natural world. The continued development of technology will worsen the situation. It will certainly subject human beings to greater indignities and inflict greater damage on the natural world, it will probably lead to greater social disruption and psychological suffering, and it may lead to increased physical suffering even in "advanced" countries. . . .

2. . . . Furthermore, if the system survives, the consequences will be inevitable: There is no way of reforming or modifying the system so as to prevent it from depriving people of dignity and autonomy. . . .

4. We therefore advocate a revolution against the industrial system. This revolution may or may not make use of violence: it may be sudden or it may be a relatively gradual process spanning a few decades. . . . This is not to be a POLITICAL revolution. Its object will be to overthrow not governments but the economic and technological basis of the present society. . . .

13.1.4.2   *The Sermon on the Mount (Matthew 5:1–12):*

[1]Now when he saw the crowds, he went up on a mountainside and sat down. His disciples came to him, [2]and he began to teach them, saying: [3]"Blessed are the poor in spirit, for theirs is the kingdom of heaven. [4]Blessed are those who mourn, for they will be comforted. [5]Blessed are the meek, for they will inherit the earth. [6]Blessed are those who hunger and thirst for righteousness, for they will be filled. [7]Blessed are the merciful, for they will be shown mercy. [8]Blessed are the pure in heart, for they will see God. [9]Blessed are the peacemakers, for they will be called sons of God. [10]Blessed are those who are persecuted because of righteousness, for theirs is the kingdom of heaven.

[11]"Blessed are you when people insult you, persecute you and falsely say all kinds of evil against you because of me. [12]Rejoice and be glad, because great is your reward in heaven, for in the same way they persecuted the prophets who were before you."

13.1.4.3   *Aristotle, Nicomachean Ethics, 1094a:*

[1094a] Every art and every investigation, and likewise every practical pursuit or undertaking, seems to aim at some good: hence it has been well said that the Good is That at which all things aim. (It is true that a certain variety is to be observed among the ends at which the arts and sciences aim: in some cases the activity of practising the art is itself the end, whereas in others the end is some product over and above the mere exercise of the art; and in the arts whose ends are certain things beside the practice of the arts themselves, these products are essentially superior in value to the activities.) But as there are numerous pursuits and arts and sciences, it follows that their ends are correspondingly numerous: for instance, the end of the science of medicine is health, that of the art of shipbuilding a vessel, that of strategy victory, that of domestic economy wealth. Now in cases where several such pursuits are subordinate to some single fac-

ulty—as bridle-making and the other trades concerned with horses' harness are subordinate to horsemanship, and this and every other military pursuit to the science of strategy, and similarly other arts to different arts again—in all these cases, I say, the ends of the master arts are things more to be desired than the ends of the arts subordinate to them; since the latter ends are only pursued for the sake of the former. (And it makes no difference whether the ends of the pursuits are the activities themselves or some other thing beside these, as in the case of the sciences mentioned.) If therefore among the ends at which our actions aim there be one which we will for its own sake, while we will the others only for the sake of this, and if we do not [20] choose everything for the sake of something else (which would obviously result in a process ad infinitum, so that all desire would be futile and vain), it is clear that this one ultimate End must be the Good, and indeed the Supreme Good. Will not then a knowledge of this Supreme Good be also of great practical importance for the conduct of life? Will it not better enable us to attain our proper object, like archers having a target to aim at? If this be so, we ought to make an attempt to determine at all events in outline what exactly this Supreme Good is, and of which of the sciences or faculties it is the object.

Now it would seem that this supreme End must be the object of the most authoritative of the sciences—some science which is pre-eminently a master-craft. But such is manifestly the science of Politics; for it is this that ordains which of the sciences are to exist in states. . . .

13.1.4.4   *Statement Regarding Values and Science*

Statement Regarding Values and Science of the Committee On Science, Engineering, And Public Policy, National Academy of Sciences, the National Academy of Engineering and the Institute of Medicine:

Scientists bring more than just a toolbox of techniques to their work. Scientists must also make complex decisions about the interpretation of data, about which problems to pursue, and about when to conclude an experiment. They have to decide the best ways to work with others and exchange information. Taken together, these matters of judgment contribute greatly to the craft of science, and the character of a person's individual decisions helps determine that person's scientific style (as well as, on occasion, the impact of that person's work). . . .

Other kinds of values also come into play in science. Historians, sociologists, and other students of science have shown that social and personal beliefs—including philosophical, thematic, religious, cultural, political, and economic beliefs—can shape scientific judgment in fundamental ways. For example, Einstein's rejection of quantum mechanics as an irreducible description of nature—summarized in his insistence that "God does not play dice"—seems to have been based largely on an aesthetic conviction that the physical universe could not contain such an inherent component of randomness. The nineteenth-century geologist Charles Lyell, who championed the idea that geological change occurs incrementally rather than catastrophically, may have been influenced as much by his religious views as by his geological observations. He favored the notion of a God who is an unmoved mover and does not intervene in His creation. Such a God, thought Lyell, would produce a world in which the same causes and effects keep cycling eternally, producing a uniform geological history.

Does holding such values harm a person's science? In some cases the answer has to be "yes." The history of science offers a number of episodes in which social or personal beliefs distorted the work of researchers. The field of eugenics used the techniques of science to try to demonstrate the inferiority of certain races. The ideological rejection of Mendelian genetics in the Soviet Union beginning in the 1930s crippled Soviet biology for decades. Despite such cautionary episodes, it is clear that values cannot—and should not—be separated from science. The desire to do good work is a human value. So is the conviction that standards of honesty and objectivity need to be maintained. The belief that the universe is simple and coherent has led to great advances in science. If researchers did not believe that the world can be described in terms of a relatively small number of fundamental principles, science would amount to no more than organized observation. Religious convictions about the nature of the universe have also led to important scientific insights, as in the case of Lyell discussed above. (Committee on Science Engineering and Public Policy. National Academy of Sciences, National Academy of Engineering, Institute of Medicine. "Values in Science" in *On Being a Scientist: Responsible Conduct in Research.* National Academy Press. 1995.)

13.1.4.5 *1996 Democratic Party Platform*

We believe parents should be able to take unpaid leave from work and choose flex time so they can do their job as parents: to do things like go to parent-teacher conferences or take a child to the doctor. We support tax credits to encourage adoption, because every child deserves a mother and father who will love them and raise them.

We believe in public support for the arts, and especially for high-quality, family-friendly programming. We are proud to have stopped the Republican attack on the Corporation for Public Broadcasting—we want our children to watch Sesame Street, not Power Rangers. And we echo the President's call to the entertainment industry: Work harder to develop and promote movies, music, and TV shows that are suitable—and educational—for children.

Cigarette smoking is rapidly becoming the single greatest threat to the health of our children. We know that 3,000 young people start smoking every day, and 1,000 of them will lead shorter lives because of it. Despite that, Senator Dole and other Republicans continue to ignore volumes of medical research to make baffling claims that cigarettes are not addictive. They even argue with distinguished Republican experts like President Reagan's Surgeon General C. Everett Koop. President Clinton and Vice President Gore understand that we have a responsibility to protect our children's future by cracking down on illegal sales of tobacco to minors and by curbing sophisticated advertising campaigns designed to entice kids to start smoking before they are old enough to make an informed decision. The President has proposed measures to cut off children's access to cigarettes, crack down on those who sell tobacco to minors illegally, and curtail advertising designed to appeal to children. We believe tobacco companies should market to adults if they wish, but take the responsibility to draw the line on children.

13.1.4.6   *1996 Republican Platform*

We are discovering as a nation that many of our deepest social problems are problems of character and belief. We will never solve those problems until the hearts of parents are turned toward their children; until respect is restored for life and property; until a commitment is renewed to love and serve our neighbor. . . .

The unborn child has a fundamental individual right to life which cannot be infringed. We support a human life amendment to the Constitution and we endorse legislation to make clear that the Fourteenth Amendment's protections apply to unborn children. Our purpose is to have legislative and judicial protection of that right against those who perform abortions. We oppose using public revenues for abortion and will not fund organizations which advocate it. We support the appointment of judges who respect traditional family values and the sanctity of innocent human life.

Our goal is to ensure that women with problem pregnancies have the kind of support, material and otherwise, they need for themselves and for their babies, not to be punitive towards those for whose difficult situation we have only compassion. We oppose abortion, but our pro-life agenda does not include punitive action against women who have an abortion. We salute those who provide alternatives to abortion and offer adoption services. Republicans in Congress took the lead in expanding assistance both for the costs of adoption and for the continuing care of adoptive children with special needs. Bill Clinton vetoed our adoption tax credit the first time around—and opposed our efforts to remove racial barriers to adoption—before joining in this long overdue measure of support for adoptive families.

Worse than that, he vetoed the ban on partial-birth abortions, a procedure denounced by a committee of the American Medical Association and rightly branded as four-fifths infanticide. We applaud Bob Dole's commitment to revoke the Clinton executive orders concerning abortion and to sign into law an end to partial-birth abortions.

13.2   ASSIGNMENT FOR ADVANCED STUDENTS: ANALYZE A PROFESSIONAL CODE OF ETHICS

There is an increasing reliance in professional ethics upon the moral intuitions of competent professionals as a source of moral principles. These moral intuitions are embodied in paradigm cases—situations taken from the actual experience of professionals—and professional codes of ethics. Cases are not used merely as tools for understanding a theory but as a source of complex yet practical ethical principles. We might even say that advocates of the case method see themselves as combating the tyranny of theory. After all, what business does a philosopher have telling a police commissioner when an act of force was unjustified? No more business than ordinary citizens would have sitting on police review boards!

What "bottom up" advocates of the case study method are asserting is that professional codes are the outgrowth of years of cooperative engagement by educated and sensitive members of a profession. According to these advocates, the closest we are going to get to ethical principles that are also practically workable is to look at the practice of competent professionals. Their practice is a means of telling us which competing ethical theory is the superior one.

But there is a great deal of disagreement about professional competence. Mayor Goode, the BATF, and Mark Fuhrman all have their supporters. Those who want to exclude them from having a voice in determining what an ethical decision is are covertly relying on either a theory or a tradition.

Also, the admirable behavior of good police officers or good business persons almost immediately leads us to ask whether they are examples of exemplary behavior or a professional standard. In other words, should their actions be merely praised or required as standard behavior? And that question moves us into a theoretical discussion.

One final warning about cases is needed. Whether the case be the short, hypothetical ones of the philosopher or the elaborate ones of the lawyer, you should be wary of concluding too much on the basis of a case. For instance, when you read about a decision to admit women to a private military academy that would enhance their careers as officers and in civilian life after the military, do not automatically conclude that it also follows that women should be deployed in infantry combat situations.

So note the limits of what a case decision implies. Also, try to see what happens to your intuitions when you add or remove details from the case.

13.2.1   Writing an Analysis of a Professional Code of Ethics

An analysis of a code of ethics is a writing exercise in which you describe the philosophical orientation of a professional code of ethics. This assignment is for advanced students of ethics, that is, students who have studied the varieties of ethical thought and the history of philosophy. Performing this sort of analysis will teach you not only practical details about the nature of ethics as they come into play in society but also about the structure of such statements. Depending on the code you select, it may be advisable to concentrate on one major part of the code. To analyze a code of ethics, you must:

- Select an appropriate statement to analyze.
- Identify the foundational ethical principles expressed or implied in the code.

- Determine the philosophical orientation of the code: the "school" or "schools" of ethics from which the code's principles have been drawn. Is the code, for example, predominantly a utilitarian, deontological, egoist, or relativist document? Or is it a combination of these or other approaches?
- Determine the philosophical genealogy of the code. Of the philosophers (psychologists, sociologists, and the like) you have read, whose ideas seem likely to have contributed, directly or indirectly, the writing of the code?

13.2.2   Contents of a Code of Ethics Analysis

An analysis of a professional code of ethics will include the following elements:

- Title page
- Text or body of the paper, including the elements listed above (foundational ethical principles, and so on)
- Reference page
- Appendices

For all of the elements above, follow the basic format directions included in Chapter 6 of this manual. It is not necessary to cite references to the target statement that you have selected. If you select a code of ethics other than the APA code given below, attach a copy of the code you have selected to your paper as an appendix. Since you will refer to philosophers, you will need to cite your sources according to reference models given in Chapter 7 of this manual. You may cite references to the APA Code by placing parenthetical references in your text that correspond to the APA section number or section title, when there is no number, for example:

> The APA code states, "Psychologists consult with, refer to, or cooperate with other professionals and institutions to the extent needed to serve the best interests of their patients, clients, or other recipients of their services" (Principle C).

13.2.3   An Ethical Controversy in Psychology: Delayed Memory Debate

The history of counseling psychology is filled with victories. Recent studies have indicated that psychotherapy indeed helps people free themselves of many varieties of emotional problems. The therapist-client relationship, however, provides the setting for many potential ethical problems. Clients are usually distressed and look to their therapists for help, support, and encouragement. Much of the success of therapy depends upon the creation of a relationship of trust involving intimately personal matters, and the client can become vulnerable to the therapist's influence. Not only is it possible for unscrupulous therapists intentionally to take advantage of clients, but ethical therapists may unintentionally mistreat clients by leading them in directions that conform more to the therapist's perspective or bias than to perspectives of greater help to the client. Psychologists are well aware of these difficulties, and the American Psychological Association (APA) helps them organize their efforts to understand and address these problems.

In the last decade one controversy related to therapy has arisen that has received substantial attention in the national news. It has become known as the "delayed memory debate." Sigmund Freud (1856–1939), the father of modern psychology, asserted that there exists a psychological phenomenon known as repression. Repression is a mental defense mechanism by which we subconsciously repress memories that are too painful or terrifying for us to deal with. Later in life these memories may resurface, having been buried in the subconscious for years or even decades. Although there is little laboratory evidence to support the concept of repression, therapists have received countless thousands of reports by clients who claim to have recovered memories of trauma, including stories by soldiers, refugees, and accident victims. Many of these recovered memories, upon further investigation, appear to be confirmed.

Reports of repressed memories of sexual abuse during childhood are particularly common. Some research indicates that as many as one in three women and one in six men will have been sexually abused in some way before they reach the age of eighteen. In the past decade, however, a controversy has arisen about the validity of many of the reports of repressed memories. A leading figure in this controversy is Dr. Elizabeth Loftus of the University of Washington, Seattle. In January 1994 Dr. Loftus and her associate Maryanne Garry published an article entitled "Repressed Memories of Childhood Trauma: Could Some of Them Be Suggested?" in *USA Today*. The article suggests that some therapists, too eager to help their clients find the root of their emotional problems, may suggest too forcefully the presence of repressed memories of sexual abuse. Clients eager to find any breakthrough to healing may then unknowingly invent memories of events that never happened. The *USA Today* article tells the following story:

Gloria Grady is the child of devil worshippers. Around an altar in their home, her family would don black robes and perform Satanic rituals led by her father, a Baptist minister. Grady's father raped her repeatedly from the time she was ten until she was in college, and her mother, brother, and grandfather sexually abused her. She was a "breeder" for the cult, providing them with aborted fetuses, and even an incestuous child when she was fourteen. The child was tossed into a fire as a sacrificial devil-offering. Now in her thirties, Grady has vivid memories of these childhood events, but, as reported in *D Magazine* (October 1991), there is no evidence that any of these memories are true.

Grady didn't have these memories until she was about twenty-seven, shortly after she began "Christian counseling" at a Dallas-area clinic to grapple with what had been a lifelong weight problem. After an intensive hospitalization, she continued with weekly individual and group counseling. At first, her therapist suggested that she write down all the bad things that had happened in her life. A friend says Grady's list originally had rather benign entries, like the time her parents refused to let her square dance as a first-grader. Eventually, however, Grady came to remember incidents that were far worse. She began to have horrifying flashbacks, claiming that her father sexually abused her. With ensuing therapy sessions, she remembered more of these previously "repressed" memories, transforming her model Baptist family into a cult of child-eating Satanic ritualistic monsters. Her accusations left virtually no one in her family unaccused except a favorite aunt.

Grady's parents denied all the allegations. Their attempts to intervene directly were unsuccessful, so they enlisted the aunt's help. When the group attempted to visit Grady at a halfway house, an altercation ensued and the police eventually ordered the relatives to leave. Shortly afterwards, the district attorney's office served the family with papers requesting a protective order to prohibit any contact with Grady.

At the hearing, Grady's charges were refuted by other evidence. Her gynecological records revealed no indication of any sexual activity, let alone abortion or childbirth, during the period of alleged systematic rape. Grady remembered her mother hitting her so hard that she broke her collarbone; her orthopedic records showed the break to be the result of a spill in her walker as a nine-month-old child. Finally, photographs of Grady taken a few days before she supposedly gave birth showed that, although overweight, she most certainly was not pregnant.

Her therapist never testified, because of what Grady said was a joint agreement to end the relationship just prior to trial. Ultimately, the protective order request was turned down for lack of evidence, but Grady and her parents have not seen each other since. Most important, there still is no evidence that her memories are real.

As a result of this and other reports of repressed memories that were later invalidated, substantial research is now being conducted concerning memories and repression. Many issues of interest to students of ethics, from how therapists should relate to clients in response to repressed memories to how much therapists should charge for their services, arise in relation to psychological therapy. The APA has studied many of these issues intensively, and the result of their efforts is the association's code of professional ethics. Selected sections of the American Psychological Association Ethical Principles of Psychologists and Code of Conduct are reprinted here for your use, if you wish, in completing this assignment. The discussion of the delayed memory debate above has been included in this chapter to provide you with a focus for your analysis, if you wish to use it. You may, for example, want to pursue the question "How well does the APA code of ethics address the problems encountered in the delayed memory debate?"

You need not analyze the APA code of ethics. You will find that most professional associations have developed statements or codes of ethics, and some of them are available on the internet. Be sure to ask your instructor if the code of ethics you have selected is appropriate for this assignment.

13.2.4 The APA Code of Ethics*

INTRODUCTION

The American Psychological Association's (APA's) Ethical Principles of Psychologists and Code of Conduct (hereinafter referred to as the Ethics Code) consists of an Introduction, a Preamble, six General Principles (A F), and specific Ethical Standards. The Introduction discusses the intent, organization, procedural considerations, and scope of application of the Ethics Code. The Preamble and General Principles are aspirational goals to guide psychologists toward the highest ideals of psychology. Although the Preamble and General Principles are not themselves enforceable rules, they should be considered by psychologists in arriving at an ethical course of action and may be considered by ethics bodies in interpreting the Ethical Standards. The Ethical Standards set forth enforceable rules for conduct as psychologists. Most of the Ethical Standards are written broadly, in order to apply to psychologists in varied roles, although the application of an Ethical Standard may vary depending on the context. The Ethical Standards are not exhaustive. The fact that a given conduct is not specifically addressed by the Ethics Code does not mean that it is necessarily either ethical or unethical.

Membership in the APA commits members to adhere to the APA Ethics Code and to the rules and procedures used to implement it. Psychologists and students, whether or not they are APA members, should be aware that the Ethics Code may be applied to them by state psychology boards, courts, or other public bodies.

This Ethics Code applies only to psychologists' work related activities, that is, activities that are part of the psychologists' scientific and professional functions or that are psychological in nature. It includes the clinical or counseling practice of psychology, research, teaching, supervision of trainees, development of assessment instruments, conducting assessments, educational counseling, organizational consulting, social intervention, administration, and other activities as well. These work related activities can be distinguished from the purely private conduct of a psychologist, which ordinarily is not within the purview of the Ethics Code.

The Ethics Code is intended to provide standards of professional conduct that can be applied by the APA and by other bodies that choose to adopt them. Whether or not a psychologist has violated the Ethics Code does not by itself determine whether he or she is legally liable in a court action, whether a contract is enforceable, or whether other legal consequences occur. These results are based on legal rather than ethical rules. However, compliance with or violation of the Ethics Code may be admissible as evidence in some legal proceedings, depending on the circumstances.

In the process of making decisions regarding their professional behavior, psychologists must consider this Ethics Code, in addition to applicable laws and psychology board regulations. If the Ethics Code establishes a higher standard of conduct than is required by law, psychologists must meet the higher ethical standard. If the Ethics Code standard appears to conflict with the requirements of law, then psychologists make known their commitment to the Ethics Code and take steps to resolve the conflict in a responsible manner. If neither law nor the Ethics Code resolves an issue, psychologists should consider other professional materials and the dictates of their own conscience, as well as seek consultation with others within the field when this is practical.

The procedures for filing, investigating, and resolving complaints of unethical conduct are described in the current Rules and Procedures of the APA Ethics Committee. The actions that APA may take for violations of the Ethics Code include actions such as reprimand, censure, termination of APA membership, and referral of the matter to other bodies. Complainants who seek remedies such as monetary damages in alleging ethical violations by a psychologist must resort to private negotiation, administrative bodies, or the courts. Actions that violate the Ethics Code may lead to the imposition of sanctions on a psychologist by bodies other than APA, including state psychological associations, other professional groups, psychology boards, other state or federal agencies, and payors for health services. In addition to actions for violation of the Ethics Code, the APA Bylaws provide that APA may take action against a member after his or her conviction of a felony, expulsion or suspension from an affiliated state psychological association, or suspension or loss of licensure.

PREAMBLE

Psychologists work to develop a valid and reliable body of scientific knowledge based on research. They may apply that knowledge to human behavior in a variety of contexts. In doing so, they perform many roles, such as researcher, educator, diagnostician, therapist, supervisor, consultant, administrator, social interventionist, and expert witness. Their goal is to broaden knowledge of behavior and, where appropriate, to apply it pragmatically to improve the condition of both the individual and society. Psychologists respect the central importance of freedom of inquiry and expression in research, teaching, and publication. They also strive to help the public in developing informed judgments and choices concerning human behavior. This Ethics Code provides a common set of values upon which psychologists build their professional and scientific work.

This Code is intended to provide both the general principles and the decision rules to cover most situations encountered by psychologists. It has as its primary goal the welfare and protection of the individuals and groups with whom psychologists work. It is the individual responsibility of each psychologist to aspire to the highest possible standards of conduct. Psychologists respect and protect human and civil rights, and do not knowingly participate in or condone unfair discriminatory practices.

The development of a dynamic set of ethical standards for a psychologist's work related conduct requires a personal commitment to a lifelong effort to act ethically; to encourage ethical behavior by students, supervisees, employees, and colleagues, as appropriate; and to consult with others, as needed, concerning ethical problems. Each psychologist supplements, but does not violate, the Ethics Code's values and rules on the basis of guidance drawn from personal values, culture, and experience.

GENERAL PRINCIPLES

Principle A: Competence

Psychologists strive to maintain high standards of competence in their work. They recognize the boundaries of their particular competencies and the limitations of their expertise. They provide only those services and use only those techniques for which they are qualified by education, training, or experience. Psychologists are cognizant of the fact that the competencies required in serving, teaching, and/or studying groups of people vary with the distinctive characteristics of those groups. In those areas in which recognized professional standards do not yet exist, psychologists exercise careful judgment and take appropriate precautions to protect the welfare of those with whom they work. They maintain knowledge of relevant scientific and professional information related to the services they render, and they recognize the need for ongoing education. Psychologists make appropriate use of scientific, professional, technical, and administrative resources.

Principle B: Integrity

Psychologists seek to promote integrity in the science, teaching, and practice of psychology. In these activities psychologists are honest, fair, and respectful of others. In describing or reporting their qualifications, services, products, fees, research, or teaching, they do not make statements that are false, misleading, or deceptive. Psychologists strive to be aware of their own belief systems, values, needs, and limitations and the effect of these on their work. To the extent feasible, they attempt to clarify for relevant parties the roles they are performing and to function appropriately in accordance with those roles. Psychologists avoid improper and potentially harmful dual relationships.

Principle C: Professional and Scientific Responsibility

Psychologists uphold professional standards of conduct, clarify their professional roles and obligations, accept appropriate responsibility for their behavior, and adapt their methods to the needs of different populations. Psychologists consult with, refer to, or cooperate with other professionals and institutions to the extent needed to serve the best interests of their patients, clients, or other recipients of their services. Psychologists' moral standards and conduct are personal matters to the same degree as is true for any other person, except as psychologists' conduct may compromise their professional responsibilities or reduce the public's trust in psychology and psychologists. Psychologists are concerned about the ethical compliance of their colleagues' scientific and professional conduct. When appropriate, they consult with colleagues in order to prevent or avoid unethical conduct.

Principle D: Respect for People's Rights and Dignity

Psychologists accord appropriate respect to the fundamental rights, dignity, and worth of all people. They respect the rights of individuals to privacy, confidentiality, self determination, and autonomy, mindful that legal and other obligations may lead to inconsistency and conflict with the exercise of these rights. Psychologists are aware of cultural, individual, and role differences, including those due to age, gender, race, ethnicity, national origin, religion, sexual orientation, disability, language, and socioeconomic status. Psychologists try to eliminate the effect on their work of biases based on those factors, and they do not knowingly participate in or condone unfair discriminatory practices.

Principle E: Concern for Others' Welfare

Psychologists seek to contribute to the welfare of those with whom they interact professionally. In their professional actions, psychologists weigh the welfare and rights of their patients or clients, students, supervisees, human research participants, and other affected persons, and the welfare of animal subjects of research. When conflicts occur among psychologists' obligations or concerns, they attempt to resolve these conflicts and to perform their roles in a responsible fashion that avoids or minimizes harm. Psychologists are sensitive to real and ascribed differences in power between themselves and others, and they do not exploit or mislead other people during or after professional relationships.

Principle F: Social Responsibility

Psychologists are aware of their professional and scientific responsibilities to the community and the society in which they work and live. They apply and make public their knowledge of psychology in order to contribute to human welfare. Psychologists are concerned about and work to mitigate the causes of human suffering. When undertaking research, they strive to advance human welfare and the science of psychology. Psychologists try to avoid misuse of their work. Psychologists comply with the law and encourage the development of law and social policy that serve the interests of their patients and clients and the public. They are encouraged to contribute a portion of their professional time for little or no personal advantage.

ETHICAL STANDARDS

1.0   General Standards

These General Standards are potentially applicable to the professional and scientific activities of all psychologists.

1.01   Applicability of the Ethics Code

The activity of a psychologist subject to the Ethics Code may be reviewed under these Ethical Standards only if the activity is part of his or her work related functions or the activity is psychological in nature. Personal activities having no connection to or effect on psychological roles are not subject to the Ethics Code.

1.02   Relationship of Ethics and Law

If psychologists' ethical responsibilities conflict with law, psychologists make known their commitment to the Ethics Code and take steps to resolve the conflict in a responsible manner.

1.03   Professional and Scientific Relationships

Psychologists provide diagnostic, therapeutic, teaching, research, supervisory, consultative, or other psychological services only in the context of a defined professional or scientific relationship or role. (See also Standards 2.01, Evaluation, Diagnosis, and Interventions in Professional Context, and 7.02, Forensic Assessments.)

1.04   Boundaries of Competence

(a) Psychologists provide services, teach, and conduct research only within the boundaries of their competence, based on their education, training, supervised experience, or appropriate professional experience.

(b) Psychologists provide services, teach, or conduct research in new areas or involving new techniques only after first undertaking appropriate study, training, supervision, and/or consultation from persons who are competent in those areas or techniques.

(c) In those emerging areas in which generally recognized standards for preparatory training do not yet exist, psychologists nevertheless take reasonable steps to ensure the competence of their work and to protect patients, clients, students, research participants, and others from harm.

1.05   Maintaining Expertise

Psychologists who engage in assessment, therapy, teaching, research, organizational consulting, or other professional activities maintain a reasonable level of awareness of current scientific and professional information in their fields of activity, and undertake ongoing efforts to maintain competence in the skills they use.

1.06   Basis for Scientific and Professional Judgments

Psychologists rely on scientifically and professionally derived knowledge when making scientific or professional judgments or when engaging in scholarly or professional endeavors.

1.07   Describing the Nature and Results of Psychological Services

(a) When psychologists provide assessment, evaluation, treatment, counseling, supervision, teaching, consultation, research, or other psychological services to an individual, a group, or an organization, they provide, using language that is reasonably understandable to the recipient of those services, appropriate information beforehand about the nature of such services and appropriate information later about results and conclusions. (See also Standard 2.09, Explaining Assessment Results.)

(b) If psychologists will be precluded by law or by organizational roles from providing such information to particular individuals or groups, they so inform those individuals or groups at the outset of the service.

1.08   Human Differences

Where differences of age, gender, race, ethnicity, national origin, religion, sexual orientation, disability, language, or socioeconomic status significantly affect psychologists' work concerning particular individuals or groups, psychologists obtain the training, experience, consultation, or supervision necessary to ensure the competence of their services, or they make appropriate referrals.

1.09   Respecting Others

In their work related activities, psychologists respect the rights of others to hold values, attitudes, and opinions that differ from their own.

1.10   Nondiscrimination

In their work related activities, psychologists do not engage in unfair discrimination based on age, gender, race, ethnicity, national origin, religion, sexual orientation, disability, socioeconomic status, or any basis proscribed by law.

1.11   Sexual Harassment

(a) Psychologists do not engage in sexual harassment. Sexual harassment is sexual solicitation, physical advances, or verbal or nonverbal conduct that is sexual in nature, that occurs in connection with the psychologist's activities or roles as a psychologist, and that either: (1) is unwelcome, is offensive, or creates a hostile workplace environment, and the psychologist knows or is told this; or (2) is sufficiently severe or intense to be abusive to a reasonable person in the context. Sexual harassment can consist of a single intense or severe act or of multiple persistent or pervasive acts.

(b) Psychologists accord sexual harassment complainants and respondents dignity and respect. Psychologists do not participate in denying a person academic admittance or advancement, employment, tenure, or promotion, based solely upon their having made, or their being the subject of, sexual harassment charges. This does not preclude taking action based upon the outcome of such proceedings or consideration of other appropriate information.

1.12   Other Harassment

Psychologists do not knowingly engage in behavior that is harassing or demeaning to persons with whom they interact in their work based on factors such as those persons' age, gender, race, ethnicity, national origin, religion, sexual orientation, disability, language, or socioeconomic status.

1.13   Personal Problems and Conflicts

(a) Psychologists recognize that their personal problems and conflicts may interfere with their effectiveness. Accordingly, they refrain from undertaking an activity when they know or should know that their personal problems are likely to lead to harm to a patient, client, colleague, student, research participant, or other person to whom they may owe a professional or scientific obligation.

(b) In addition, psychologists have an obligation to be alert to signs of, and to obtain assistance for, their personal problems at an early stage, in order to prevent significantly impaired performance.

(c) When psychologists become aware of personal problems that may interfere with their performing work related duties adequately, they take appropriate measures, such as obtaining professional consultation or assistance, and determine whether they should limit, suspend, or terminate their work related duties.

1.14   Avoiding Harm

Psychologists take reasonable steps to avoid harming their patients or clients, research participants, students, and others with whom they work, and to minimize harm where it is foreseeable and unavoidable.

1.15   Misuse of Psychologists' Influence

Because psychologists' scientific and professional judgments and actions may affect the lives of others, they are alert to and guard against personal, financial, social, organizational, or political factors that might lead to misuse of their influence.

1.16   Misuse of Psychologists' Work

(a) Psychologists do not participate in activities in which it appears likely that their skills or data will be misused by others, unless corrective mechanisms are available. (See also Standard 7.04, Truthfulness and Candor.)

(b) If psychologists learn of misuse or misrepresentation of their work, they take reasonable steps to correct or minimize the misuse or misrepresentation.

1.17   Multiple Relationships

(a) In many communities and situations, it may not be feasible or reasonable for psychologists to avoid social or other nonprofessional contacts with persons such as patients, clients, students, supervisees, or research participants. Psychologists must always be sensitive to the potential harmful effects of other contacts on their work and on those persons with whom they deal. A psychologist refrains from entering into or promising another personal, scientific, professional, financial, or other relationship with such persons if it appears likely that such a relationship reasonably might impair the psychologist's objectivity or otherwise interfere with the psychologist's effectively performing his or her functions as a psychologist, or might harm or exploit the other party.

(b) Likewise, whenever feasible, a psychologist refrains from taking on professional or scientific obligations when preexisting relationships would create a risk of such harm.

(c) If a psychologist finds that, due to unforeseen factors, a potentially harmful multiple relationship has arisen, the psychologist attempts to resolve it with due regard for the best interests of the affected person and maximal compliance with the Ethics Code.

1.18   Barter (with Patients or Clients)

Psychologists ordinarily refrain from accepting goods, services, or other nonmonetary remuneration from patients or clients in return for psychological services because such arrangements create inherent potential for conflicts, exploitation, and distortion of the professional relationship. A psychologist may participate in bartering only if (1) it is not clinically contraindicated, and (2) the relationship is not exploitative. (See also Standards 1.17, Multiple Relationships, and 1.25, Fees and Financial Arrangements.)

1.19   Exploitative Relationships

(a) Psychologists do not exploit persons over whom they have supervisory, evaluative, or other authority such as students, supervisees, employees, research participants, and clients or patients. (See also Standards 4.05–4.07 regarding sexual involvement with clients or patients.)

(b) Psychologists do not engage in sexual relationships with students or supervisees in training over whom the psychologist has evaluative or direct authority, because such relationships are so likely to impair judgment or be exploitative.

1.20   Consultations and Referrals

(a) Psychologists arrange for appropriate consultations and referrals based principally on the best interests of their patients or clients, with appropriate consent, and subject to other relevant considerations, including applicable law and contractual obligations. (See also Standards 5.01, Discussing the Limits of Confidentiality, and 5.06, Consultations.)

(b) When indicated and professionally appropriate, psychologists cooperate with other professionals in order to serve their patients or clients effectively and appropriately.

(c) Psychologists' referral practices are consistent with law.

1.21   Third Party Requests for Services

(a) When a psychologist agrees to provide services to a person or entity at the request of a third party, the psychologist clarifies to the extent feasible, at the outset of the service, the nature of the relationship with each party. This clarification includes the role of the psychologist (such as therapist, organizational consultant, diagnostician, or expert witness), the probable uses of the services provided or the information obtained, and the fact that there may be limits to confidentiality.

(b) If there is a foreseeable risk of the psychologist's being called upon to perform conflicting roles because of the involvement of a third party, the psychologist clarifies the nature and direction of his or her responsibilities, keeps all parties appropriately informed as matters develop, and resolves the situation in accordance with this Ethics Code.

1.22   Delegation To and Supervision of Subordinates

(a) Psychologists delegate to their employees, supervisees, and research assistants only those responsibilities that such persons can reasonably be expected to perform competently, on the basis of their education, training, or experience, either independently or with the level of supervision being provided.

(b) Psychologists provide proper training and supervision to their employees or supervisees and take reasonable steps to see that such persons perform services responsibly, competently, and ethically.

(c) If institutional policies, procedures, or practices prevent fulfillment of this obligation, psychologists attempt to modify their role or to correct the situation to the extent feasible.

1.23   Documentation of Professional and Scientific Work

(a) Psychologists appropriately document their professional and scientific work in order to facilitate provision of services later by them or by other professionals, to ensure accountability, and to meet other requirements of institutions or the law.

(b) When psychologists have reason to believe that records of their professional services will be used in legal proceedings involving recipients of or participants in their work, they have a responsibility to create and maintain documentation in the kind of detail and quality that would be consistent with reasonable scrutiny in an adjudicative forum. (See also Standard 7.01, Professionalism, under Forensic Activities.)

1.24   Records and Data

Psychologists create, maintain, disseminate, store, retain, and dispose of records and data relating to their research, practice, and other work in accordance with law and in a manner that permits compliance with the requirements of this Ethics Code. (See also Standard 5.04, Maintenance of Records.)

1.25   Fees and Financial Arrangements

(a) As early as is feasible in a professional or scientific relationship, the psychologist and the patient, client, or other appropriate recipient of psychological services reach an agreement specifying the compensation and the billing arrangements.

(b) Psychologists do not exploit recipients of services or payors with respect to fees.

(c) Psychologists' fee practices are consistent with law.

(d) Psychologists do not misrepresent their fees.

(e) If limitations to services can be anticipated because of limitations in financing, this is discussed with the patient, client, or other appropriate recipient of services as early as is feasible. (See also Standard 4.08, Interruption of Services.)

(f) If the patient, client, or other recipient of services does not pay for services as agreed, and if the psychologist wishes to use collection agencies or legal measures to collect the fees, the psychologist first informs the person that such measures will be taken and provides that person an opportunity to make prompt payment. (See also Standard 5.11, Withholding Records for Nonpayment.)

1.26   Accuracy in Reports to Payors and Funding Sources

In their reports to payors for services or sources of research funding, psychologists accurately state the nature of the research or service provided, the fees or charges, and where applicable, the identity of the provider, the findings, and the diagnosis. (See also Standard 5.05, Disclosures.)

1.27   Referrals and Fees

When a psychologist pays, receives payment from, or divides fees with another professional other than in an employer employee relationship, the payment to each is based on the services (clinical, consultative, administrative, or other) provided and is not based on the referral itself.

3.0   ADVERTISING AND OTHER PUBLIC STATEMENTS

3.01   Definition of Public Statements

Psychologists comply with this Ethics Code in public statements relating to their professional services, products, or publications or to the field of psychology. Public statements include but are not limited to paid or unpaid advertising, brochures, printed matter, directory listings, personal resumes or curriculum vitae, interviews or comments for use in media, statements in legal proceedings, lectures and public oral presentations, and published materials.

3.02   Statements by Others

(a) Psychologists who engage others to create or place public statements that promote their professional practice, products, or activities retain professional responsibility for such statements.

(b) In addition, psychologists make reasonable efforts to prevent others whom they do not control (such as employers, publishers, sponsors, organizational clients, and representatives of the print or broadcast media) from making deceptive statements concerning psychologists' practice or professional or scientific activities.

(c) If psychologists learn of deceptive statements about their work made by others, psychologists make reasonable efforts to correct such statements.

(d) Psychologists do not compensate employees of press, radio, television, or other communication media in return for publicity in a news item.

(e) A paid advertisement relating to the psychologist's activities must be identified as such, unless it is already apparent from the context.

3.03   *Avoidance of False or Deceptive Statements*

(a) Psychologists do not make public statements that are false, deceptive, misleading, or fraudulent, either because of what they state, convey, or suggest or because of what they omit, concerning their research, practice, or other work activities or those of persons or organizations with which they are affiliated. As examples (and not in limitation) of this standard, psychologists do not make false or deceptive statements concerning (1) their training, experience, or competence; (2) their academic degrees; (3) their credentials; (4) their institutional or association affiliations; (5) their services; (6) the scientific or clinical basis for, or results or degree of success of, their services; (7) their fees; or (8) their publications or research findings. (See also Standards 6.15, Deception in Research, and 6.18, Providing Participants with Information About the Study.)

(b) Psychologists claim as credentials for their psychological work, only degrees that (1) were earned from a regionally accredited educational institution or (2) were the basis for psychology licensure by the state in which they practice.

3.04   *Media Presentations*

When psychologists provide advice or comment by means of public lectures, demonstrations, radio or television programs, prerecorded tapes, printed articles, mailed material, or other media, they take reasonable precautions to ensure that (1) the statements are based on appropriate psychological literature and practice, (2) the statements are otherwise consistent with this Ethics Code, and (3) the recipients of the information are not encouraged to infer that a relationship has been established with them personally.

3.05   *Testimonials*

Psychologists do not solicit testimonials from current psychotherapy clients or patients or other persons who because of their particular circumstances are vulnerable to undue influence.

3.06   *In Person Solicitation*

Psychologists do not engage, directly or through agents, in uninvited in person solicitation of business from actual or potential psychotherapy patients or clients or other persons who because of their particular circumstances are vulnerable to undue influence. However, this does not preclude attempting to implement appropriate collateral contacts with significant others for the purpose of benefiting an already engaged therapy patient.

4.0   THERAPY

4.01   Structuring the Relationship

(a) Psychologists discuss with clients or patients as early as is feasible in the therapeutic relationship appropriate issues, such as the nature and anticipated course of therapy, fees, and confidentiality. (See also Standards 1.25, Fees and Financial Arrangements, and 5.01, Discussing the Limits of Confidentiality.)

(b) When the psychologist's work with clients or patients will be supervised, the above discussion includes that fact, and the name of the supervisor, when the supervisor has legal responsibility for the case.

(c) When the therapist is a student intern, the client or patient is informed of that fact.

(d) Psychologists make reasonable efforts to answer patients' questions and to avoid apparent misunderstandings about therapy. Whenever possible, psychologists provide oral and/or written information, using language that is reasonably understandable to the patient or client.

4.02   Informed Consent to Therapy

(a) Psychologists obtain appropriate informed consent to therapy or related procedures, using language that is reasonably understandable to participants. The content of informed consent will vary depending on many circumstances; however, informed consent generally implies that the person (1) has the capacity to consent, (2) has been informed of significant information concerning the procedure, (3) has freely and without undue influence expressed consent, and (4) consent has been appropriately documented.

(b) When persons are legally incapable of giving informed consent, psychologists obtain informed permission from a legally authorized person, if such substitute consent is permitted by law.

(c) In addition, psychologists (1) inform those persons who are legally incapable of giving informed consent about the proposed interventions in a manner commensurate with the persons' psychological capacities, (2) seek their assent to those interventions, and (3) consider such persons' preferences and best interests.

4.03   Couple and Family Relationships

(a) When a psychologist agrees to provide services to several persons who have a relationship (such as husband and wife or parents and children), the psychologist attempts to clarify at the outset (1) which of the individuals are patients or clients and (2) the relationship the psychologist will have with each person. This clarification includes the role of the psychologist and the probable uses of the services provided or the information obtained. (See also Standard 5.01, Discussing the Limits of Confidentiality.)

(b) As soon as it becomes apparent that the psychologist may be called on to perform potentially conflicting roles (such as marital counselor to husband and wife, and then witness for one party in a divorce proceeding), the psychologist attempts to clarify and adjust, or withdraw from, roles appropriately. (See also Standard 7.03, Clarification of Role, under Forensic Activities.)

4.04   *Providing Mental Health Services to Those Served by Others*

In deciding whether to offer or provide services to those already receiving mental health services elsewhere, psychologists carefully consider the treatment issues and the potential patient's or client's welfare. The psychologist discusses these issues with the patient or client, or another legally authorized person on behalf of the client, in order to minimize the risk of confusion and conflict, consults with the other service providers when appropriate, and proceeds with caution and sensitivity to the therapeutic issues.

4.05   *Sexual Intimacies with Current Patients or Clients*

Psychologists do not engage in sexual intimacies with current patients or clients.

4.06   *Therapy with Former Sexual Partners*

Psychologists do not accept as therapy patients or clients persons with whom they have engaged in sexual intimacies.

4.07   *Sexual Intimacies with Former Therapy Patients*

(a) Psychologists do not engage in sexual intimacies with a former therapy patient or client for at least two years after cessation or termination of professional services.

(b) Because sexual intimacies with a former therapy patient or client are so frequently harmful to the patient or client, and because such intimacies undermine public confidence in the psychology profession and thereby deter the public's use of needed services, psychologists do not engage in sexual intimacies with former therapy patients and clients even after a two year interval except in the most unusual circumstances. The psychologist who engages in such activity after the two years following cessation or termination of treatment bears the burden of demonstrating that there has been no exploitation, in light of all relevant factors, including (1) the amount of time that has passed since therapy terminated, (2) the nature and duration of the therapy, (3) the circumstances of termination, (4) the patient's or client's personal history, (5) the patient's or client's current mental status, (6) the likelihood of adverse impact on the patient or client and others, and (7) any statements or actions made by the therapist during the course of therapy suggesting or inviting the possibility of a post termination sexual or romantic relationship with the patient or client. (See also Standard 1.17, Multiple Relationships.)

4.08   *Interruption of Services*

(a) Psychologists make reasonable efforts to plan for facilitating care in the event that psychological services are interrupted by factors such as the psychologist's illness, death, unavailability, or relocation or by the client's relocation or financial limitations. (See also Standard 5.09, Preserving Records and Data.)

(b) When entering into employment or contractual relationships, psychologists provide for orderly and appropriate resolution of responsibility for patient or client care in the event that the employment or contractual relationship ends, with paramount consideration given to the welfare of the patient or client.

4.09   *Terminating the Professional Relationship*

(a) Psychologists do not abandon patients or clients. (See also Standard 1.25e, under Fees and Financial Arrangements.)

(b) Psychologists terminate a professional relationship when it becomes reasonably clear that the patient or client no longer needs the service, is not benefiting, or is being harmed by continued service.

(c) Prior to termination for whatever reason, except where precluded by the patient's or client's conduct, the psychologist discusses the patient's or client's views and needs, provides appropriate pretermination counseling, suggests alternative service providers as appropriate, and takes other reasonable steps to facilitate transfer of responsibility to another provider if the patient or client needs one immediately.

5.0   PRIVACY AND CONFIDENTIALITY

These Standards are potentially applicable to the professional and scientific activities of all psychologists.

5.01   *Discussing the Limits of Confidentiality*

(a) Psychologists discuss with persons and organizations with whom they establish a scientific or professional relationship (including, to the extent feasible, minors and their legal representatives) (1) the relevant limitations on confidentiality, including limitations where applicable in group, marital, and family therapy or in organizational consulting, and (2) the foreseeable uses of the information generated through their services.

(b) Unless it is not feasible or is contraindicated, the discussion of confidentiality occurs at the outset of the relationship and thereafter as new circumstances may warrant.

(c) Permission for electronic recording of interviews is secured from clients and patients.

5.02   *Maintaining Confidentiality*

Psychologists have a primary obligation and take reasonable precautions to respect the confidentiality rights of those with whom they work or consult, recognizing that confidentiality may be established by law, institutional rules, or professional or scientific relationships. (See also Standard 6.26, Professional Reviewers.)

5.03   *Minimizing Intrusions on Privacy*

(a) In order to minimize intrusions on privacy, psychologists include in written and oral reports, consultations, and the like, only information germane to the purpose for which the communication is made.

(b) Psychologists discuss confidential information obtained in clinical or consulting relationships, or evaluative data concerning patients, individual or organizational clients, students, research participants, supervisees, and employees, only for appropriate scientific or professional purposes and only with persons clearly concerned with such matters.

5.04   *Maintenance of Records*

Psychologists maintain appropriate confidentiality in creating, storing, accessing, transferring, and disposing of records under their control, whether these are written, automated, or in any other medium. Psychologists maintain and dispose of records in accordance with law and in a manner that permits compliance with the requirements of this Ethics Code.

5.05   *Disclosures*

(a) Psychologists disclose confidential information without the consent of the individual only as mandated by law, or where permitted by law for a valid purpose, such as (1) to provide needed professional services to the patient or the individual or organizational client, (2) to obtain appropriate professional consultations, (3) to protect the patient or client or others from harm, or (4) to obtain payment for services, in which instance disclosure is limited to the minimum that is necessary to achieve the purpose.

(b) Psychologists also may disclose confidential information with the appropriate consent of the patient or the individual or organizational client (or of another legally authorized person on behalf of the patient or client), unless prohibited by law.

5.06   *Consultations*

When consulting with colleagues, (1) psychologists do not share confidential information that reasonably could lead to the identification of a patient, client, research participant, or other person or organization with whom they have a confidential relationship unless they have obtained the prior consent of the person or organization or the disclosure cannot be avoided, and (2) they share information only to the extent necessary to achieve the purposes of the consultation. (See also Standard 5.02, Maintaining Confidentiality.)

5.07   *Confidential Information in Databases*

(a) If confidential information concerning recipients of psychological services is to be entered into databases or systems of records available to persons whose access has not been consented to by the recipient, then psychologists use coding or other techniques to avoid the inclusion of personal identifiers.

(b) If a research protocol approved by an institutional review board or similar body requires the inclusion of personal identifiers, such identifiers are deleted before the information is made accessible to persons other than those of whom the subject was advised.

(c) If such deletion is not feasible, then before psychologists transfer such data to others or review such data collected by others, they take reasonable steps to determine that appropriate consent of personally identifiable individuals has been obtained.

5.08   *Use of Confidential Information for Didactic or Other Purposes*

(a) Psychologists do not disclose in their writings, lectures, or other public media, confidential, personally identifiable information concerning their patients, individual or organizational clients, students, research participants, or other recipients of their services that they obtained during the course of their work, unless the person or organization has consented in writing or unless there is other ethical or legal authorization for doing so.

(b) Ordinarily, in such scientific and professional presentations, psychologists disguise confidential information concerning such persons or organizations so that they are not individually identifiable to others and so that discussions do not cause harm to subjects who might identify themselves.

5.09   Preserving Records and Data

A psychologist makes plans in advance so that confidentiality of records and data is protected in the event of the psychologist's death, incapacity, or withdrawal from the position or practice.

5.10   Ownership of Records and Data

Recognizing that ownership of records and data is governed by legal principles, psychologists take reasonable and lawful steps so that records and data remain available to the extent needed to serve the best interests of patients, individual or organizational clients, research participants, or appropriate others.

5.11   Withholding Records for Nonpayment

Psychologists may not withhold records under their control that are requested and imminently needed for a patient's or client's treatment solely because payment has not been received, except as otherwise provided by law.

8.0   RESOLVING ETHICAL ISSUES

8.01   Familiarity with Ethics Code

Psychologists have an obligation to be familiar with this Ethics Code, other applicable ethics codes, and their application to psychologists' work. Lack of awareness or misunderstanding of an ethical standard is not itself a defense to a charge of unethical conduct.

8.02   Confronting Ethical Issues

When a psychologist is uncertain whether a particular situation or course of action would violate this Ethics Code, the psychologist ordinarily consults with other psychologists knowledgeable about ethical issues, with state or national psychology ethics committees, or with other appropriate authorities in order to choose a proper response.

8.03   Conflicts Between Ethics and Organizational Demands

If the demands of an organization with which psychologists are affiliated conflict with this Ethics Code, psychologists clarify the nature of the conflict, make known their commitment to the Ethics Code, and to the extent feasible, seek to resolve the conflict in a way that permits the fullest adherence to the Ethics Code.

8.04   Informal Resolution of Ethical Violations

When psychologists believe that there may have been an ethical violation by another psychologist, they attempt to resolve the issue by bringing it to the attention of that individual if an informal resolution appears appropriate and the intervention does not violate any confidentiality rights that may be involved.

8.05   Reporting Ethical Violations

If an apparent ethical violation is not appropriate for informal resolution under Standard 8.04 or is not resolved properly in that fashion, psychologists take further action appropriate to the situation, unless such action conflicts with confidentiality rights in ways that cannot be resolved. Such action might include referral to state or national committees on professional ethics or to state licensing boards.

8.06   *Cooperating with Ethics Committees*

Psychologists cooperate in ethics investigations, proceedings, and resulting requirements of the APA or any affiliated state psychological association to which they belong. In doing so, they make reasonable efforts to resolve any issues as to confidentiality. Failure to cooperate is itself an ethics violation.

8.07   *Improper Complaints*

Psychologists do not file or encourage the filing of ethics complaints that are frivolous and are intended to harm the respondent rather than to protect the public.

14

History of Philosophy Papers

Nothing so absurd can be said, that some philosopher has not said it.

—Marcus Tullius Cicero, 106–43 BCE

14.1 THOMAS HOBBES, JOHN LOCKE, AND MICHAEL GREESON

If you mention British philosophers Thomas Hobbes (1588–1679) or John Locke (1632–1704) to philosophy student Michael Greeson, be prepared for a lecture. When it comes to philosophy, Mike Greeson, is a natural. Philosophy is as necessary to Mike's daily life as oxygen; pizza; his wife, Jennifer; and his vivacious children, Madeleine and Jasmine. Because philosophy is Mike's passion it is possible that, generations from now, students will be reading his writings along with those of Hobbes and Locke.

Mike's paper entitled "Hobbes, Locke, and the State of Nature Theories: A Reassessment" is included in this chapter as a sample history of philosophy papers. Written during Mike's junior year at the University of Central Oklahoma, the paper, as Mike readily admits, is not free from error. The authors of this book specifically asked Mike for his original paper, and it is presented here.

Mike was a philosophy major who wrote this paper to fullfill the requirements of a political philosophy class taken through the university's Political Science Department. When the semester was completed, Mike's professor nominated his paper for two awards, both of which he won: The Best Undergraduate Paper Award of the Oklahoma Political Science Association, and the Best Undergraduate

Paper Award of the Southwest Political Science Association. On the basis of these awards and other achievements, Mike was offered entrance to the Master of Arts program in social theory at the University of Chicago, a program he has now completed.

The point of telling you about Mike and his paper is to make it clear that a well-written paper may have benefits beyond those that are immediately foreseeable.

Before presenting Mike's paper, we shall first provide a brief tour of the history of philosophy and some directions that will help you write your own history of philosophy papers. As you read this chapter, think about the topics in philosophy that most interest you and the questions you would most like to tackle.

14.2   A VERY SHORT HISTORY OF THE GREAT PHILOSOPHERS

Music magazines such as *Rolling Stone* and *Living Blues* regularly print "best of" lists that report the choices of magazine readers and, separately, those of music critics. One can spend many delightful hours in conversation trying to understand why readers prefer one guitarist and critics another. The historical figures that you are about to be introduced to would not all appear on my personal list of the ten greatest philosophers. While Emerson and Josiah Royce would be on my personal list, many philosophers would not even include them in their top fifty. So think of the list that follows as analogous to the music critics' list, but remember you can tell quite a bit about philosophers by their references to other philosophers.

One of the earliest philosophers, Xenophanes of Colphon, was born sometime around 565 BCE. Xenophanes was concerned with the nature of god:

> But if cattle or lions had hands, so as to paint with their hands and produce works of art as men do, they would paint their gods and give them bodies in form like their own—horses like horses, cattle like cattle. Ethiopians make their gods black and snub-nosed, Thracians red-haired and with blue eyes. God is one, supreme among gods and men, and not like mortals in body or in mind. (Milton C. Nahm. *Early Greek Philosophy*. New York: Appleton-Century-Crofts, 1964. 84–85.)

What makes Xenophanes a philosopher, and not a satirist or a critic, is that his criticism of received beliefs is coupled with an attempt to provide a reasoned substitute for them. Xenophanes attempts to answer a major question of human existence without appealing to a historical text or tradition. And his attempt at an answer then becomes a suggestion for all reasoning beings and not just for Ethiopians and Thraceans. The god he proposes is a monotheistic god that is identical with the universe. Xenophanes, in other words, was a pantheist. Like Xenophanes, the important historical philosophers are those who propose important alternative answers to one or more of the major questions of human existence.

Buddha is the name by which most of us refer to Siddhartha Gautama. Born around 565 BCE in India, Buddha preached the Four Noble Truths:

- Life is suffering.
- Suffering involves a chain of causes.
- Suffering can cease.
- There is a path to the cessation of suffering.

The path to happiness, or at least to the end of bodily reincarnation and the suffering that accompanies it, can be reached through following the Buddhist ethic called the eightfold path. The eightfold path is based on the view that suffering can be eliminated through the disappearance of the self. And moral selflessness is the path toward eliminating the psychological self and avoiding bodily reincarnation. Buddhist philosophy may be the first example of a religion, a system of beliefs, that includes immortality without the mediation of a god. It certainly does base its ethics upon the human concern to avoid suffering and not upon a version of god's commandments.

Lao-Tzu lived, if he lived at all, during the sixth or fifth century BCE. Lao-Tzu may, like Homer, simply be the name given to serve as the place holder for the authors of a collection of writings derived from a preexisting oral tradition—the Tao. Taoist literature consists of both philosophical and religious writings. You may be familiar with Sun Tzu's *The Tao of War* from your management or political theory courses. The writings ascribed to Lao-Tzu tend to be deterministic in nature, meaning that Lao-Tzu is concerned with the ways in which human beings are inextricably led through their lives by natural forces beyond their control.

Chuang-Tzu lived in the fourth century BCE. His writings are more epistemological than those attributed to Lao-Tzu. Chuang-Tzu was less concerned with determinism and more concerned with the ethical implications of skepticism. Chaung-Tzu seems to recommend skepticism as a road to detachment that occasions happiness. And both his skepticism and the detachment he recommends are radical and nonconformist.

Plato lived between 428 and 347 BCE. He was a student of Socrates, and much of what we attribute to Socrates comes from Plato's depiction of his teacher in his early dialogues. It is difficult to pinpoint what was most important about Plato because he wrote upon so many important topics. Plato constructed a blueprint for a utopian state, attempted to put his theoretical views into practice in Sicily, and eventually, in *The Laws*, wrote another blueprint for the best state possible for human beings. Plato wrote on the nature of art and the implications of artistic freedom for a well-ordered state, and Plato was the first philosopher explicitly to formulate the question of the nature of knowledge. The school he founded, the Academy, guaranteed the continued influence of his thought on Western culture and is still considered by many to be the proper model for a university.

A student of Plato, Aristotle (384–322 BCE) was more empirically minded than his teacher, perhaps because his father was a doctor. Alexander the Great sent Aristotle new animals for study that he encountered in his world conquest. Aristotle's empiricism led him to question Plato's idealist realm of the forms. The forms were the objects in a realm existent beyond sense perception that corresponded to the essential natures of particular items in this world. For instance, the truth that we are all human is guaranteed by our sharing an essential form—humanity. Aristotle believed that the forms existed in particulars and not in an ideal realm. Like Plato, Aristotle wrote on a wide variety of important topics, including the nature of the tragic character and the nature of friendship. His great intelligence, however, did not prevent him from defending slavery and the inequality of the sexes.

Thomas Aquinas lived in Italy from 1225 until 1275. Aquinas, who became a saint of the Catholic Church, tried to demonstrate that the Christian faith was compatible with reason. Revelation provides the details that fill in the religious truth available to all humans through the natural light of reason. He wrote many philosophical commentaries and included Aristotle prominently in his studies. Aquinas provided five proofs of the existence of god. And his ethics, still influential today in secular law as well as Christian ethics, was based on the notion of a natural law revealed to all humans by reason. Aquinas's lasting importance, however, is in two areas: the demonstration of a concern to make religious truth compatible with reason, and the emphasis of Greek concepts of the deity within Christian religion.

When we reach the period that philosophers call modern philosophy, it is more difficult to decide whom to include in our short history of the great philosophers. René Descartes (1596–1650), the French philosopher and mathematician, is an obvious choice. In previous chapters we have noted his views on several important issues. Modern philosophy is usually presented as an ongoing dialogue between representatives of empiricism and rationalism. Locke, Berkeley, and Hume are the empiricists; Descartes, Spinoza, and Leibniz are the rationalists. A good case could be made for including any of these five thinkers, in addition to Descartes, in our list of major philosophers. John Locke is especially important to Americans since, to a large extent, the United States of America is constructed along Lockean lines.

Thomas Hobbes (1588–1679) is the most committed physicalist of the modern philosophers. An Englishman, he wrote an effective set of objections to Descartes's *Meditations* in which Hobbes criticized Descartes's attempt to prove that the mind was made of a mental substance. But Hobbes' primary importance is in his attempt to justify government on the ground that it makes us better off than we would be in a state of nature. And he carefully circumscribes the responsibility of government as protecting lives and property. All advocates of more extensive government responsibilities must confront Hobbes' political thought. And anyone who wonders why nations are justified in interfering in the affairs of other nations to advance their own national interest at the expense of the client state's interest should consult Hobbes' work *Leviathan.*

David Hume (1711–1776), a Scot, was both a philosopher and a historian. Hume is known for his rigorous view of the sources of knowledge. An empiricist, he argued that all knowledge is based in impressions and their faded images, which may be called ideas. Hume's empiricism led him to deny that we have an impression of what men call causality, that is, that one phenomenon causes another. Hume reinterpreted causality to mean a constant conjunction that has become a customary expectation. Hume also posed the philosophical problem of the justification of induction. Basically, Hume noted that induction cannot be used to justify induction, that induction cannot be deductively demonstrated, and that there are no other forms of justification. Hume also formulated an ethics based on empathy that has had a great deal of influence on contemporary ethics, including feminism.

I have now included eight philosophers on the list of the ten most significant historical philosophers. No list of the top ten philosophers should leave out Kant and Hegel. Immanuel Kant (1724–1804), who lived and worked in the Prussian city of Konisberg, wrote important works in every area of philosophy and originated the idea of a universal political body that is embodied in today's United Nations. Kant was concerned with delimiting the role of reason in human knowledge and in religion and ethics. His *Critique of Pure Reason* sought to answer skeptics and empiricists by providing an account of knowledge that is not wholly dependent upon the senses. Kant argued, in part, that for experience to exist at all, some prior knowledge must be brought to experience by a rational creature. Sensation may serve as the occasion for activating this innate knowledge, but it is not the source of the knowledge itself. Kant also argued that although we cannot know objects in themselves independently of our representations of them, we still possess a form of knowledge of the external world. Knowledge, then, is not of objects, but of objects as they conform to our faculty of knowledge.

In ethics, Kant argued for a universal morality based in the categorical imperative. He believed that some moral rules could be shown to imply something like a contradiction, and that such rules must never be accepted. Just as the denial of a contradiction must be true, the denial of a self-refuting moral maxim must be accepted. So if I consider lying to you and saying that I have read every book that Kant wrote, I must first consider whether my moral maxim could be universalized. Could there be lying in a world in which everyone lied? The answer, of course, is no. In such a world people would be unable to lie since no one would believe anything anyone said. Lying, then, is always morally wrong regardless of any consequences that might convince us it is permissible in some special circumstances. Obviously, Kant had a strong sense of the importance of moral duty in living a good life and respecting other human beings.

Finally, the German philosopher Georg Wilhelm Hegel (1770–1831) deserves mention for provoking the incorporation of history into philosophical thought. Hegel sought to acquire metaphysical knowledge of God, or Spirit, in its historical manifestations in social institutions such as the political state. Hegel portrayed human history as passing through necessary stages of advancing and extending human freedom as the Spirit progressed through history. His writings provoked the historical sensitivity of the early work of Karl Marx and the situational commitment of both Christian and atheist existentialists such as Kierkegaard and Nietzsche.

This discussion of philosophers is the barest sort of introduction to the history of philosophy. It is provided only to help you think of the broad range of topics available to you as you set out to find a topic for your paper and to help you select a historically important philosopher whose work may interest and inspire you.

14.3 HOW TO WRITE A HISTORY OF PHILOSOPHY PAPER

Before writing your history of philosophy paper, be sure to read Parts One and Two of this manual. (Reading this material will save you much more time than it takes to read it.) When you do, you will find there is not one set pattern or process for writing papers. A set of basic tasks (described in Chapters 1 and 2) needs to be completed, but you need to experiment to find out how you can best accomplish them.

The first thing to remember when writing a history of philosophy paper is that your paper must make a point, and it must defend it. In other words, your paper must have a clearly defined thesis, and then it must provide the arguments and supporting materials necessary to defend your thesis. As you read Mike Greeson's paper below, you will discover that he has a thesis:

> It is my contention that although Locke painstakingly attempts to disassociate himself with the Hobbesian notion of the "self-interested man" in a perpetual "state of war," the execution of this attempt falls short, and can even be recognized to implicitly (if not explicitly) contain the very reasoning that Hobbes utilizes to advocate the movement of man from the "state of nature" to civil society.

Notice that Mike's thesis is very explicit. His thesis is not "Locke is a good guy," nor is it "Locke is better than Hobbes." Mike has set out to compare the state-of-nature theories of the two philosophers, and his thesis is a definition of the difference between the two theories. Mike has read the commentaries on Locke and Hobbes and on their concepts of the state of nature, and in his paper he discovers a different way of understanding the topic than is present in the literature.

Do not be alarmed! Thousands of interpretations of the works of the great philosophers have been published. You do not need to generate a new interpretation in order to write a good paper. You merely need to evaluate the interpretations that are available and present your reasons for claiming that some are better than others. Mike's interpretation, however, was sufficiently different from previously published ones that he won recognition in the form of state and regional awards. Originality is important, but the most important qualities of a history of philosophy paper are clarity and precision in stating and defending a thesis.

Note that after Mike states his thesis, he immediately tells the reader how he will go about supporting his argument:

> In order to demonstrate the truth of this contention, I will briefly outline the development of their philosophies, and offer both a reinterpretation of the Hobbesian state of nature, and a critical analysis of Locke's view of the state of nature in the Second Treatise.

Although all good history of philosophy papers will define and defend a thesis, they may take any one of three approaches, offering either (1) a study of one aspect of a writer's philosophy, (2) a comparison of two or more philosophers on a selected topic, or (3) a study of a philosophical concept.

If you take the first approach and study a single writer's philosophy, you will want to select a philosopher who has written something you find interesting. Let's suppose that you are interested in discrimination. You may want to investigate Aristotle's view of slavery, or John Stuart Mill's attitude toward women.

The second approach is a comparison of two or more philosophers on a selected topic. In the paper below, Mike Greeson compares the idea of a state of nature in the writings of John Locke and Thomas Hobbes. If you decide to compare, say, Hegel and Kant on the subject of ethics, your paper topic will be too broad, but if you select a particular aspect of ethics, such as the permissible uses of violence, you will be able to get a grasp on the topic.

The third way to write a history of philosophy paper is to select a particular topic, such as freedom, medical ethics, or sexual ethics, and to describe the variety of attitudes toward that subject that are available. If you take this approach, your paper will be much less specific than if you had used one of the first two approaches, but you will be able to sort through many different ideas about a subject and place them in relationship to each other. A paper that describes different concepts of justice, for example, will provide you with an overview that will help you to select more specific topics, such as recidivism or distributive justice, for further research.

14.4   THE CONTENTS OF A HISTORY OF PHILOSOPHY PAPER

History of philosophy papers vary widely in subject matter and approach, but your paper should include the following three elements:

1. Title page
2. Body of the paper

3. Reference page or bibliography

Abstracts, tables of contents, and appendices are not normally needed.

14.5   A SAMPLE HISTORY OF PHILOSOPHY PAPER

Hobbes, Locke, and the State of Nature Theories:

A Reassessment*

Michael P. Greeson

University of Central Oklahoma

Most of the great works in political philosophy were written as a response to or as a result of a particular historical context. As Hegel points out, whatever happens to the philosopher, each individual is "a child of his time."[1] If this be true, the 17th century provided ample cause for philosophic reflection: the turmoil of civil war and violent shifts of political power, combined with a new intellectual climate that emphasized science and reason over supernatural explanation helped to cultivate the thoughts and passions of many brilliant political philosophers.

Two of the most critical and influential of these thinkers were Thomas Hobbes and John Locke. For both philosophers, political society, in its most general sense, was the result of certain fundamental human motivations, a natural extension of certain metaphysical first principles of the universe. Natural rights theorists from Hobbes to Kant (and

*This is the original paper submitted as a class assignment. A substantially revised version of this paper was published as "Hobbes, Locke, and the State of Nature Theories: A Reassessment" in Episteme Vol. 5, May 1994, 1–15.

even more recently Rawls) typically have claimed to discover the most universal features of human beings by means of a kind of thought experiment, hypothetically stripping or peeling away everything we have acquired through the influence of custom, history, and tradition in order to discover the pre-political state of nature and the natural man behind it.[2]

Both Hobbes and Locke utilize this "state of nature" construct to elucidate their views on human nature and politics.[3] Yet the common conception of their views of man's original condition in the state of nature is usually contrasted: the political philosophy of the Second Treatise paints man as a "pretty decent fellow," far removed from the quarrelsome, competitive, selfish creatures found in Hobbes' Leviathan. Lockean man seems to be more naturally inclined to civil society, supposedly more governed by reason. From this interpretation of human nature, it follows logically that the state of nature was no "condition of war" and anarchy as Hobbes has argued.[4]

Locke states in the Second Treatise:

> Where we have the plain difference between the state
> of nature and the state of war, however some men have
> confounded [Locke's reference here is probably to
> Hobbes' concept of the state of nature as being
> "identical" with the state of war], are as far dis-
> tant as a state of peace, goodwill, mutual assistance
> and preservation, and a state of enmity, malice, vio-
> lence, and mutual destruction are one from another.[5]

It is my contention that although Locke painstakingly attempts to disassociate himself with the Hobbesian notion of the "self-interested man" in a perpetual "state of war," the execution of this attempt falls short, and can even be recognized to implicitly (not explicitly) contain the very reasoning that Hobbes utilizes to advocate the movement of man from the "state of nature" to civil society.

In order to demonstrate the truth of this contention, I will briefly outline the development of their philosophies, and offer both a reinterpretation of the Hobbesian state of nature, and a critical analysis of Locke's view of the state of nature in the Second Treatise.

1. Hobbes: Method and Problem

Thomas Hobbes is thought to have been influenced by such Enlightenment luminaries as Galileo, René Descartes, and Francis Bacon. Though the influence of Bacon is often held in highest standing, his teachings left little trace on Hobbes' own matured thought. Hobbes barely mentions Bacon in his own writings and has no real place for "Baconian induction" in his own concept of scientific method.[6]

Scientific method, for Hobbes, has two branches: synthesis, or deductive logic, and analysis, or inductive logic [this is contrary to contemporary logical distinctions, in that "synthetic" truths are usually said to be the result of inductive argument--"analytic" truths are said to be the result of deductive relations]; only the former, the purely deductive type of reasoning, is rigidly certain and yields "perfectly determinate" conclusions.[7] Hobbes was particularly taken with the resolutio-compositive method, which he appropriated from Galileo. According to this method, complex phenomena are broken down into their simplest natural mo-

tions and components. Once these elements are understood,
the workings of complex wholes are easily derived. Hobbes'
intent was to develop a systematic study in three parts,
starting with simple motions in matter (De Corpore), moving
to the study of human nature (De Homine), and finally to
politics (De Cive), each based, respectively, on a lower
level of analysis.[8] Hence, reality for Hobbes is reducible
to mechanistic and material principles, or, simply stated,
bodies in motion. If we are to understand politics, we
should look at such phenomena in terms of the relationships
between men in motion.

   Furthermore, Hobbes adopted the Galilean proposition
that that which is in motion continues in motion until altered by some other force [of course, this is a theoretical
assumption which, independently, cannot be proven true or
false, since all we do observe are bodies that are acted upon
by such forces]. Likewise, Hobbes assumed that human beings
act voluntarily based upon their passions, until resisted by
another force or forces. This outward motion of the individual is the first beginning of voluntary motion, which Hobbes
calls "endeavor." Insofar as this voluntary motion creates
vital, physical motion, endeavor is directed toward an object, as so is called "appetite" or "desire." Insofar as this
voluntary motion hinders vital motion, endeavor is directed
away from the object, and is called "aversion."[9]

   The several passions of man are "species" of desires and
aversion, and directed toward those objects whose effects
enhance vital motion, and away from those objects which im-
pede vital motion. Thus, Hobbes conceives men to be self-

maintaining engines whose motion is such that it enables them to continue to "move" as long as continued motion is possible.[10]

From this account of vital and voluntary motion, it logically follows, at least according to Hobbes, that each man in the state of nature seeks, and seeks only, to preserve and strengthen himself. A concern for continued well-being is both the necessary and sufficient ground of human action; hence, man is necessarily selfish.[11]

It is this perpetual endeavor for self-preservation within the state of nature which gives rise to a condition of war. Hobbes believes that men, being originally all equal in the "faculties of the body and mind,"[12] equally hope to fulfill their ends of vital motion. Hence, if "two men desire the same thing, which nevertheless they cannot both enjoy, they become enemies,"[13] for both, knowing natural law (i.e., natural moral law, as opposed to natural physical law), would be privy to the unconditional, absolute, and categorical command (or right) to preserve oneself at all cost. This state of war encompasses all, "everyone against everyone."[14] And without a common power to police them and settle disputes, man is in a perpetual condition of war; "war consisting not only in battle, or in the act of fighting, but in a willingness to contend by battle being sufficiently recognized."[15] The state of nature is seen as a condition in which the will to fight others is known, fighting not infrequent, and each individual perceives that his life and well-being are in constant danger.[16] Accordingly, men in the state of nature live without security, other than their own strength; this is argued to be the natural condition of mankind, and leads Hobbes to the conclusion that such existence is "natural" to man, but not rational [whereas society is seen as rational, but not natural, contra Aristotle].[17]

It is within this irrational condition of "war," or Hobbesian "fear" or "despair," in which human beings find little hope of attaining their ends without conflict, that mortal men are compelled to elect a sovereign and move out of the state of nature; only then can the imperative of self-preservation be truly fulfilled through peace.[18] It is important to note that the "state of nature," for Hobbes, is a philosophic device employed as a means of hypothesizing about human behavior in a pre-political and pre-social state, i.e., a state without any external constraint on behavior. As Hobbes indicates, it is not necessary to presume such a state actually existed, only that it captures essential features human beings would naturally exhibit.

Hobbes political philosophy was greeted in his own day by nearly universal rejection, being more often renounced than actually read. Hobbes was labeled an atheist, the "monster of Malmesbury," a schemer, a heretic, and a blasphemer.[19] His advocacy of an absolute monarch as the solution to man's inherent condition further distanced him from the "enlightened" mainstream of 17th century political thought, including the philosophy of John Locke. It is a commonly held view that although Locke makes no specific mention of Hobbes in the <u>Second Treatise,</u> it may nonetheless be interpreted as an attempt to systematically refute both the notion of absolute monarchy and Hobbes' description of the state of nature.[20]

2. John Locke: Method and Problem

In the words of George Santayana, John Locke "at home was the ancestor of that whole school of polite moderate opinion, which can unite liberal Christianity with mechanical science and psychological idealism. He was invincibly rooted in prudential morality, in a rationalized Protestantism, in respect for liberty and law."[21] Locke adopted what he himself called a "plain, historical method," fit, in his own words, "to be brought into well-bred company and polite conversation."[22] (Not the personality to let truth be an offending factor!)

Philosophy, Locke tells the reader in the introduction of his Essay Concerning Human Understanding, is "nothing but true knowledge of things." Properly, philosophy contains the whole of knowledge, which Locke himself divides into three parts: a physics or natural philosophy (the study of things as they are), practice or moral philosophy, and logic, the "doctrine of signs." The aim of the philosopher is to erect as complete a system as he possibly can within these three categories.[23]

Yet Locke persuasively argues in the Essay that mankind's ability to gain true knowledge is significantly limited, and set himself the task of determining the demarcations of human knowledge. To help mankind rid itself of this "unfortunate" failing, he argues that man has been blessed with capacities and talents sufficient to enable him to live a useful and profitable life. The <u>Essay</u> is severely practical and utilitarian: we should concentrate on what we can know, and not waste our energy or effort searching for knowledge of things which lie beyond us.[24] (For Locke, there exists very little knowledge that is certain.)

It is exactly these practical and utilitarian ends that motivated the construction of his moral and political philosophy; although political and moral philosophy are not reducible to metaphysical principles that apply outside of their respective herds of inquiry, in all of his writings Locke assumes, fundamentally, that man knows enough to live a good and righteous life if he so chooses.

Locke's political philosophy is to be found in his <u>Two Treatises of Civil Government</u>. Locke directs his writing against two lines of absolutist argument: the <u>First Treatise</u> was directed against the patriarchal theory of divine right monarchy given by Sir Robert Filmer; the <u>Second Treatise</u>, as previously indicated, against the line of argument for absolutism presented in Hobbes' <u>Leviathan</u>.[25] My focus will concern itself primarily with Locke's <u>Second Treatise</u>.

Locke argued that the state of nature was not identical to the state of war, and that although it was "inconvenient," nature was governed by a natural law known by reason, the "common rule and measure God has given mankind." Furthermore, the natural law "teaches all mankind who will but consult it that, being all equal and independent, no one ought to harm another in his life, health, liberty or property."[26] If the law of nature is observed, the state of nature remains peaceful; conventional wisdom defines this condition as one of mutual-love (via the "judicious" Hooker), from whence are "derived the great maxims of justice and charity."[27]

Yet, according to Locke, God has instilled in natural man "strong obligation of necessity, convenience, and inclination to drive him into society"[28]; hence, men quit their "natural power, resigned it up into the hands of the community"[29] for the assurance that property, in the Lockean sense, will be preserved, for that is the aim of all government.[30]

Men being, as has been said, by nature free, equal, and independent, no one can be put out of this estate and subjected to the political power of another without his own consent. The only way whereby any one divests himself of his natural liberty and puts on the bonds of civil society is by agreeing with other men to join and unite into a community for their comfortable, safe, and peaceable living one amongst another, in a secure enjoyment of their properties and a greater security against any that are not of it.[30] (A classic statement of libertarianism!)

An equally important factor motivating men to forfeit the perfect freedom of the state of nature, is that within this environment, each man has a right to interpret natural law for himself, and to punish what he judges to be violations of it.[32] Anyone who violates another's right to life, liberty, or property, has placed himself in a state of war, and the innocent party has the right to destroy those who act against him because those that are waging war do not live under the rule of reason, and, as a result, have no other rule but that of force and violence;[34] furthermore, this state of war would be perpetual if justice could not be fairly administered.[35]

Therefore, in order to avoid a state of war, Locke suggests that one must forfeit the state of nature, creating an environment where disputes can be decided upon by an impartial authority.[36] It would seem, at least upon prima facie analysis, that although both thinkers utilize a "state of nature" device to demonstrate political necessity, their similarities would end there. Hobbes' state of nature would seem to be populated by self-interested egoists whose personal gain is ultimately important; whereas, Locke appears to suggest that a "civil" nature permeates pre-civil society to such an event that man is voluntarily obliged to respect his fellow human beings, and the formation of civil society soon follows.

The common conception regarding the state of nature theories of Thomas Hobbes and John Locke is thus presented. I shall now turn to the arguments as to why this conception is invalid, beginning with a reassessment of Hobbes' position, followed by specific arguments regarding Locke's notion of pre-political man's motivation to pursue civil ends.

3. Reassessing Hobbes

To understand morality and politics, Hobbes argues that you must understand man qua man: hence, psychology becomes the necessary foundation of moral and political science. And the only way to view mankind in its most natural condition is to assume a hypothetical state of nature in which men act purely out of passion, void of reason (at least initially).

Hobbes' account of the state of nature, as shown in Chapter Seventeen of <u>Leviathan</u>, was expressly designed to provide a glimpse of man without the garb of convention, tradition, or society, so as to uncover the underlying principles of the mundane equity of natural man, without assuming an transcendent purpose or will.[37]

Therefore, Hobbes' prescription for stability was a deduction from the necessary behavior of man in a theoretical society, not emphasizing how men ought to act, but rather how they would act void of any relationships, whatsoever. It is in this condition that our endeavors dispose us towards pleasure or pain, man, being concerned with only those endeavors which serve to preserve himself, chooses those objects which meet this condition. Hence, man would find himself often in competition with others for the same objects, and a state of war would ensue, with each having the 'right to everything' he wishes. (Keep in mind, the aim of Hobbes is not to suggest that we can actually observe such a condition, or that it is even remotely possible; this is merely a fundamental axiom in Hobbes' thought experiment.)

Historically, the negative interpretation of this condition of nature, being a "war of all against all," has been dominant in political and philosophical circles. Sterling Lamprecht defines the common conception of Hobbes' descriptive psychology as follows:

God made man such a beast and a rascal that he inclines universally to malice and fraud. Man's typical acts, unless he is restrained by force, are violent and ruthless, savagely disregarding the persons and property of his fellows. His greatest longing is to preserve himself by gaining power over others and exploiting others for his own egoistic ends.[38]

Lamprecht labels this view "Hobbism" and argues that in this view of human nature, Hobbes is far from being a Hobbist. Hobbes gives, to be sure, a picture of man in the state of nature which is far from flattering. But, Lamprecht argues, Hobbes did not intend to say that his picture of man in the state of nature is a complete account of human nature. The concept of man in the state of nature enables us to measure the extent to which reason and social pressures qualify the expression of human passions. The idea of man in the state of nature is for social science like that of natural body in physical science. Physical science holds that a body continues in a state of rest or uniform motion in a straight line unless influenced by outside forces. Actually, there is no body which is not influenced by outside bodies; but the idea of such a body enables us to measure the outside forces.[39]

Such a "natural man" would be observable whenever one operates wholly under the dominion of passion, without the "restraint," or to use Hobbes' language, "the opposing force" of reason. Man, acting on his own, with no concern for others' self-preservation, guided by short-term considerations only, is doomed to failure in a state of nature. But if long-term moral, political, or social arrangements enable them to maintain themselves without facing a war of all against all, then the basic cause for hostility is removed.[40] In fact, the whole concern of Hobbes' moral and po-

litical philosophy is to show men the way out of this short-
term condition of war and into a long-term condition of
peace. Whatever we may think of Hobbes' theoretical view of
human nature, it must not be forgotten for a moment that its
object is not the repudiation of law and morality, but the
vindication of them as the only safeguards against general
anarchy and misery.[41]

David Gauthier, in his treatise entitled <u>The Logic Of
Leviathan</u>, states this argument most eloquently:

> In the beginning everyman has an unlimited right to do,
> conceiving it to be for his preservation. But the exer-
> cise of this unlimited right is one of the causes of the
> war of all against all, which is inimical to preserva-
> tion. Thus the unlimited right of nature proves contra-
> dictory in its use; the man who exercises his right in
> order to preserve himself contributes thereby to the war
> of all against all, which tends to his own destruction.
> And so it is necessary to give up some part of the unlim-
> ited natural right.[42]

The fundamental law of nature is

that every man ought to endeavor peace, as far as he has
hope of obtaining it. The law is the most general conclusion man derives from his experience of the war of all
against all. Clearly it depends on that experience,
whether real or imagined. Although hypothetically a man
might conclude that it was necessarily inimical to human
life, only an analysis of the human condition with all
social bonds removed shows that peace is the primary req-
uisite for preservation.[43]

The salvation of mankind, for Hobbes, depends on the fact that though nature has placed him in an unpleasant condition, it has also endowed him with the possibility to come out of it, as revealed through the use of reason! It is not merely the passion of fearing death, but the rational desire to pursue those avenues ending in commodious living, in an environment in which the hope of actually obtaining them is real. Furthermore, reason suggests convenient articles of peace, upon which men may be drawn to agreement and social contract; to argue that the state of nature, for Hobbes, is devoid of rationality or reason is to miss the point: it is a necessary ingredient to lead man out of the state of nature and into a civil society. Hobbes' vision of nature might be but a limited guide; his picture shows us an important, but partial truth. It is a truth which we must endeavor to overcome--but we shall not overcome it if we misunderstand it, deny it, or ignore it.

4. Locke and Political Motivation

What follows are several arguments which independently suggest that the Lockean state of nature implicitly admits of a Hobbesian condition of war, for Locke himself views conflict as the primary motivating factor that necessarily compels man to leave the state of nature, and enter civil society. Initially, is important to establish a fundamental point of difference between these two theories: Locke's "state of nature" was pre-political (i.e., prior to common authority), whereas, for Hobbes, it was pre-social. Locke refers to a situation in which a collection of men living within a given region are not subject to political author-

ity, not a situation in which there exists no form of rudi-
mentary organization, much less an organized society.[44]
Hobbes uses the expression "state of nature" to denote a
situation in which men do not live in any form of society at
all, regardless of how fundamental. Furthermore, his definition tells us what people would be like if they could be di-
vested of all their learned responses or culturally induced
behavior patterns, especially those such as loyalty, patrio-
tism, religious fervor or class honor that frequently could
override the "fear" that Hobbes speaks of so dramatically in
pre-civil society.[45]

　　If we were to assume man as existing pre-socially, as
Hobbes does (a condition without trade, without the arts,
without knowledge, without any account of time, without society itself), it seems a rather intuitive implication that
he might be motivated by only self-centered drives, for that
would be the extent of his learned behavior within this condition. Locke, on the other hand, takes social and cultural
bonds for granted, and argues purely from a pre-political
position. Even a hypothetical Lockean might act a bit more
selfishly in a Hobbesian state of nature; once semantic dis-
crepancies are taken into account, these definitions already
begin to appear closer to agreement.[46]

　　Secondly, Locke's position seems to be a normative prescription, as opposed to a factual or theoretical description. For example: in Chapter 11, Section 6 of the Second
Treatise, Locke argues that through reason, those who consult the law of nature will learn that no one "ought" to
harm another's life, liberty or possessions. This phrasing
seems to suggest a normative position, prescribing how man

should live in a state of nature, versus the descriptive account that Hobbes constructs upon his theoretical premises. These positions are not mutually exclusive: one can still observe pre-civil man in a Hobbesian state of nature, and morally prescribe a Lockean state of nature as a more "civil" alternative.

Thirdly, Locke seems to provide evidence for the Hobbesian assumption that man often acts out of selfishness and criminal intent.

Initially, Locke seems somewhat ambiguous about precisely what motivates the man of nature to move to civil society: he states that God has instilled a "strong obligation of necessity, convenience and inclination to drive him into society." But why would man leave a state of nature that, at least according to Locke, provides him the ultimate liberty and power over his destiny, a condition that he likens to "a state of peace, good-will, mutual assistance and preservation"?

If man in the state of nature be so free, as has been said, if he be absolute lord of his own person and possessions, equal to the greatest, and subject to nobody, why will he part with his freedom, why will he give up his empire and subject himself to the dominion and control of any other power? To which it is obvious to answer that though in the state of nature he has such a right, yet the enjoyment of it is very uncertain and constantly exposed to the invasion of others; for all being king as much as he, every man his equal, and the greater part no strict observers of equity and justice, the enjoyment of property he has in this state is very unsafe, very unsecure. This makes him willing to quit a condition which, however free, is full of fear and continual dangers.[47]

He continues: "Were it not for the corruption and viciousness of degenerate men, there would be no need of any other [law], no necessity that men should separate from this great and natural community."[48]

If Locke's state of nature is truly as "rational" and "concerned" as he suggests, why is the only motivating factor powerful enough to move men out of this condition that which he so vehemently denies exists: a Hobbesian condition of "war"? Locke clearly states in the Second Treatise that one of the natural rights that must be granted to all men in the state of nature, equally, is that since there exists no common judge to settle controversies between men, man should interpret this natural law for himself and decide upon appropriate punishment for the offenders. This is a fundamental natural right for Locke, and it is precisely this intuitive and pre-political knowledge of the natural law that is said to enlighten man to the burdens of civil society.

Yet Locke argues persuasively that any knowledge of a natural law is more often than not hindered due to mankind's inherent epistemic limitations. Man's own unquenchable and boundless curiosity itself becomes a hindrance. Richard Aaron uses the words of Locke's Essay to demonstrate this point:

Thus men, extending their inquiries beyond their capacities and letting their thoughts wander into these depths where they can find no sure footing, 'tis no wonder they raise questions and multiply disputes, which never coming to any clear resolution, are proper only to continue and increase their doubts and to confirm them at last in perfect skepticism.[49]

Even if one accepted that a natural law existed, Locke's clear rejection of man's ability to know this law with any degree of certainty, combined with his suggestion that foreknowledge of such a law does not guarantee moral action, would seem to suggest a condition of skepticism and disagreement. (Note: this position is strikingly similar to Hobbes' argument that although human reason is capable of discerning the laws of nature, mankind is unable to consistently follow the dictates of such reason.[50]) In fact, one of the strongest arguments that Locke proposes to reject the divine right theory of Sir Robert Filmer in the First Treatise is based upon the notion that even if a right of succession had been determined by a law of nature, our knowledge of natural law is limited to such a degree that there remains no persuasive reason to accept one explanation over another.

Furthermore, such subjective interpretations of the natural law would logically imply an unfairly administered and inconsistent justice. Locke continues:

For every one in the state of nature being both judge and executioner, of the laws of nature, men being partial to themselves, passion and revenge is very apt to carry them too far with too much heat in their own cases, as well as negligence and unconcernedness to make them remiss in other men's.[51]

This seems contradictory to an environment of peace and fellowship, and Locke strongly suggests that a state of war would exist if justice could not be fairly administered.

Consider this: for Locke, in the absence of a neutral judge, no one can accurately know truthfully whether his cause is right or wrong. Thus, everyone is at liberty to believe himself right. Patrick Colby provides a case in point:

> If one person fears his neighbor, whether with cause or without (for only an individual can judge), by this partial and subjective determination the neighbor becomes a wild beast and is lawfully destroyed But when the neighbor, now the target of attack, might understandably conclude that his assailant is the wild beast and so endeavor to execute the law of nature against him.[52]

But this means that Locke's state of nature will not divide neatly into groups of "upright law-abiders and selfish malefactors." And if a distinction cannot be made between such individuals, it would seem impossible for justice to be administered effectively. Locke provides such a conclusion: "The inconveniences that they are therein exposed by the irregular and uncertain exercise of the power every man has of punishing the transgressions of others make them take sanctuary under the law of government."[53]

Locke makes it clear from the beginning of his argument and increasingly as he progresses that because judgment and punishment are in the hands of every man, the state of nature works very poorly.[54] And in the state of nature, conflict (or a willingness to contend by conflict), once begun, and once unable to achieve a satisfactory resolution, would tend to continue to a harsh ending, because there exists no authority to subject both parties to the fair determination of the law.[55]

This potential inconsistency in the application of natural law seems, for Locke, to create significant enough hardships to motivate man to civil society:

> I easily grant that civil government is the proper remedy
> for the inconveniences of the state of nature, which must
> certainly be great where men may be judges in thief own
> case; since it is easy to be imagined that he who was to
> be unjust as to do his brother an injury will scarce be
> so just as to condemn himself for it.[56]

Clearly, Locke's state of nature, if not absolutely equivalent to Hobbes' state of nature, is at the very least a place of extreme anxieties, inconveniences, inequality, and fear of the potential outbreak of war. Locke provides convincing evidence that the state of nature would be so dangerous and unhappy, and the preservation of one's right to life so precarious, that the law of nature commands that the state of nature be abandoned for civil society.[57] Though Locke suggests that his state of nature is not a Hobbesian condition of "war," a closer examination of this argument would tend to suggest that without the failure of nature to guarantee a secure peace, mankind would never voluntarily choose to forfeit his absolute freedom. Jean Faurot provides support:

> But [Locke's] state of nature also includes a condition
> scarcely distinguishable from that which Hobbes describes

as a state of war--all that is needed is for some man to act contrary to reason, because in the state nature every man is obligated to punish evildoers in this way, war begins, with the right on the side of the innocent to destroy the evildoer, or, if he prefers, to enslave him. Nor is there any end to this condition in the state of nature, where every man is both judge and executioner. The slightest disagreement is enough to set men fighting, and the victory of the righteous is never secure. Therefore, men have the strongest reasons for leaving the state of nature and entering civil society.[58]

Hence, not only do I argue that this state of nature corresponds to Hobbes' notion of a condition of perpetual fear, or the "state of war," but it actually becomes the identical catalyst by which Lockean man justifies movement to civil society.

Conclusion

The point of this presentation is clear: the common conception of John Locke as the political propounder of the polite school of positive, optimistic descriptive psychology is an inaccurate characterization. Furthermore, the also-common contrasting of Locke's view of man in the state of nature with Hobbes' theoretical consideration of natural man has traditionally been misunderstood. Hobbes did not concern himself with a "plain, historical method," or with impressing "well-bred company" with "polite conversation." His concerns were with discovering the true nature of mankind so as to devise a system of government (albeit monarchial) that would best serve mankind's inherent drive for both self-preservation and peace.

Men enter civil society because the state of nature tends to deteriorate into a condition of unrest and insecurity if all men were rational and virtuous, apprehending and obeying a natural law, there would be no problem. The presence of merely a few men acting in opposition to reason creates a condition of instability and provides the necessary impetus for, in Locke's words, "reasonable part of positive agreement," a social contract.[59]

Whether one accepts a reinterpretation of Hobbes' theoretical state of nature construct, or a closer examination of Locke's arguments, it is clear that, although not identical, their analyses offer many striking similarities. And, more importantly, without the instability and fear in the state of nature, neither philosopher could logically infer movement from nature to civil society: it becomes the necessary, perhaps sufficient cause for any social contract.

Therefore, the classical juxtaposition of Hobbes' and Locke's "state of nature" theories is at best questionable, and far from convincing.

Notes

1. G. W. F. Hegel, <u>Hegel's Philosophy of Right</u>, trans. T. M. Knox (Oxford: Oxford Univ. Press, 1967), 2.

2. The use of terminology such as "man" or "mankind" within the context of this paper is not intended to be gender-specific (i.e, to exclude feminine denotations). Due to the language of both Hobbes and Locke in their discussion of political philosophy, I felt it best to likewise utilize such wording.

3. Lewis P. Hinchman, "The Origin of Human Rights: A Hegelian Perspective," Western Political Quarterly 37 (March 1984): 9.

4. John Locke, The Second Treatise of Government, ed. Thomas P. Peardon (New York: Bobbs-Merill, 1952), XII.

5. Ibid., 12.

6. A. E. Taylor, Thomas Hobbes (Port Washington, NY: Kennikat Press, 1970), 6.

7. Ibid., 34.

8. Joseph Lasco and Leonard Williams, Political Theory: Classic Writings, Contemporary Views (New York: St Martin's, 1992), 230.

9. David P. Gauthier, The Logic of Leviathan (Oxford: Clarendon Press, 1969), 6.

10. Ibid., 10.

11. Ibid., 7.

12. Thomas Hobbes, Leviathan, intro. Richard S. Peters (New York: Macmillan, 1962), 100.

13. Ibid., 98.

14. Roman M. Lemos, Hobbes and Locke (Atlanta: Univ. of Georgia Press, 1978), 73.

15. Hobbes, Leviathan, 100.

16. Ibid., 100.

17. Gregory S. Kavka, "Hobbes' War Against All," Ethics 83 (1983): 292.

18. Lemos, 24.

19. Sterling P. Lamprecht, Introduction to De Cive, by Thomas Hobbes (New York: Appleton-Century-Krofts, 1949), xx.

20. Lemos, 74.

21. George Santayana, "Locke and the Frontiers of Common Sense" in <u>Some Turns of Thought in Modern Philosophy</u> (New York: Books for Libraries Press, 1933), 4.

22. Ibid., 6.

23. Richard Aaron, <u>John Locke</u> (Oxford: Clarendon Press, 1967), 77.

24. Ibid., 77.

25. Though conventional wisdom validates this line of reasoning, recent scholarship has brought forth historical, biographical, and philosophic evidence to suggest that both Treatises were written as a call to revolution prior to the Glorious Revolution of 1688, and not as a response to Hobbes' philosophy. See Peter Laslett's introduction to Locke's <u>Two Treatises</u> (Cambridge, 1967), and Ruth Grant's <u>John Locke's Liberalism</u> (Chicago, 1987).

26. Locke, 4.

27. Ibid., 4.

28. Ibid., 44.

29. Ibid., 48.

30. Ibid., 53.

31. Ibid., 53.

32. Lemos, 85.

33. Locke, 11.

34. Ibid., 11.

35. Ibid., 13.

36. Ibid., 14.

37. Lasco and Williams, 252.

38. Lamprecht, xx.

39. Ibid., xi.

40. Gauthier, 18.

41. Ibid., 161; Taylor, 71.

42. Gauthier, 51.

43. Ibid., 52.

44. Lemos, 89.

45. Hinchman, 10.

46. A. John Simmons, "Locke's State of Nature," <u>Political Theory</u> 17 (1989): 450.

47. Locke, 71.

48. Ibid., 72.

49. Aaron, 77.

50. Lamprecht, 37.

51. Ibid., 71.

52. Patrick Colby, "The Law of Nature in Locke's Second Treatise," <u>Review of Politics</u> 49 (Winter 1987): 3.

53. Locke, 71.

54. Robert Godwin, "Locke's State of Nature in Political Societies," <u>Western Political Quarterly</u> 29 (March 1976): 126.

55. Ibid., 127.

56. Locke, 9.

57. Lemos, 18.

58. Jean H. Faurot, <u>Problems of Political Philosophy</u> (Scranton, PA: Chandler Publishing, 1970), 75.

59. Ibid., 75.

Glossary of Philosophic Terms

Act Utilitarianism   The belief that the expected consequences of an action should be weighed in each situation before embracing one option as the moral one (see *Rule Utilitarianism*)

ad hoc   Latin for "to this" or "to this purpose"; in philosophy, a part of an argument that is fabricated only to serve an immediate purpose and has not been demonstrated to have independent value through added explanatory power or testable predictions

ad hominem   Latin for "to the man"; an informal fallacy committed in an argument by attacking one's opponent personally instead of attacking his or her position

aesthetics   The branch of philosophy that attempts to define, describe, and evaluate art

agnosticism   Conviction that, while a deity may exist, there can be no absolute proof of the deity's existence or non-existence. An agnostic suspends judgment on the existence or non-existence of God as opposed to an atheist who denies God's existence

agape   In Christian philosophy, the term describing the unconditional love that God feels toward humanity; contrasts with other forms of love

akrasia   Greek for "lack of self control"; an inability to do what one knows is right, due to lack of will

altruism   The belief that one should do what is best for others; usually accompanied by the belief that humans may have altruistic motives; holds that unselfish acts are accomplished for unselfish, rather than selfish, reasons

anarchism   The belief that no organized government has the right to coerce its citizens into any action; a rejection of all forms of externally imposed authority

animism   The belief, found in many primitive religions and some philosophical religions, that all things, animate and inanimate, possess a soul

a posteriori   Latin for "from what follows"; arrived at from experience and observation; a method of reaching a conclusion through reasoning from particular facts to general principles; see also *a priori*

a priori   Latin for "from before"; a method of reaching a conclusion independently of experience. Sometimes a priori knowledge is based on the meanings of terms, as when one knows from the meaning of the word triangle—independently of experiencing an actual triangle—that is has three angles and three sides. Such tacit knowledge is constitutive of experience; see also *a posteriori*.

Aristotle   384–322 B.C.E.; Plato's student, thought by some to be the greatest philosopher; concerned with formalizing the approach to argument begun by Plato and Socrates; a major influence on medieval Christian thought

artificial intelligence   Also commonly known as "A. I."; a field of study which builds or theorizes about machines capable of mimicking human thought. Some A.I. advocates believe that intelligent machines must exhibit human thought; others believe that machines are intelligent if they exhibit any kind of problem solving ability.

atheism   The belief that there is no deity

begging the question   Another term for "circular reasoning," a type of faulty argument in which a form of the conclusion to be established is used in the premises

behaviorism   An approach to the study of the mind that focuses on the observation of external behavior

best of all possible worlds   A phrase from the German mathematician and philosopher Gottfried Leibniz (1646–1716), who argued that, since the world was created by a deity who was perfect and whose works were perfect, then despite all appearances the world is the best of all possible worlds; an idea often treated with derision, as in Voltaire's fantasy novel *Candide*. Leibnitz believed that free will was a condition of the best of all possible worlds and explained why the best world contained suffering and evil.

bioethics   Ethical positions and arguments concerning biological and medical issues, such as abortion and genetic engineering

Buddha   Siddharta Gautama, the Buddha, 563–483 B.C.E.; founder of the philosophical and religious tradition known as Buddhism, based on the Four Noble Truths. Buddhism seeks to transcend the suffering and contingency of human life through the elimination of the individual self and human desires to attain the state of enlightenment or nirvana.

Buridan's ass   The central actor in a story designed to illustrate a problem inherent in the concept that one should do only what seems to be of the greatest good: the hungry ass who, finding itself equidistant from two sources of hay, finds neither source more desirable and so, unable to move in either direction, starves to death

Cartesian doubt   Referring to Descartes' process of assuming that any belief capable of being doubted is false—the first step toward discovering a point of certainty

categorical imperative   Immanuel Kant's phrase for an absolute command, something one must always do regardless of circumstance, such as "Tell the truth"

circular reasoning   See *begging the question;* reasoning that is faulty because it assumes without reasonable evidence the truth of the statement, in whole or in part, which it is trying to defend

civil disobedience   An act contrary to the law, performed in the belief that it is morally acceptable to disobey civil authority in matters where it comes in conflict with one's perceived notions of the moral law, which is generally held to follow from the authority of God or personal conscience.

consequentialism   An ethical position which holds that the consequences of an action determine whether that action is morally right or wrong

contemplation   The act of meditating in a manner that reveals ultimate reality and value

cosmology   Theorizing about the origins, the elements, and the structure of the cosmos

creationism   A would-be theory, common to many fundamentalist religions, that the world was created by a deity who intended its elements to be as they are, in opposition to the theory of evolution, which argues for the random beginning and development of life through natural selection

deduction   A form of argument which holds that if the premises of an argument are true, its conclusion must be true, in contrast to inductive argument, which argues that in such a case, the conclusion is only probably true. Example of deduction: All bulldogs breathe air; Iris is a bulldog; therefore, Iris breathes air. Example of induction: All bulldogs heretofore observed breathe air; Iris is a bulldog; therefore, Iris probably breathes air.

deontology   A system of ethical theories which emphasize the importance of duty to making the moral choice

Descartes, René   1596–1650; French philosopher who, by contending that philosophy, independently of revealed religion, could discover the foundations of truth, founded modern philosophy (see *Cartesian doubt*)

determinism   The position that all things (actions, personality traits, natural phenomena) are caused by antecedent factors which are, perhaps, knowable but beyond mediation, so that all things must be as they are

dilemma   A problem in which there is a choice between two or more unpleasant alternatives

dualism   A belief in the existence of two and only two separate classes of phenomena: spirit and matter, for example. Most dualists are really committed to three substances: matter, mind, and abstract objects such as numbers (see also *monism* and *pluralism*).

dystopia   An imagined society in which conditions are as bad as they can be; the reverse of a utopia

Eightfold Path   In Buddhism, the practice of life that aids in the attainment of enlightenment: Right View, Right Aim, Right Speech, Right Action, Right Living, Right Effort, Right Mindfulness, Right Contemplation

empiricism   A belief that experience alone generates all knowledge, and that there is no such thing as inherent or innate knowledge; opposed to rationalism

ends versus means   An argument which holds that there are some actions which, as means, are themselves so morally wrong or bad that their consequences, no matter how good, cannot compensate

epistemology   The study of the nature and origins of knowledge

ethics   The collection of beliefs by which a person determines whether an action is right or wrong; a person's set of moral principles. Philosophical ethics inquires into the foundation of such principles and seeks to offer rational justification for them.

eudaimonia   Greek for "living well"; refers to the Aristotelian belief that the true aim of life is happiness, attained by the proper balance of intellectual and moral virtues

euthanasia   Greek for "a happy death"; the act of killing someone for his or her own good, to relieve suffering due to a fatal illness, for example

existentialism   A modern philosophy which argues for the total freedom of the individual from external or inherited controls on his or her behavior, and, therefore, for the complete responsibility the individual assumes for his or her own actions. You must figure this philosophy out for yourself; we will not explain it to you.

foundationalism   The view that there is a privileged class of belief from which springs the justification of all other beliefs or statements in a particular belief system

Four Noble Truths   From Buddhist teachings: (1) Suffering exists, (2) Suffering has identifiable causes, (3) There is a way to end suffering, (4) The way is to follow the Eightfold Path.

freedom   In terms of political freedom, the degree to which the actions of people within a society are allowed by law and sometimes facilitated by government. Philosophers generally refer to *negative freedom* as those areas of human activity allowed by law, and they use the term *positive freedom* to mark areas in which government facilitates human action by offering assistance. For instance, most people would agree that you have a right to pursue a college degree (negative freedom) without suffering discrimination. Fewer people would agree that the government has a right to tax society to provide free college educations (positive freedom).

free will   A characteristic, assumed in certain philosophies, by which people may choose their actions without the influence of internal or external constraints; a troublesome term, since philosophers sometimes redefine free will in a manner that makes it difficult to separate it from the account of choice given in determinism

happiness   In some philosophies, the single basic element necessary for living the good life; usually a pluralistic concept involving a variety of intrinsic goods such as knowledge and pleasure. There are monistic eudamonists, called hedonists, who argue that happiness is ultimately reducible to pleasure.

hedonism   A philosophic position that the pursuit of pleasure is the highest aim in life

historicism   The view that it is impossible to arrive at an understanding of human behavior without understanding its historical context; also, the understanding that one's interpretation of reality is conditioned to an extent by one's historical environment

humanism   Any philosophical position that centers on the innate worthiness of humans and human values

hypothetico-deductive model   A three-step model of scientific justification in which (1) a hypothesis is developed in response to an unexpected observation, (2) statements about reality are deduced from the hypothesis, initial conditions, and other background knowledge, and (3) the hypothesis is confirmed through observation

idealism   The theory that ultimate reality exists only in a non-physical realm of ideas, and that physical objects in the world are imperfect copies of ideal objects; also, a theory that ultimate reality exists only in the mind

ideal observer theory   A process of ethical reasoning that subjects conclusions to the views of an ideal (and imagined) observer who, possessed of all the facts relating to the conclusion, should be able to make judgments about it that are free of bias

ideology   Any systematic collection of beliefs infected with ethical or religious values, but especially one relating to politics or sociological matters

induction   See *deduction*

infinite regress   A system in which one event is caused by a past event, which in turn was caused by an earlier past event, and so on, backward into eternity. Showing that an opponent's position is committed to an infinite regress is generally considered an effective refutation of the position.

innateness   The condition of being inherent or inborn, as opposed to originating externally, as through experience or education; an intrinsic quality or object; in philosophy, a term generally referring to questions about the mind, such as whether ways of classifying objects or the ability to learn a language or to reason are innate or learned

intrinsic   Partaking of the essential nature of a thing; also, the quality of having value for itself, rather than for its relationship to something else

introspection   To explore one's own consciousness deeply, looking for self-knowledge. Some introspectionists hold that one cannot be mistaken about the contents of one's own mind; you can lie to others about what you think and feel but not to yourself.

intuition   The human faculty of believing something, often suddenly, without subjecting it to argumentation or testing; in philosophy, a general term referring to the having of an experience whether it be sensory, religious, aesthetic, rational, or a combination of these

mean   A center point between two extremes; in ethics, a term referring to Aristotle's view that a virtue is always the mean between two extremes, as courage is half way between cowardice and foolhardiness

metaphysics   The branch of philosophy that focuses on the ultimate components of existence, such elements as time, free will, the nature of matter, etc.

Mill, John Stuart   1806–1873; classical liberal English philosopher who defended and popularized Utilitarianism. His father, John Mill, and Jeremy Bentham were the major proponents of Utilitarianism before him.

mind-body problem   The focal point for any attempt to understand the relationship between the physical and the mental substances

monism   A belief in the existence of only one ultimate kind of substance; for example, a belief that existence is comprised of one organic spiritual whole, with no independent elements; a tenet argued in the work of Spinoza (see *dualism* and *pluralism*)

mysticism   Any belief system that relies on direct experience as a means of connecting with ultimate reality, which is usually held to be supernatural truth or God

natural law   In some philosophies, the set of innate constraints that should govern human action. Note that *unnatural* does not mean in violation of the laws of nature in a physical sense. One cannot violate the laws of nature unless, of course, one is God. *Unnatural* means in violation of the proper purposes of nature, as exhibited in nature and apprehendible through reasoning. St. Thomas did not deny that sex outside of marriage was physically possible, but he did deny that it was natural, since it did not attend to the proper function of sex: procreation and the raising of children to adulthood.

nihilism   The position that all traditional beliefs and belief systems are unfounded and that life itself is meaningless

nothing   Emptiness, complete void, nonexistence; a philosophical puzzle, since the naming of "nothing" confers upon it an existence. In nonwestern philosophy, the term *nothing* names the unnamable and undifferentiated source of all being and has a positive role to play. The usefulness of the bowl is accounted for by the material out of which it is constructed and the emptiness that provides its shape. Consider the haiku:

> No one spoke.
> Not the host. Nor the guest.
> Nor the pink chrysanthemum.

omnipotent   All powerful; capable of any action; a characteristic often assigned to God regardless of such paradoxical facts as that God cannot build a stone so heavy that God cannot pick it up

paternalism   A system in which an authority provides for the needs of its constituents and regulates their conduct, thus, in effect, assuming responsibility for them. Even libertarians such as John Stuart Mill argue for instances in which paternalism is justified.

personal identity   The combination of personal elements that distinguishes one person from all other people; those characteristics which provide a person with his or her individuality over time

Plato   428?–348 B.C.E.; a student of Socrates and thought by some to be the greatest philosopher of all time; author of the Socratic dialogues and famous for his three theories of forms, which consistently hold that physical reality is composed of imperfect copies of ideal forms of which we can become conscious only through the mystical leap at the penultimate step of the dialectic process of reasoning

pluralism   A belief that there are many equally valid, though incompatible, classes of ultimate ethical or political values; in metaphysics, the belief that there is more than one type of substance, which leads to such questions as the mind-body problem, which questions how the substances interact (see *dualism* and *monism*)

problem of evil   The ancient question of why evil exists in a world built by a benevolent God who has the power to eliminate evil and the knowledge that it will occur

problem of induction   A reference to the difficulty of proving the "principle of reasoning," which holds that all the past and present observable properties of nature will continue into the future.

Pyrrhonism   Skeptical philosophy that draws its name from Pyrrho (306–270 B.C.E.) and is preserved in the writings of Sextus Empiricus (second–third centuries C.E.), who advocates the attainment of happiness through the suspension of judgments. Pyrrhonists engage in philosophical argument to establish the truth of skepticism and to cure others of the sickness of belief.

rationalism   A belief that some knowledge is attainable through the processes of reason alone, unaided by experience or education; opposed to empiricism

Rule Utilitarianism   The belief that general policies should be the focus of our attempt to determine which options will have the best overall consequences. Rule Utilitarians generally argue against allowing exceptions in contexts where the consequences would be better if we broke the generally beneficial rules (see *Act Utilitarianism*).

skepticism   The doctrine that knowledge in general or knowledge in certain areas, such as ethics or the question of existence of the external world, cannot be considered certain beyond a doubt. Some skeptics deny that humans have knowledge, thus seeming to refute themselves with the knowledge claim. Others suspend judgment about whether there is knowledge.

sense-data   Those sensations or impressions received through the senses and which, according to empirical philosophers, may serve as the bases of all our understanding of external objects

social contract   The actual or hypothetical agreement between the government or ruler and the governed that outlines the rights of citizens and duties of citizens and the government. Social contract theorists differ on the question of whether the governmental authorities are parties to the contract or are constituted as authorities on the basis of a contract between citizens. The concept is often invoked as a way of legitimizing a government.

Socrates   470?–399 B.C.E.; teacher of Plato and the principal speaker in the Socratic dialogues; a master of the dialectical method of argument, in which opponents are led by a series of questions into revealing the weaknesses in their own positions

solipsism   The theory that the only thing in existence is the self

state of nature   The real or hypothetical condition in which humanity existed before the establishment of government or laws regulating behavior

Tao   Originating in Chinese thought, the name for the unnamable and ineffable unity of all existence and nonexistence

Taoism   Philosophical tradition originating in China which believes that humans can find peace and tranquillity through following the Tao. Major figures in Taoism are Lao Tzu (sixth century B.C.E.) and Chuang-Tzu (fourth century B.C.E.).

theism   Opposite of atheism; the belief in a deity

utilitarian ethics   A philosophical tradition that places the ultimate moral justification of an action in the overall balance of good consequences over bad ones. Utilitarians differ over the nature of the good. Some believe that the only good is pleasure; others prefer the more pluralistic term *happiness*. But they all accept the principle of equality of interests embodied in Jeremy Bentham's statement that each counts for one, and no one counts for more than one.

utopia   Greek for "nowhere"; an imagined society of ideal perfection; the reverse of a dystopia.

Index